ENGAGING
—*the*—
CIVIL WAR

Chris Mackowski and Brian Matthew Jordan, Series Editors

A Public-History Initiative of Emerging Civil War
and Southern Illinois University Press

ENTERTAINING HISTORY
THE CIVIL WAR IN LITERATURE, FILM, AND SONG

Edited by Chris Mackowski

Southern Illinois University Press
Carbondale

Southern Illinois University Press
www.siupress.com

23 22 21 20   4 3 2 1

Cover illustrations (*clockwise from top left*): Historian Frank Jastrzembski attends
the twenty-fifth-anniversary showing of *Gettysburg* at Gettysburg's
Majestic Theater (photo by Asha Jastrzembski); Shelby Foote's classic
trilogy *The Civil War: A Narrative* still draws browsers to Civil War
bookshelves (photo by Chris Mackowski); historian Douglas Ullman Jr.
pays homage to the iconic cover of Tony Horwitz's *Confederates in the Attic*
(photo by Jennifer Ullman); and Jackson Mackowski prepares to pick a
Civil War tune on a modern banjo (photo by Chris Mackowski).

Library of Congress Cataloging-in-Publication Data
Names: Mackowski, Chris, editor.
Title: Entertaining history : the Civil War in literature, film, and song / edited
by Chris Mackowski.
Description: Carbondale : Southern Illinois University Press, [2020] | Series:
Engaging the Civil War | Includes bibliographical references and index.
Identifiers: LCCN 2019019660 | ISBN 9780809337576 (paperback) | ISBN
9780809337583 (ebook)
Subjects: LCSH: War in literature. | War films—United States—History and
criticism. | Music—United States—History and criticism. | United
States—History—Civil War, 1861–1865—Literature and the war. |
United States—History—Civil War, 1861–1865—Motion pictures and
the war. | United States—History—Civil War, 1861–1865—Music and
the war.
Classification: LCC PS374.C53 E58 2020 | DDC 973.7—dc23
LC record available at https://lccn.loc.gov/2019019660

Printed on recycled paper ♻

This paper meets the requirements of ANSI/NISO Z39.48-1992 (Permanence
of Paper). ♾

For Jack Vernon,
Jaimee Wriston Colbert, Maria Maziotti Gillan,
Wulf Kansteiner, Libby Tucker, Joe Weil,
and most especially,
Leslie Heywood

Contents

Table and Figures

Acknowledgments

This might be the most complex publishing project I've ever worked on, and it's certainly the most complex project Emerging Civil War has undertaken to date. I have been fortunate to work with a highly talented and extremely generous collection of historians who were all delighted to have the chance to talk about their favorite books, films, TV shows, and songs. My interactions with them often had the feel of a book club—swapping reactions, insights, and ideas with great enthusiasm—which made the book tremendous fun to curate. My sincere thanks to each of them for the lively, entertaining discussions.

Our contributors, in turn, tapped into a wide array of sources and expertise as they wrote their essays. Collectively, we thank the American Battlefield Trust, Paige Gibbons Backus, Jack Davis, Bert Dunkerly, the Friends of Grant Cottage, the Friends of the *Hunley*, the Gettysburg Foundation, Susan Hellman, John Hennessy, Bobby Horton, Tony Horwitz, Caroline Keinath, Michael Lesser, Rebekah Oakes, Kristen Pawlak, Nick Sacco, Jeff Shaara, Timothy B. Smith, Jay Ungar, Craig Warren, and Jake Wynn. Thanks, too, to Ken Burns and his assistants, Cauley Powell and Michael McCormack.

Sylvia Frank Rodrigue, the true guiding light behind the Engaging the Civil War series, patiently waited for me to get this collection in order, which took much longer than I had ever imagined it would. That she didn't strangle me with an old film reel from *Gone with the Wind* or bludgeon me with all three volumes of Shelby Foote's narrative speaks to her patience, good humor, and commitment to the creative process.

Her colleagues at Southern Illinois University Press remain supportive partners of the Engaging the Civil War series, and I appreciate all the work they do for us.

I am also grateful to Jack Vernon, Leslie Heywood, and the rest of the creative writing faculty at Binghamton University, as well as Libby Tucker in the English Department and Wulf Kansteiner in the History Department. The genesis of this book came about as part of my doctoral studies under their guidance. (I also offer my thanks to a still-unknown anonymous second reader for my field exam in Civil War literature.) Jack Vernon, a wonderful historical novelist, gave me wide latitude to explore—exploration that continues to this day, currently exemplified by this volume. My dean at St. Bonaventure University at the time, Dr. Pauline Hoffmann, made those doctoral studies possible through encouragement and logistical support.

Thanks, finally, to my colleagues at Emerging Civil War; to my series coeditor, the inspiring historian Brian Matthew Jordan; to my frequent collaborator, Kris White, who helped me brainstorm this project off the ground; and to my family, especially my wife, Jennifer, and my children, Steph, Jackson, and Maxwell.

ENGAGING
—*the*—
CIVIL WAR

For additional content that will let you engage this material further, look for unique QR codes at the end of the introduction and at the start of each part. Scanning them will take you to exclusive online material, additional photos and images, links to online resources, and related blog posts at www.emergingcivilwar.com.

A QR scanner is readily available for download through the app store on your digital device. Or go to www.siupress.com/entertaininghistory for links to the digital content.

Entertaining History

❄ Prologue
The Ken Burns Effect

Chris Mackowski

As former battlefield guides at Fredericksburg and Spotsylvania National Military Park (FSNMP), my colleague Kris White and I frequently spoke with visitors who had read *The Killer Angels*, which in turn inspired them to come see a Civil War battlefield.[1] Michael Shaara's 1974 novel is about the Battle of Gettysburg and has nothing to do with any of the battlefields at FSNMP (Fredericksburg, Chancellorsville, Wilderness, and Spotsylvania). However, it was also nice to see that the novel—or perhaps its film version, *Gettysburg*—had stimulated people's interest enough to bring them through the front door.

Gods and Generals, by Shaara's son, Jeff, features Fredericksburg and Chancellorsville prominently. It also chronicles the death of Confederate general "Stonewall" Jackson. Visitors come to the Jackson Shrine, the building where Jackson died, and say, "Hey, this isn't what it looked like in the movie" or "This isn't the way I pictured it from the book," and they sometimes feel disappointed that sublime reality doesn't live up to Hollywood slick.

For that reason, some colleagues would roll their eyes at the mention of "Gods and Jacksons"—a derisive nickname they'd given the film because of its adoring treatment of Robert E. Lee and Stonewall Jackson. They grumbled the word *novelist* as an epithet, and they dismissed the cinematic splendor of *Gone with the Wind* because it's too drenched in magnolias and moonlight— Oscars be damned. Likewise, *The Killer Angels'* Pulitzer Prize has often carried little weight with them. "I am a historian," historian D. Scott Hartwig, widely acknowledged as the National Park Service's authority on the Battle of Gettysburg, once wrote about the novel. "Consequently, I originally looked down upon Shaara's work. After all, it was fiction."[2]

Similarly, artists like Shelby Foote and Ken Burns—whose major Civil War works are ostensibly creative nonfiction—draw scorn for their research methods or their historical interpretation.

1

Yet creative works undeniably teach Americans about the Civil War, says academic historian Gary Gallagher—"to a lamentable degree in the minds of many academic historians."[3] History, some suggest, should be left to the historians.

Lest anyone underestimate the importance of movies, books, or other forms of popular media in getting people interested in Civil War history, take a second to study the table, which presents visitation numbers for several Civil War battlefields administered by the National Park Service.

Notice the spike in 1991. PBS first aired Ken Burns's film *The Civil War* on September 23–27, 1990, so 1991 served as the first full season of fair weather for tourists to get out onto the battlefields following the film—and they went out in droves. "The real war will never get in the books," said poet Walt Whitman, quoted in the documentary. But after *The Civil War*, people flocked to battlefields across the country to get as close to "the real war" as they could. (You'll notice a jump again in 1994, which we'll talk about in a minute.)

I call this the Ken Burns Effect. Ken Burns did for the Civil War in one eleven-hour film what thousands of well-intentioned history teachers across America could never do: *The Civil War* made people pay attention to the Civil War. It made them care about it. It made them fall in love with it. Some 40 million viewers tuned in over nine nights, making *The Civil War* the most watched program ever to air on public television.[4]

The most visited Civil War battlefield, Gettysburg, coming off its 125th anniversary in 1988, saw its numbers start to dip by 1990, but up they jumped in the season after *The Civil War*. Then, in 1993, visitation saw a similar bump when Ted Turner adapted Shaara's novel *The Killer Angels* into the movie *Gettysburg* (fig. 0.1). The film inspired a second, even bigger bump the following year when it appeared on Turner's TNT cable network, where it attracted 34 million viewers, making it the most watched cable TV show ever at the time.[5] It has since become a perennial favorite. If you refer to the table above, you can see the corresponding bump in 1994 at the other parks, too. *Gettysburg*'s reach went well beyond Gettysburg.

In 1996, following the airing of the television movie *Andersonville*—another Ted Turner production, based on MacKinlay Kantor's 1955 novel of the same name—visitation at Andersonville National Historic Site jumped by forty-one thousand visitors—a 20.6 percent increase. Figure 0.2 clearly shows that *The Civil War* (1991) and the cable airing of *Gettysburg* (1994) also affected Andersonville's attendance.

* * *

Visitation Statistics for Selected Civil War–Related Sites, 1989–94

	1989	1990	1991	1992	1993	1994
Andersonville	136,068	131,406	151,408	143,025	136,567	162,279
Antietam	147,007	217,249	263,110	243,707	181,909	237,707
Chickamauga–Chattanooga	851,534	955,084	1,002,285	995,622	1,015,945	1,015,610
Fort Sumter	256,455	249,552	309,927	337,236	341,794	345,345
Fredericksburg-Spotsylvania	448,985	449,004	471,311	472,623	472,239	493,643
Gettysburg	1,352,728	1,243,642	1,415,840	1,299,203	1,411,453	1,674,532
Manassas	767,138	799,972	905,485	867,606	614,897	917,534
Petersburg	370,735	250,289	293,874	299,146	254,617	218,561
Shiloh	338,946	337,191	400,983	407,986	341,220	363,441
Vicksburg	571,862	530,733	864,799	910,493	1,010,001	801,381

Source: National Park Service, "Visitor Use Statistics," https://irma.nps.gov/Stats/.

Note: Any number of other parks could have been included on this list. A large park notably absent is Kennesaw Mountain, which I did not include because of its popularity as one of the largest green spaces in the metro Atlanta area, making it impossible to distinguish recreational users from visitors there to explore the park's Civil War history. At a time when other parks experienced the Ken Burns Effect, visitation at Kennesaw held steady between 1990 and 1991, with 784,310 and 787,400 visitors, respectively. In 1992, visitation jumped to 926,748, marking the start of an upward climb and exceeding 2.36 million in 2016.

Visitation numbers fluctuate from year to year and from park to park for a variety of reasons, including whether a park charges user fees and which procedures it uses for counting visitors. Other external factors may also come into play. For instance, the population of the city of Petersburg continued to decline from the mid-1960s, when more than a million people visited the battlefield, to less than a quarter of that number by 1990. The Ken Burns Effect appears to have arrested that decline for a couple of years, but then the downward trend continued.

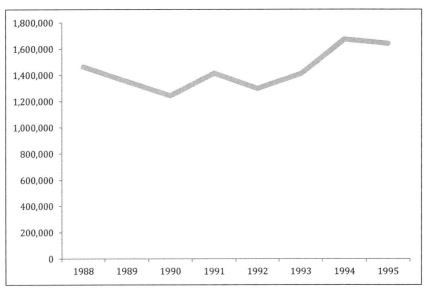

Fig. 0.1. Visitation at Gettysburg National Military Park, 1988–95. *Graph by Chris Mackowski based on National Park Service, "Visitor Use Statistics," https://irma.nps.gov/Stats/.*

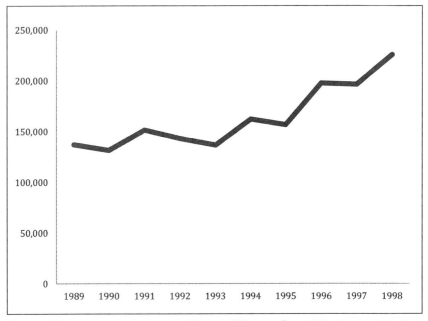

Fig. 0.2. Visitation at Andersonville National Historic Site, 1989–98. *Graph by Chris Mackowski based on National Park Service, "Visitor Use Statistics," https://irma.nps.gov/Stats/.*

A more recent example of the Ken Burns Effect comes from 2016, when PBS TV premiered the Civil War hospital drama *Mercy Street*. By the end of the year, many sites related to Civil War medicine saw increased traffic. Most notable was Carlyle House Historic Park in Alexandria, Virginia—the site that served as the basis for the show (fig. 0.3). Between January 2016 and September 2016, Carlyle House saw a 38.6 percent increase in visitation over the same period the year before.

"Prior to January of 2016, our tour focused exclusively on the eighteenth-century story of John Carlyle and his family, although we did have a small [Civil War] Sesquicentennial exhibit in our cellar space that opened in 2011," explained Susan Hellman, historic site manager for Carlyle House. "With the advent of *Mercy Street* and the anticipated press and visitor interest, we converted the entire second floor of the museum in the fall of 2015 to tell the tale of the Civil War Mansion House Hospital. We opened the exhibit in January 2016 to coincide with the premier of *Mercy Street*."[6]

The effect at the National Museum of Civil War Medicine in Frederick, Maryland, was less pronounced. Director of interpretation Jake Wynn said the museum experienced "a slight uptick in visitation," although he cautioned it was still too early to tell what the lasting results might be, if any. "It's been a

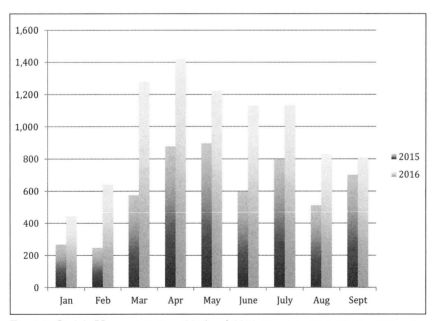

Fig. 0.3. Carlyle House visitation, 2015 and 2016. *Graph by Chris Mackowski based on National Park Service, "Visitor Use Statistics," https://irma.nps.gov/Stats/.*

positive for the museum," he said. "People have seen the show and have been really curious to know more about Civil War medicine."[7]

The demographics of the visitors have been quite specific. "It's been the *Downton Abbey* crowd that stuck around for *Mercy Street* as its replacement," Wynn explained. "These are people who haven't heard our story before. From that standpoint, the show has been beneficial [in] connecting with lay audiences that don't know much about Civil War medicine."

People who *do* know about Civil War medicine, Wynn said, have tended to pan the show, "but they're mostly not the audience the producers are going for." Such criticism also misses the point. "They miss the opportunity that's now here," he noted. The museum capitalizes on that with special programs and viewing parties. "We interpret scenes and talk about what had a historical basis and what was based in creative license," he said.

The Ben Lomond Plantation in Prince William County, Virginia, site of an 1861 Civil War hospital, has likewise done special *Mercy Street*–themed programming, including a popular bus tour. The site's seasonal operating schedule meant it was closed when *Mercy Street* first aired, but Ben Lomond "did see a decent increase in visitation" once they opened, said site manager Paige Gibbons-Backus. "We had a lot of [visitors] ask about *Mercy Street* and how we compared to what people saw on the show. It brought Civil War medicine into the spotlight."[8]

Not all medical-related sites experienced similar benefits. National Park Service historian Robert Dunkerly said Richmond National Battlefield Park's Chimborazo Medical Museum did not enjoy any noticeable increase since *Mercy Street* first aired. "I'm at Chimborazo regularly and can't recall a single person saying they came because of the show," he said, "nor has it seemed to generate many questions from visitors who do come."[9]

One explanation might be that the Museum of Civil War Medicine and Ben Lomond Plantation have actively capitalized on *Mercy Street* in their marketing, tapping into the public's raised consciousness. In any case, Wynn and Gibbons-Backus both said it was too early to get a sense of how visitation numbers would ultimately play out.

What's obvious, though, is that the Ken Burns Effect is not a magic bullet: not every book or movie or show sparks a rush to battlefields and historic sites. *The Killer Angels*, published in 1974 and winner of the Pulitzer Prize for fiction in 1975, made nary a blip on the attendance at Gettysburg National Military Park. In 1974, the park saw 3,774,900 visitors; in 1975, that number actually dropped, significantly, to 2,242,700 visitors. In 1976, visitation rose to 3,070,200.[10] While it's doubtful the novel bears any blame for the drop in attendance, it certainly didn't send people to Gettysburg in droves, either. Even the movie version of the novel, as we've seen, had only a moderate impact, and it wasn't until *Gettysburg* found its legs on cable that it made its true mark.

Even Burns's *The Civil War* didn't have a universal impact. Visitation at Pea Ridge National Military Park, a lesser-known battlefield in the oft-overlooked Trans-Mississippi Theater, actually dropped from 109,972 visitors in 1990 to 103,034 in 1991—a 6.5 percent decrease. Similarly, visitation at Wilson's Creek, another Trans-Mississippi site, dropped from 156,676 to 146,947 visitors—a 6.2 percent decrease. The Trans-Mississippi received little attention in Burns's documentary, which might explain why the sites didn't benefit from a bump.

"But I wonder how many people living in Missouri, Kansas, [and] Arkansas were inspired to learn more about the Civil War in their hometowns as a result of Ken Burns?" asked Kristen Pawlak, former programming coordinator of the Missouri Civil War Museum in St. Louis. She cited her father, the founder of the museum, as an example. "My dad was inspired to learn more about the war on the Missouri-Kansas Border while he was a police officer in Kansas City, Missouri, as a direct result of that documentary."

If Burns breezed past the Trans-Mississippi Theater, a number of other films, such as *Outlaw Josey Wales* and *Ride with the Devil*, and novels, such as *Enemy Women*, have been set there—specifically in Missouri. "Since our museum was not open when those movies were released, we never had visitor traffic directly in response to the popularity of those films," Pawlak said. "Honestly, I had maybe two people in my career with the museum say that they had an interest in Missouri as a result of seeing *The Outlaw Josey Wales* or *Ride with the Devil*. However, because visitors enjoyed our museum, it led them to watch *Ride with the Devil*, *The Outlaw Josey Wales*, or the Wide Awake documentaries, as well as read *Enemy Women*, *Uncle Tom's Cabin*, *The Civil War in Missouri: A Military History*, and many others."[11]

* * *

While I've described the Ken Burns Effect in terms of the Civil War, it certainly shows up in other contexts. For comparison, look at the attendance figures at Adams National Historic Site (now Adams National Historical Park), outside of Boston, which rose after David McCullough's best-selling, Pulitzer-winning John Adams biography came out in 2001—a bump that has never gone down (fig. 0.4).[12] Assistant superintendent Caroline Keinath described the increase in visitation as "very significant."[13]

So powerful is this effect that visitation numbers even suggest spillover. Readers who enjoyed McCullough's *John Adams* looked for other books he'd written, including his first, *The Johnstown Flood*. That site celebrated its centennial in 1998, but numbers began falling off in the two years afterward (fig. 0.5). Then in 2002—the year after *John Adams* fans started reading other McCullough books—attendance spiked dramatically, nearly matching the centennial's visitation.

In what could be an instance of six degrees of Civil War separation, McCullough's second book was *The Great Bridge* (1972), about the Brooklyn Bridge. McCullough returned to the bridge in 1981, narrating a film about it directed by a young filmmaker named Ken Burns (fig. 0.6). The movie, *The Brooklyn Bridge*, was Burns's first. The narrator and filmmaker collaborated again nearly two decades later for *The Civil War*.

McCullough's butterscotch voice stands out as one of the film's many wonderful features: gorgeous, patient shots of beautiful landscapes; primary source material voiced by recognizable actors; close-up examination of period photographs; a haunting, now iconic theme song and a period music soundtrack.

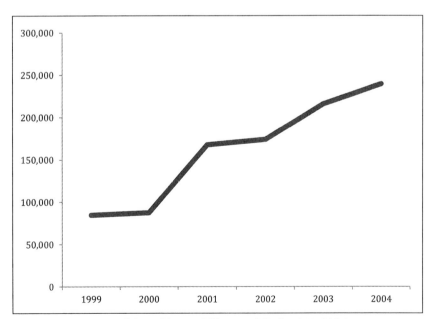

Fig. 0.4. Visitation at Adams National Historical Park, 1999–2004. *Graph by Chris Mackowski based on National Park Service, "Visitor Use Statistics," https://irma.nps.gov/Stats/.*

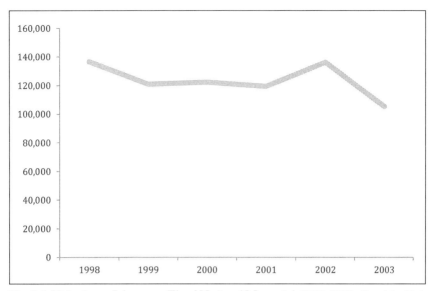

Fig. 0.5. Visitation at Johnstown Flood National Memorial, 1998–2003. *Graph by Chris Mackowski based on National Park Service, "Visitor Use Statistics," https://irma.nps.gov/Stats/.*

Fig. 0.6. Filmmaker Ken Burns fundamentally changed the way America looks at—and engages with—its own history. *Florentine Films.*

Burns found so many ways to let the documents and the battlefields tell the story. His final product was artful, moving, and personal in a way most "pure" history fails to be, and it redefined the genre of documentary filmmaking.

And look at the results: *The Civil War* brought people to the battlefields and into museums. It inspired them to buy books and learn more about the war. Suddenly, opportunity existed for hundreds of historians to reach hundreds of thousands of visitors who otherwise never would have stepped onto their sites or into their museums and bookstores. Many of those visitors have been coming back, over and over, ever since.

It's worth noting, too, that the Ken Burns Effect isn't limited to visitation. Popular entertainment can affect the public's interaction with history in a number of ways. When Alex Haley published *Roots* in 1976, it sparked "a new era in genealogical research," wrote historian Gary B. Mills and genealogist Elizabeth Shown Mills, who also pointed out that the book "served as the foundation for a host of education courses, seminars, and lecture series, all labelled 'Black Studies' or 'Afro-American History.'" Although ultimately critical of the book, they admitted that "no published work of the seventies, and perhaps none of the century, has had the social or cultural impact of Alex Haley's *Roots*."[14]

Historian Nicolaus Mills, writing in 2004, credited the completion of the embattled National World War II Memorial in Washington, D.C., in large part to a surge in media events related to the war, including the movie *Saving Private Ryan* and the appearance of its star, Tom Hanks, as the national spokesperson for the memorial's fund-raising campaign. "We are living in a period in which the re-evaluation of World War II has not come, as we might have expected, at the opportune historic moments presented by the fiftieth anniversary of D-Day in 1994 and the fiftieth anniversary of the war's end in 1995," Mills wrote. "The re-evaluation has come about as a result of the public response to an outpouring of books, films, and television programs about the war that appeared between 1997 and 2001 and included Stephen Ambrose's *Citizen Soldiers*, Tom Brokaw's *The Greatest Generation*, Steven Spielberg's *Saving Private Ryan*, James Bradley's *Flags of Our Fathers*, and the HBO series *Band of Brothers*."[15]

More recently, when Lin-Manuel Miranda's *Hamilton* hit the stage on Broadway in 2015—and later raked in the season's Tony Award for Best Musical, a Grammy Award for Best Musical Theater Album, and the Pulitzer Prize for Best Drama—sales of the Ron Chernow biography on which the show was based soared. According to the *New York Times*, "Paperback sales spiked after the musical opened, from 3,300 copies in 2014 to 106,000 in 2015." In March of that year—eleven years after the biography was first published—the paperback hit number one on the *New York Times* best seller list and has sold well over a million copies.[16]

The resultant success turned Chernow into a Burns-like force of his own with the 2018 publication of his biography *Grant*. At Ulysses S. Grant National Historic Site in St. Louis, where attendance had already been on the rise for several years, Chernow's biography gave an additional boost to the numbers. "I have talked with a good number of people who visited the site after reading Chernow and can say that it's had some sort of effect on our attendance," said historian Nick Sacco. "Chernow's book has had a sort of 'gateway drug' effect for those visitors. They read the book, and it inspired them to continue their learning journey by seeing history with their own two eyes at a historic site."[17] Grant Cottage State Historic Site in upstate New York, where Grant died after completing his memoirs, has likewise enjoyed a bump. Tour guide Michael Lesser said the site was on track for its second consecutive record-breaking annual attendance. "We're hearing from many of our visitors who have read *Grant* and can attribute much (albeit not all) of this growth to the Chernow book."[18]

Such is the power of popular entertainment: it can spark the national consciousness in a way that gets people's attention, gets them excited, gets them invested, and gets them to battlefields and museums and historic sites where they can engage with history on a deeper level. Once they come through the front door, no matter how incomplete their historical literacy, the frontline historians who await them have a remarkable opportunity to carry the story forward.

Endnotes

1. Portions of this essay have been adapted from a paper coauthored by Chris Mackowski and Kristopher D. White, "Making History Something Someone Would Want to Know," presented 8 June 2008, at the "Beyond the Academy" Conference, George Mason University.
2. D. Scott Hartwig, *A Killer Angels Companion* (Gettysburg, PA: Thomas Publications, 1996), v.
3. Gary Gallagher, *Causes Won, Lost, & Forgotten: How Hollywood and Popular Art Shape What We Know about the Civil War* (Chapel Hill: University of North Carolina Press, 2008), 9.
4. Robert Brent Toplin, ed. *Ken Burns's The Civil War: Historians Respond* (New York: Oxford University Press, 1996), v.

5. Thomas A. Desjardin, *These Honored Dead: How the Story of Gettysburg Shaped American Memory* (New York: Da Capo, 2003), 180.

6. Susan Hellman, interview by the author, 10 January 2017.

7. Jake Wynn, interview by the author, 3 January 2017.

8. Paige Gibbons-Backus, interview by the author, 5 January 2017.

9. Robert Dunkerly, interview by the author, 3 January 2017.

10. National Park Service, "Visitor Use Statistics," accessed 15 January 2017, https://irma.nps.gov/Stats/.

11. Kristen Pawlak, interview by the author, 25 January 2018.

12. Visitation did go down in 2010, when the site was closed for part of the year for restoration work, but it jumped back up in 2011, and in 2012, the site attracted a record number of visitors: 336,031.

13. Caroline Keinath, assistant superintendent, Adams National Historic Site (now Adams National Historical Park), interview by the author, 3 June 2008.

14. Gary B. Mills and Elizabeth Shown Mills, "Roots and the New 'Faction,'" *Virginia Magazine of History and Biography* 89, no. 1 (January 1981): 24, 22.

15. Nicolaus Mills, *Their Last Battle: The Fight for the National World War II Memorial*, (New York: Basic Books, 2004), 218. See also pp. 166–68.

16. Alexandra Alter, "'Hamilton: The Revolution' Races out of Bookstores, Echoing Musical's Success," *New York Times*, 3 May 2016.

17. Nick Sacco, park ranger, Ulysses S. Grant National Historic Site, email message to the author, 4 September 2018.

18. Michael Lesser, tour guide, Ulysses S. Grant Cottage State Historic Site, email message to the author, 3 September 2018.

Introduction

Chris Mackowski

Of the five books assigned for my undergraduate Civil War class, I read—I am now ashamed to admit—only two. Of the three I did not read, one never even made it out of the plastic wrapper it came in, and I sold it back new at semester's end. The other two somehow remained with me all these years and occupy places in my Civil War library, and I've since, out of guilt, gone back to read them. Better late than never.

The two I read at the time were Michael Shaara's *The Killer Angels* and Bruce Catton's *A Stillness at Appomattox*. It probably comes as no surprise to Civil War buffs that those two books in particular caught my eye—but at the time, I was no Civil War buff. As a college junior, I had enrolled in Rick Frederick's Civil War class because he was an amazing storyteller and "funnier 'n hell," as we said. His seventy-five-minute lectures doubled as stand-up comedy routines, and by the end of each one, our hands cramped from note-taking and our sides stitched from laughing. And lo and behold, after that laughter died down, we discovered in the midst of all that shtick we'd learned a lot, too. (I'm fortunate to have Rick among the contributors to this volume.)

Beyond Rick's wonderful talent as a professor, though, I had no particular interest in the Civil War. *Glory* had come out the year before, but Ferris Bueller as Colonel Robert Shaw had been hard to get past.

Shaara and Catton had both grabbed my attention, though. Both wrote in easily accessible styles—Shaara's more literary and Catton's more journalistic. I knew little about Appomattox beyond what I'd see in the TV miniseries *The Blue and the Gray*, but Catton took me there and helped me appreciate the poignancy and gravity of the event. Gettysburg I knew much more about, having grown up not too far from the battlefield, but Shaara helped me appreciate events in an entirely new way.

These storytellers—Shaara, Catton, and Frederick—made a profound impact on me without my even realizing it. Only two decades later, when I began writing Civil War history myself, did I come to understand that impact. Even then, it didn't click until I heard David McCullough's 2003 Jefferson Lecture for the National Endowment for the Humanities. "No harm's done to history by making it something someone would want to read," McCullough said.[1] I figured that as a two-time Pulitzer winner and *New York Times* best seller, he knew what he was talking about.

I came to history writing sideways, through my professional work as a journalist, my avocational work as a creative writer, and my academic work in English. I've long understood the value of—and been inspired by—a good story. And in my Civil War adventures, I've heard from so many other people hooked by Shaara or Catton or *Gone with the Wind* or *Glory*.

This book, then, in a way, is a celebration of the great books, movies, TV shows, and songs that have hooked so many of us and brought us to the Civil War. Our hope is that in reading this collection, you will feel as if you're sitting down with a bunch of folks who like a lot of the same books and movies you do and having an enjoyable conversation about them. I hope, too, that you discover a gem that you might otherwise not have encountered before, or that you'll discover something new in a work you *thought* you knew. I hope this collection leads to new appreciations for you.

This collection is not intended as a comprehensive survey, although we've tried to hit most of the most influential works. We've divided them into three sections: print, film, and music. Each section offers an example or two of a Civil War–era work that still enjoys modern popularity and then moves in roughly chronological order toward the present. We've organized the collection this way for easier apples-to-apples discussions so that, for instance, essays about movies are in conversation with other essays about movies. After all, that is the way movie fans tend to discuss movies (unless they're comparing a movie to the book it was adapted from). An alternative approach would have been to forgo the subdivisions and just offer a single chronological approach as a way to show an evolution in the way we remember the war. An online appendix provides a chronological listing.

The print section begins with a pair of authors most of us have read in middle school or high school, offering us our first taste of Civil War litera-ture—and, for many of us, our first taste of the war itself. Then we look at some of the other heavy hitters of Civil War writing: Ulysses S. Grant, Bruce Catton, MacKinlay Kantor, Shelby Foote, Michael and Jeff Shaara, and more. We've arranged them in order of first publication, intermingling works of fic-tion and nonfiction. The section wraps up by looking at Civil War magazines.

The film section begins with photography—done on glass plates rather than actual film, if we're getting technical—because images from the battlefield had a powerful visual impact unrivaled by anything else the media could offer. We then look at cycloramas—which are giant works of art on canvas, not film—but as visual spectacles, they were all the rage in their day as the equivalent of today's 3-D IMAX movies. Then we get into movies and TV shows, putting some essays and movies into conversation with each other in ways that we hope will help you see them a little differently.

The music section starts with what's probably the most recognizable Civil War–era song, followed by a piece that looks at other pop music of the day along with some modern musicians who help keep that music alive. We'll touch on some modern favorites, including what's probably the most recognizable modern Civil War song, and we'll finish under the lights of Broadway with a story that might well be the exception that proves our larger rule: sometimes Civil War–themed popular entertainment does *not* necessarily translate into wider interest.

You'll find a wide variety of voices and styles in this book, which is true of any group conversation but something that's a particular hallmark of Emerging Civil War. Our writers have diverse backgrounds, experiences, perspectives, and approaches, which helps keep the conversation fresh—an approach that's served our readers well at www.emergingcivilwar.com and an approach we've tried to replicate here.

Aside from a great collection of contributors—whose bios are all in the back—we're also excited about the lineup of "guest stars" we have in this book. William C. "Jack" Davis, the legendary former editor of *Civil War Times*, took time to talk with us. So did Pulitzer Prize–winning writer Tony Horwitz, best-selling author Jeff Shaara, noted historians John Hennessy and Timothy B. Smith, and beloved Civil War musician Bobby Horton. A half dozen other experts also lent their voices to our conversation, for which we're grateful.

Beyond the book, you'll find additional web-exclusive content at www.emergingcivilwar.com, including essays about other movies, books, TV shows, songs, poems, and writers. You can access that material using the QR codes at the beginning of each section. And next year, a companion volume will look at some of the connections between history and popular culture in broader contexts, touching on such things as reenacting, commemoration, politics, genealogy, memoir, and more.

We've tried to keep this collection as engaging as the examples we discuss. The resulting conversation—with its varied voices, perspectives, and styles—will, we hope, prove lively, entertaining, eclectic, and thoughtful. After all, we love these books and movies and shows and songs. They're fun and cool. They're beloved. They capture our imagination. While giving you plenty to think about, we hope we also honor that spirit.

Note

1. David McCullough, "The Course of Human Events," Jefferson Lecture in the Humanities, 2003, accessed 19 August 2012, https://www.neh.gov /about/awards/jefferson-lecture/david-mccullough-biography.

Part One

THE WAR OF WORDS:
THE CIVIL WAR IN LITERATURE

The real war will never get in the books.
—Walt Whitman, *Specimen Days*

Scan to see exclusive online material related to this part of the book.

1. Ambrose Bierce and Stephen Crane: A "First Look" at the Civil War through Fiction

Amelia Ann and Chris Mackowski

While it might have been history class where many of us first learned about the Civil War, it has often been in English class where we discovered the war consisted of more than names, dates, and places. For decades, that was largely due to a pair of works by Ambrose Bierce and Stephen Crane: "An Occurrence at Owl Creek Bridge" and *The Red Badge of Courage.* As mainstays on middle and high school reading lists, they provided insight into the war that history textbooks, by their nature, couldn't offer.

However, like other once-expected reads, both titles are now, at least to some degree, fondly remembered by historians but often unfamiliar to middle and high school readers.

Bierce was born in 1842 and served in the Civil War; Stephen Crane was born in 1871, six years after the war ended. Yet they were contemporaries in the late nineteenth-century literary scene, where both men achieved success. Bierce reportedly said of Crane, "This young man has the power to feel. He knows nothing of war, yet he is drenched in blood. Most beginners who deal with this subject spatter themselves merely with ink."[1] Crane, meanwhile, deeply admired Bierce's short stories and favorably critiqued Bierce's most notable work, "An Occurrence at Owl Creek Bridge," by saying, "Nothing better exists. That story contains everything."[2]

But privately, Crane irked Bierce—the veteran did not like the nonveteran garnering acclaim for a realistic war story when the younger man had not experienced combat.[3] When the *New York Journal* compared *The Red Badge of Courage* unfavorably to Bierce's work in May 1896, Bierce responded by thanking the paper more for "its just censure of the Crane freak than for its too kindly praise of me."[4] On another occasion, he told a literary confident, "I had thought there could be only two worse writers than Stephen Crane;

namely, two Stephen Cranes."[5] Bierce biographer Roy Morris Jr. attributed the private vitriol to jealously: "Crane made no secret of his admiration for Bierce, but while his work does show traces of the Biercian style, Crane was inarguably the better writer, which may have provoked the older man's spleen."[6] Contemporary newspapers and literary circles played up the rivalry. "Bierce is hot on the track of Stephen Crane," wrote the *Atlanta Constitution* in 1897. "There is no doubt about one thing, however: Everything that Crane writes is red."[7] The two have been linked ever since.

Bierce published "An Occurrence at Owl Creek Bridge" in 1890, and Crane published *The Red Badge of Courage* in 1895. For more than a century after, the stories were must-reads among school-aged children.

"An Occurrence at Owl Creek Bridge" follows the thoughts and actions of Peyton Farquhar, a thirty-something plantation owner, as he is precariously positioned to be hanged from a railroad bridge he had earlier planned to sabotage. Union infantry stand watch as they wait for his sentence to be carried out. The narrative point of view switches to Farquhar's mind as he reminisces about his home life with his wife and children. The loud ticking of his watch suddenly brings him back, and he considers jumping and swimming away.

Once again his mind flashes back to a time when he learned Northern troops had seized Owl Creek Bridge and then repaired it. Farquhar, with Southern loyalty, heads out with plans to burn the bridge—but is then caught in a trap after deciding to turn around.

Farquhar once again hangs from the side of the bridge. The rope breaks, and he falls into the water below, freeing his hands and swimming downstream, away from the soldiers' shots from the bridge. He heads home, several miles away, before spending the night hallucinating. The following day, he arrives at his plantation, just as there is a heavy blow to the back of his neck, and everything goes black.

Readers learn Farquhar never escaped the bridge hanging and that the heroic escape was merely a figment of his imagination before he fell to his death at the end of a noose.

However, it's this dramatic, suspenseful, unexpected ending that likely contributed to the immediate popularity of Bierce's story, said Dr. Craig Warren, founder and editor of the Ambrose Bierce Project, a digital humanities archive. Warren added that it has become one of the author's most famous works solely because of the short story's last few sentences.[8]

"'An Occurrence at Owl Creek Bridge' made for engaging junior high and high school reading because of its brevity, dramatic subject matter . . .

surprise ending, and themes such as life and death, justice, self-deception, and the power of the imagination, " said Warren, who is a professor of English at Pennsylvania State University's Behrend campus in Erie.

"Owl Creek Bridge" was originally published in the *San Francisco Examiner* on July 13, 1890, before being included in Bierce's collection of short stories, *Tales of Soldiers and Civilians*, the following year.[9] Owl Creek is located on the Shiloh battlefield, where the armies fought in April 1862. "A number of Bierce's short stories were based on real incidents remembered from this battle," explained literary critic Edmund Wilson, who pointed out that Bierce "transposed the Owl Creek from Tennessee to Alabama and made use of a hanging that took place at this time."[10]

However, both Warren and Dr. Timothy Smith, a historian at the University of Tennessee at Martin and one of the foremost experts on the Battle of Shiloh, said it may not have been simply the Civil War that made the short story so popular but also Bierce's focus on the human mind, especially during the story's ending.[11] "It's a long story that's really happening in 25 or 30 seconds," said Smith. "It's an interesting literary technique."

The power of the ending, Warren contended, gave the story its heft. "The ending comments on the power and speed with which the human mind can operate when under stress," he said. "Far more to the point, the shrewd ending emphasizes the self-defensive nature of human fantasy; hope springs eternal, even in the last moments of life."

Almost a century later, the story's ending made it a perfect candidate for *Twilight Zone* treatment. Turned into a short film for the 1962 Cannes Film Festival, which then won the Academy Award for Live Action Short Film in 1963, "An Occurrence at Owl Creek Bridge" found its way to Rod Serling's program—famous for its bizarre stories and twist endings—on February 28, 1964. "Here is a haunting study of the incredible, from the past master of the incredible, Ambrose Bierce," Serling said in his introduction.[12]

Bierce's work made perfect sense in the Twilight Zone, said historian Ron Soodalter. "The author's sinister genius lies in his ability to surprise and shock," Soodalter wrote. "Irony abounds and endings are anything but predictable."[13]

Warren would not necessarily recommend the book as an introduction to Civil War literature because, as he explained, the details about the war that surround the story are not crucial to the plot. "Although the piece has a Civil War setting and features a slave-owning protagonist, the story is mostly concerned with the human mind and human nature more generally," said Warren, whose published books include *Scars to Prove It: The Civil War Soldier and American*

Fiction and *The Rebel Yell: A Cultural History.*[14] "One could argue convincingly, in fact, that the Civil War is only incidental to the narrative, and that the same plot would function well in nearly any historical or cultural setting."

Despite this universal resonance, the book has begun disappearing from school libraries and class lists in recent decades, now finding its most frequent home on historians' or Civil War buffs' shelves. In Warren's opinion, this is largely just due to a quickly changing cultural landscape in the United States. "The story declined in popularity among junior high and high school educators during the 1990s, when schools increasingly emphasized multicultural literature at the expense of 'classic' works of American fiction," said Warren. "I'm not suggesting that this is a negative trend, particularly given the educational rewards of multiculturalism."

Warren added that in the last few years, fewer of his freshman students have read the text before beginning college—and fewer read it in college, too. "It's also the case that today few college and university faculty require students to read the story, the exception being in courses devoted to American short fiction," he said. "I would suggest that this has almost always been the case at the college level, as 'Owl Creek Bridge' is often—and unfairly—regarded as secondary school reading."

But Smith, who has worked as a historian at Shiloh, said visitors to the battlefield often recognize Bierce and "An Occurrence at Owl Creek Bridge"— many remembering them fondly. "A lot of people have heard of Ambrose Bierce and 'An Occurrence at Owl Creek Bridge,' and so people are interested," Smith said. "The younger generation, though, is maybe not if they are not reading it in school anymore, but certainly some older generations did read it and are interested to see where he was on the battlefield and all that."

Bierce's time on the battlefield had been dark. He had enlisted right after the war's beginning, joining the 9th Indiana Volunteers, Elkhart's company, for the Union. Bierce worked his way through the ranks, finally being promoted to first lieutenant and surviving a serious head injury. As a result, said Soodalter, Bierce "came away with a jaded vision of war—and of man—that colored his writings for the remainder of his life."[15] He added, "Nothing in Bierce's writing justifies war or grants mercy to those who wage it."[16]

While the Civil War itself may not have been crucial to the plot of "An Occurrence at Owl Creek Bridge," historian Allen Guelzo argued the war had nonetheless highly influenced Bierce's writing because "the Civil War haunted him. The finest of his short stories were those he drew from his memories of the war.... These stories were more than merely recollections of an old soldier."[17]

Literary critics have agreed. "His accounts of battles he took part in are among the most attractive of his writings, because here he is able to combine a ceaseless looking Death in the face with a delight in the wonder of the world," said Edmund Wilson.[18] Eric Solomon noted that same contradiction: "Bierce expertly invokes, by superb selection of detail and response, war's paradoxes and enigmatic agonies."[19]

That's where Bierce and Crane, as writers, begin to overlap. More than any other writer, Solomon said, "Bierce resembles Crane in technique—in the treatment of time, nature, religion, and the theme of growth through combat. . . . But Crane's more ambitious fiction surpasses Bierce's bitter portraits of combat." That concentration on literary quality, he said, made Crane's *The Red Badge of Courage* "the first work of any length . . . purely dedicated to an artistic reproduction of war, and it has rarely been approached in craft or intensity."[20]

Crane grew up writing, working as a journalist, short story author, and novelist, but not as a soldier. Yet *The Red Badge of Courage* was so well written that many former soldiers thought Crane was a fellow veteran, said historian John Hennessy, who has done many programs on Crane's book.[21] Hennessy is the chief of interpretation and chief historian at Fredericksburg and Spotsylvania National Military Park, which includes the battlefield at Chancellorsville, where Crane's story takes place. Crane never mentioned the battle by name in the book, although in a short story, "The Veteran," published as a sequel a year later, he identified it as such.[22]

Crane's story opens with on cold day as Private Henry Fleming waits with his Union regiment to go into battle. He reflects on his reason for enlisting and questions his bravery. In the middle of the battle, he deserts his fellow soldiers right before he hears someone announce a Union victory. He heads to a forest and finds a body before stumbling upon a group of men. In the group is Jim Conklin, one of Henry's old friends, who soon dies, causing Henry to once again flee.

After a run-in with another group, Henry returns to his regiment, wounded from the interaction, and the other men care for him. With relief that his cowardice has not yet been made public, he performs his duty in the ensuing fight. In the final battle scene, Henry, who has taken over the position of color-bearer—carrying the regimental flag—charges with his fellow Union soldiers after realizing they have been spotted by hidden Confederate troops. With the thought of Jim on his mind, Henry takes the lead and is somehow unhurt in the successful charge—particularly noteworthy because color-bearers served as particular targets.

Author Stephen Crane

The Red Badge of Courage and Chancellorsville

Henry Fleming, the main character in Stephen Crane's classic *The Red Badge of Courage*, did not name the battle that was his baptism of fire in that book, but in another short story, he did. "That was Chancellorsville," Fleming declared.

Historians agree that the fighting depicted in *The Red Badge of Courage* reflects the intense combat at Chancellorsville on the morning of May 3, 1863. Though born after the Civil War, Crane grew up around Civil War veterans and took an intense interest in their experiences. Crane's prose and descriptive abilities were so powerful that some doubted that the book could have been written by one who was not there.

Fig. 1.1. An exhibit at the Chancellorsville Battlefield Visitor Center highlights the connection between the battle and Crane's *The Red Badge of Courage*. The display includes an early edition of the book. *Chris Mackowski.*

Henry reflects on his time in battle, and while he remembers his recent success, he cannot forget his earlier instances of cowardice. However, he finally moves past that feeling and realizes his manhood.

Like Bierce's work, Crane's *The Red Badge of Courage* quickly grew popular among the American public, including many younger readers. Unlike his first book, *Maggie: A Girl of the Streets*, which he had financed himself and published under a pseudonym, Crane's 1895 story of Henry Fleming won him international fame.[23]

The story soon began to appear in school reading lists, often for middle or junior high school students. According to National Park Service historian Rebekah Oakes, who works at the Chancellorsville battlefield and does programs on *The Red Badge of Courage*, Crane's inventive style contributed to the story's wide use and success.[24]

"Another, more practical reason could be that *Red Badge* is a fairly easy read—it's short, digestible, with an easy-to-understand plot and few main characters," said Oakes. "As far as a very teachable example of American realism goes, Crane's work is about as good as it gets."

Although younger students often read the book as an introduction to Crane and the Civil War, Hennessy recommended that adults give it a second read, not just "chalking it up on their list of books" that they read in middle school.

Like Bierce, Crane uses the power of the human mind as the focus of his story, rather than specific battle or regiment details, said Oakes. "Crane wanted readers to delve into both Fleming's internal and external struggles, and the true philosophical challenges presented by fear and courage, without being distracted by the details and minutiae of an actual battle. He wanted the focus to be individual and emotional, and creating this fictional world helps us to understand decades later why the individual experiences of real soldiers were so important."

But Crane never had the experience of being a real soldier. In fact, he wasn't even born until 1871—six years after the war had ended—and by the time *The Red Badge of Courage* hit bookstores, the war was three decades in the past. Despite this, Civil War veterans praised Crane's work for its "realism and ability to capture the true feelings and images of combat."[25] Scholar Eric Solomon said the novel "stands by itself in nineteenth-century English and American war fiction. Indeed, it is still the masterwork in English among the abundance of war novels that two world conflicts and dozens of smaller wars have produced."[26]

According to Oakes, who believes the novel remains a good introduction to Civil War literature, Crane conducted extensive research on his topic. And Crane had something else on his side, Hennessy pointed out: incredible literary talent. "He had an intuitive understanding," Hennessy said. "[He had] a perceptive magic that great novelists have."

However, both Oakes and Hennessy said that despite its success, *The Red Badge of Courage* received its fair share of criticism—which may have led to its decreased popularity on reading lists, added Oakes. "Some of the critics of Crane's work may have had an influence," she said. "Throughout the twentieth century, *Red Badge* has been criticized as unpatriotic or as an antiwar statement, although Crane intended neither. For those reasons, perhaps the novel would not have been as popular of an item on a course syllabus during times of war."

Crane himself didn't think of his story as anything special, once saying, "I don't think *The Red Badge* to be any great shakes."[27] But readers, even more than a hundred years later, disagree. The New York Public Library said the book is "long considered to be the definitive Civil War novel."[28] And according to a December 2011 article in the *Wall Street Journal*, *The Red Badge of Courage* ranks as one of the five best novels about the war and is "still taught to young readers as a tale of initiation to manhood and triumph over fear."[29]

In Bierce's case, Kurt Vonnegut, author of famed stories such as *Slaughterhouse Five*, perhaps summed it up best: "I consider anybody a twerp who hasn't read the greatest American short story, which is 'Occurrence at Owl Creek Bridge,' by Ambrose Bierce. It isn't remotely political. It is a flawless example of American genius, like 'Sophisticated Lady' by Duke Ellington or the Franklin stove."[30]

Like "Owl Creek Bridge," *Red Badge* has made it to the movies, first appearing on screen in 1951. It starred World War II hero-turned-actor Audie Murphy, one of the most decorated American soldiers of all time. Of director John Huston's adaptation of Crane's work, a *New York Times* movie reviewer said, "In most respects, Mr. Huston has put 'The Red Badge of Courage' on the screen, and that means a major achievement that should command admiration for years and years."[31] A made-for-television version starring Richard Thomas of *Waltons* fame appeared in 1974.

Neither Crane, who died of tuberculosis at only age twenty-eight, nor Bierce, who disappeared under uncertain circumstances in 1914, lived to see their well-read works adapted for screen use. Nonetheless, their fiction gave them each a kind of extended literary life span. While readers' familiarity with them has diminished in the twenty-first century, Bierce and Crane served as the point of first contact between generations of readers and the Civil War. They still offer much for future generations to discover, too.

Notes

1. "Story of the Week: Chickamauga, Ambrose Bierce," Library of America, 16 June 2017, http://storyoftheweek.loa.org/2017/06/chickamauga.html.
2. M. E. Grenander, *Ambrose Bierce* (New York: Twayne, 1971), 161; "An Occurrence at Owl Creek Bridge," the Ambrose Bierce Project, http://www.ambrosebierce.org/owlcreekbridge.html.
3. R. W. Stallman, *Stephen Crane: A Biography* (New York: George Braziller, 1968), 265.
4. Grenander, *Ambrose Bierce*, 65.
5. Stallman, *Stephen Crane*, 592.
6. Roy Morris Jr., *Ambrose Bierce: Alone in Bad Company* (New York: Oxford University Press, 1995), 224.

7. Stallman, *Stephen Crane*, 265.

8. This and other direct and indirect quotes from Craig Warren come from an interview conducted by Amelia Ann on 22 June 2017.

9. "Occurrence at Owl Creek Bridge," Ambrose Bierce Project.

10. Edmund Wilson, *Patriotic Gore: Studies in the Literature of the American Civil War* (New York: W. W. Norton, 1994), 618.

11. This and other direct and indirect quotes from Timothy Smith come from an interview conducted by Amelia Ann on 8 June 2017.

12. Rod Serling, "An Occurrence at Owl Creek Bridge," *Twilight Zone*, 28 February 1964.

13. Ron Soodalter, "'Bitter Bierce' and the Macabre Side of War," *Civil War Times* (November 2009): 21.

14. Craig Warren, *Scars to Prove It: The Civil War Soldier and American Fiction* (Kent, OH: Kent State University Press, 2009); *The Rebel Yell: A Cultural History* (Tuscaloosa: University of Alabama Press, 2014).

15. Soodalter, "'Bitter Bierce,'" 20.

16. Ibid, 21.

17. Allen Guelzo, "Ambrose Bierce's Civil War: One Man's Morbid Vision," *Civil War Times* (October 2005), http://www.historynet.com/ambrose -bierces-civil-war-one-mans-morbid-vision.htm.

18. Wilson, *Patriotic Gore*, 623.

19. Eric Solomon, "A Definition of the War Novel," in *The Red Badge of Courage: A Norton Critical Edition*, ed. Sculley Bradley, Richmond Croom Beatty, and E. Hudson Long (New York: W. W. Norton, 1976), 170.

20. Ibid.

21. This and other direct and indirect quotes from John Hennessy come from an interview conducted by Amelia Ann on 4 May 2017.

22. "That was Chancellorsville," says an elderly Henry Fleming, the protagonist from *Red Badge*. First published in *McClure's Magazine* in August 1896, "The Veteran" is available online at http://www.online-literature .com/crane/2543/.

23. "Stephen Crane: American Writer," *Encyclopaedia Britannica*, https://www. britannica.com/biography/Stephen-Crane.

24. This and other direct and indirect quotes from Rebekah Oakes come from an interview conducted by Amelia Ann on 24 June 2017.

25. "Stephen Crane," American Literature, https://americanliterature.com /author/stephen-crane/bio-books-stories.

26. Solomon, "Definition of the War Novel," 167.

27. "The 100 Best Novels," *Guardian*, 14 April 2014, https://www.theguardian.com/books/2014/apr/14/100-best-novels-red-badge-courage-stephen-crane.

28. "Ambrose Bierce: Civil War Stories," *NYPL Blogs*, New York Public Library, 18 April 2013, https://www.nypl.org/blog/2013/04/18/ambrose-bierce-civil-war-stories.

29. David W. Blight, "Five Best: Novels about the Civil War," *Wall Street Journal*, 31 December 2011, https://www.wsj.com/articles/SB10001424052970204879004577108562134895388.

30. The Ambrose Bierce Site, http://donswaim.com.

31. Bosley Crowther, "The Screen in Review; 'Red Badge of Courage,' Based on Stephen Crane's Novel, at Trans-Lux 52d St.," *New York Times*, 19 October 1951, https://www.nytimes.com/1951/10/19/archives/the-screen-in-review-red-badge-of-courage-based-on-stephen-cranes.html.

2. ❧ Interpreting the Man: General Ulysses S. Grant and His *Personal Memoirs*

Nick Sacco

In my work as a public historian, I've learned that interpreters at Civil War historic sites must be careful not to fall in love with the subjects they interpret. The temptation to do so exists since these sites often provide jobs and financial profits for local communities through "heritage tourism." Places dedicated to historic figures such as Andrew Johnson, Abraham Lincoln, Robert E. Lee, and many others like them must nevertheless proceed with caution and avoid excessive hero worship. When interpreters become defense attorneys looking to exonerate their dead clients of all charges against them, the result leads to sloppy narratives that flatten the complexity of the past.

I am reminded of this truth on a daily basis working at Ulysses S. Grant National Historic Site in St. Louis, Missouri. At this site, I am tasked with interpreting the history of White Haven, a slave plantation where Grant lived with his family from 1854 to 1859 and where his wife, Julia Dent Grant, grew up. General Grant's reputation among visitors to White Haven is wide-ranging. To some, Grant was an incompetent general who unnecessarily sacrificed lives on the battlefield and a bad president with a corrupt administration. To others, he was the savior of the Union, an honorable president who protected the rights of black Americans during Reconstruction, and perhaps the greatest American of the nineteenth century. And for many, the most recognizable trait in Grant that they learned in school isn't that he was a general or president, but that he was allegedly an alcoholic. These comments are reflective of historical scholarship about Grant, which has swung from negative assessments that existed for most of the twentieth century to now overwhelmingly positive assessments in the twenty-first century. How do I, as an interpreter, strike a balance in my educational programming that accounts for these many understandings of Ulysses S. Grant's life?

An important element of my interpretive philosophy is that I don't seek to portray Grant as a sinner or a saint so much as I intend to humanize him. I aim to highlight not just Grant's accomplishments but also the hopes, fears, and mistakes that marked the life of a person far more complex than the one visitors encounter in public statues and history textbooks. Fitting Grant's perspective within the circumstances of his times can help visitors consider how debates over nationalism, citizenship, slavery, and race that sparked the Civil War still shape our own political debates today.

A central interpretive tool for telling Grant's story is his much-heralded *Personal Memoirs of Ulysses S. Grant.* Written during the last few months of his life and completed days before his death on July 23, 1885, the *Personal Memoirs* highlight Grant's recollection of his experiences during the American Civil War in clear, lucid prose. The *Memoirs* became an instant best seller after their release and have never been out of print.[1] They also provide unique insights into his personal character and the underlying motivations that strengthened him during tough times. What follows are three insights from Grant's *Memoirs* that I discuss with visitors when interpreting his life.

Nationalism

Young students learning about the American Civil War are often exposed to Confederate general Robert E. Lee's conflicted loyalties at the outbreak of the war. A career army officer who expressed a strong devotion to the Union before the war, Lee resigned his commission following his native Virginia's secession, arguing, "I have been unable to make up my mind to raise my hand against my native state, my relations, my children and my home."[2] For Lee, loyalty to state trumped loyalty to the Union and guided his decision to fight for the Confederacy. Grant's *Memoirs* provide an intriguing counterargument to Lee's perspective. In the very first sentence of the book, he proclaimed, "My family is American, and has been for generations, in all its branches, direct and collateral."[3] In other words, Grant boldly asserted that he was not an Ohioan, a Missourian, an Illinoisan, or a New Yorker. Grant, as a native Ohioan, did not possess a separate nationality from a person born in Virginia or Massachusetts. He never felt a sense of divided loyalty between state and nation. The Grant family were not members of a state within a compact of states, but members of a single political community dedicated to promoting a more perfect Union. He and his family were *American.*

Fig. 2.1. Photographed on June 27, 1885, Ulysses S. Grant sat in a wicker chair, propped up with a pillow, wearing a robe and stocking cap. He usually worked on his memoirs in the morning, rested, then edited and made notes in the afternoon between calls from visitors. *Library of Congress.*

Grant conceded in his *Memoirs* that "each colony considered itself a separate government" when the United States was first established. He argued, however, that new states admitted to the Union were creations of the people. Texas, for example, was "purchased with both blood and treasure" of the American people through their service in the Mexican-American War and public revenues held in the U.S. Treasury.[4] The states added after the original thirteen owed their existence to the Union, and their residents should likewise value their allegiance to the entire country above their state. Likewise, the development of railroads, telegraphs, and steamboats in Grant's lifetime bound the states into a stronger economic union of interstate commerce and global trade. America, in Grant's view, had experienced "a commingling of the people" that diminished regional distinctions as "railroads connect the two oceans and all parts of the interior," and laws were passed promoting political equality during the Reconstruction era.[5] While some nineteenth-century Americans did value their state allegiance, Grant's words convey a strong sense of nationalism that many of his fellow Americans shared.

Tenacity

Grant's persistence and determination helped him accomplish important personal goals in both public and private life. Two anecdotes in the *Memoirs* highlight his dogged tenacity.

On graduating from the West Point Military Academy in 1843, Grant was stationed with the 4th U.S. Infantry at Jefferson Barracks in St. Louis. While there, he met and began courting Julia at White Haven, five miles north of the barracks. When word came in May 1844 that the 4th Infantry would be transferring to Fort Jessup, Louisiana, in preparation for a potential conflict with Mexico over U.S. plans to annex Texas, the young soldier immediately set his sights toward White Haven to propose marriage to Julia. On the way there, he crossed the Gravois Creek, typically "an insignificant creek" with hardly any water in it. On this day, however, heavy rains nearly overflowed the Gravois. Grant considered holding off on his proposal but recalled, "One of my superstitions had always been when I started to go anywhere, or to do anything, not to turn back, or stop until the thing intended was accomplished."[6] Leaving St. Louis without expressing his feelings to Julia was an unacceptable outcome for Grant.

This superstition did not always lead to positive outcomes during the Civil War. One may recall the battle of Cold Harbor, or the Crater, or other conflicts where turning back or stopping would have worked better for Grant's forces than a frontal attack.[7] But this episode nevertheless reinforced Grant's determination never to turn his back when a potential challenge threatened his plans. While Grant lost his clothes and almost his life in successfully crossing the Gravois, he ultimately won his future wife's hand. Although this story might sound silly to modern readers, it resonated with Victorian-era readers, who appreciated the romanticism of a man risking his life to express his feelings to his true love.

Grant also learned a lesson in tenacity while a colonel of the 21st Illinois Infantry at the beginning of the Civil War. Colonel Grant had been ordered to march his troops to Florida, Missouri, to engage Confederate colonel Thomas Harris.[8] As Grant's troops began moving toward Florida from Quincy, Illinois, he felt fear and anxiety. "I had been in all the engagements in Mexico that it was possible for one person to be in" during that war, he recalled, "but not in command." Now that he was a commanding officer facing what could be his first combat of the Civil War, Grant remembered, "My heart kept getting higher and higher until it felt to me as though it was in my throat" as they approached Florida. Much like when he had felt trepidation at the Gravois Creek, Grant had the urge to turn back. "I would have given anything then to have been back [home] in Illinois, but I had not the moral courage to halt and consider what to do," he said.[9]

Despite his fears, Grant led his men to Harris's encampment. On arrival, they discovered that Harris had recently abandoned the area. Grant learned an important lesson from this experience, however. He realized that for all his fears in that moment, "Harris had been as much afraid of me as I had been of him." For the rest of the war, Grant still occasionally felt anxious about his troops and their battles, but, he noted, "I never [again] experienced trepidation upon confronting an enemy."[10] Realizing that Confederate commanders were just as nervous as he was gave strength to Grant's tenacious approach to his military strategy.

An Evolving Attitude on Slavery and Race

When Abraham Lincoln stated in his "House Divided" speech that the United States could not permanently endure half slave and half free, Grant looked at the claim with skepticism. As he admitted in his *Memoirs*, "I took no part in any such view of the case at the time."[11] For Grant, the possibility of further compromises on slavery's westward expansion still existed and could help maintain the Union.

Left unsaid in the *Memoirs*, however, was his intimate connection to slavery while living at White Haven. During these years, Grant toiled as a farmer growing fruit and vegetable crops. He worked alongside his father-in-law's enslaved laborers in the fields and at one point even owned one enslaved man named William Jones. Little is known about Jones and his relationship to Grant; the only primary source document that exists is an 1859 manumission paper Grant signed at the St. Louis Courthouse giving Jones his freedom.[12]

Whatever Grant's personal views toward the "peculiar institution" may have been before the Civil War, he participated in and benefited from a slave plantation lifestyle during those years until it was no longer economically feasible. The coming of the Civil War and the evolution of the Union war effort toward a policy of emancipation, however, triggered an evolution in Grant's own thinking about slavery.

By the time Grant began writing the last lines of his *Memoirs* a few days before his death, he could confidently assert in the first sentence of the conclusion that "the cause of the great War of the Rebellion against the United States will have to be attributed to slavery."[13] Looking back at the political debates surrounding slavery in the years before the war, Grant argued that the 1850 Fugitive Slave Act marked a significant turning point in Northern political thought. Before the passage of that law, "the great majority of the people of the North had no particular quarrel with slavery, so long as they were not forced to have it themselves." When the law mandated that Northern residents, police officers, and courts help federal agents capture runaway slaves and return them to their enslavers, many Northerners felt outraged. They were "not willing to play the role of police for the South in the protection of this particular institution," argued Grant.[14] The Fugitive Slave Act—combined with future debates over slavery after passage of the 1854 Kansas-Nebraska Act, the creation of the antislavery Republican Party, and the 1857 Dred Scott Supreme Court decision—helped create the political conditions in which civil war would break out between the United States and the Confederacy over slavery and its westward expansion in 1861.

Grant also argued in his *Memoirs* that African Americans were entitled to citizenship and equal rights in America. By the time the *Memoirs* were published in 1885, the country had begun a long retreat from the egalitarian ideals of the Reconstruction era. The U.S. Supreme Court had decided two years earlier that a civil rights law passed during Grant's presidency was unconstitutional. That law had barred racial discrimination in public accommodations, public transportation, and jury service. The court ruled, however, that the government could not prevent racial discrimination by private businesses and individuals. Meanwhile, voter disenfranchisement and racial terrorism increased in the South as the federal government turned a blind eye to such outrages.[15]

Within this context, Grant argued that "the colored man . . . was brought to our shores by compulsion, and he now should be considered as having as good a right to remain here as any other class of our citizens." African

Americans had been forcibly brought to America in the early seventeenth century, endured more than two hundred years of enslavement, and fought loyally in the U.S. military during the Civil War. For this service, they had earned their emancipation and the right to enjoy the same political privileges as any other American. Grant was hopeful that future political debates would not be based on the color line, but he predicted that "the question of a conflict between races may come up again in the future" and continue to be "a source of anxiety" for the country. To stop such a conflict, Grant called on white Americans to stop their persecution of their fellow black citizens. While the *Personal Memoirs* quickly gained widespread popularity, far too many readers failed to heed this sage advice in the years after its release.[16]

Conclusion

Like any expression of historical memory, Ulysses S. Grant's *Personal Memoirs* must be taken with proper caution. Military historians poring over his descriptions of Civil War battles and leaders have simultaneously praised his recollections of the war while, in some cases, criticizing the *Memoirs* as "so riddled with flaws as to be unreliable," as one historian said.[17] Grant's *Memoirs* are his last word on the history of the American Civil War, but he recognized that his perspective could not be *the* last word on the war's history. With the passage of time and the knowledge that he needed to finish the book before inoperable throat cancer claimed his life, mistakes regarding the number of troops engaged in a particular battle or the actions of one general or another were bound to occur. Although his son Frederick and a team of fact-checkers aided Grant, he confessed in the book's preface that "there must be many errors of omission in this work, because the subject [of the Civil War] is too large to be treated [completely] in two volumes."[18] Complementing Grant's *Memoirs* with the recollections of other Civil War figures and modern scholarship is therefore necessary when studying the Civil War more holistically.

Despite these potential issues, the *Personal Memoirs* are a fascinating and enlightening recollection that must be read by all students of the American Civil War. And to understand the man who led the United States to victory on the battlefield, one must analyze the personal characteristics, beliefs, and motivations that drove him to enlist on the side of the Union during the nation's deadliest conflict. As an interpreter who makes his living discussing Ulysses S. Grant's life with visitors from all over the world, I believe the *Personal Memoirs of Ulysses S. Grant* provide important insights that enable me to tell the story of not just the victorious U.S. general and eighteenth president, but also a nineteenth-century slaveholding society enmeshed in a deadly conflict over the fate of its peculiar institution and the very meaning of freedom itself.

Notes

1. In fact, an annotated version of the *Personal Memoirs* was released in 2017. See John F. Marszalek, David S. Nolen, and Louie P. Gallo, eds., *The Personal Memoirs of Ulysses S. Grant: The Complete Annotated Version* (Cambridge, MA: Harvard University Press, 2017).
2. Elizabeth Brown Pryor, *Reading the Man: A Portrait of Robert E. Lee through His Private Letters* (New York: Viking, 2007), 276.
3. Ulysses S. Grant, *Personal Memoirs of Ulysses S. Grant* (New York: Charles L. Webster, 1885), 1:17.
4. Ibid., 1:218–21.
5. Ibid., 2:552.
6. Ibid., 1:48–51.
7. See Gordon Rhea, *Cold Harbor: Grant and Lee, May 26-June 3, 1864* (Baton Rouge: Louisiana State University Press, 2007); Robert M. Dunkerly, Donald C. Pfanz, and David R. Ruth, *No Turning Back: A Guide to the 1864 Overland Campaign, from the Wilderness to Cold Harbor, May 4–June 13, 1864* (El Dorado Hills, CA: Savas Beatie, 2014); Gary Gallagher and Caroline Janney, eds., *Cold Harbor to the Crater: The End of the Overland Campaign* (Chapel Hill: University of North Carolina Press, 2015).
8. Florida, Missouri, was the birthplace of Grant's good friend later in life, Mark Twain.
9. Grant, *Memoirs*, 1:250.
10. Ibid.
11. Ibid., 2:542.
12. The two best treatments of Grant's life before the Civil War are by Lloyd Lewis and Brooks D. Simpson. Lloyd Lewis, *Captain Sam Grant* (New York: Little, Brown, 1950); Brooks D. Simpson, *Ulysses S. Grant: Triumph Over Adversity, 1822–1865* (New York: Houghton Mifflin Harcourt, 2000), 1–77. The transcript of William Jones's manumission paper is published in John Y. Simon, ed., *The Papers of Ulysses S. Grant*, vol. 1, *1837–1861* (Carbondale: Southern Illinois University Press, 1967), 347.
13. Grant, *Memoirs*, 2:542.
14. Ibid., 2:542–43. For more info on the Fugitive Slave Act, see Stanley Harrold, *Border War: Fighting over Slavery before the Civil War* (Chapel Hill: University of North Carolina Press, 2010).

15. For an extended discussion of the Civil Rights Act of 1875 and its eventual overturn, see William Gillette, *Retreat from Reconstruction, 1869–1879* (Baton Rouge: Louisiana State University Press, 1980); see also Eric Foner, *Reconstruction: 1863–1877* (New York: HarperCollins, 1988); Richard White, *The Republic for Which It Stands: The United States during Reconstruction and the Gilded Age* (New York: Oxford University Press, 2017).

16. Grant, *Memoirs*, 2:550.

17. Frank P. Varney, *General Grant and the Rewriting of History: How the Destruction of General William S. Rosecrans Influenced Our Understanding of the Civil War* (El Dorado Hills, CA: Savas Beatie, 2013).

18. Grant, *Memoirs*, 1:7–9.

3. ✵ Glory Road: Bruce Catton's *Army of the Potomac* Series

Meg Groeling

If anyone had asked me about the Civil War when I was a child, I might not have had any information ready to offer, but I certainly knew where to get some: my dad's study, in one of the three volumes with paper covers of red, white, or blue. Inside those books was . . . the Civil War. They were right next to an oversize book of Mathew Brady's photographs. Close by was an album set of *Songs of the Civil War* by, if I remember correctly, Pete Seeger. I was pretty sure everything I'd ever need to know was right there, on that shelf, somewhere in the photos, songs, and those three volumes titled *Mr. Lincoln's Army* (1951), *Glory Road* (1952), and *A Stillness at Appomattox* (1953).

For many readers in the 1950s, Bruce Catton's Pulitzer Prize–winning series was, indeed, *the* Civil War. Until Catton published his trilogy, most written-for-the-public accounts of the war came from *Battles and Leaders of the Civil War*. There were Lincoln scholars like James G. Randall and academic historians like Allan Nevins, but neither wrote for the "middle-brow" reader. Bruce Catton changed all that. Public historian Patrick Murfin puts it succinctly: instead of "swoons over Lee's alleged military genius and the daring-do [*sic*] of brilliant subordinates like J.E.B. Stuart and Stonewall Jackson by the creators of the Lost Cause myth," Bruce Catton wrote about the Army of the Potomac, from its beginnings after the First Battle of Bull Run to the surrender of Lee's Army of Northern Virginia in Wilmer McLean's farmhouse at Appomattox.[1]

Catton was born in Petosky, Michigan, on October 9, 1899. His family soon moved to Benzonia, Michigan, where his father, a Congregationalist minister, took a teaching position at the Benzonia Academy. The family patriarch soon became headmaster there.[2]

Growing up, Catton was used to seeing Civil War veterans. The local Benzonia post of the Grand Army of the Republic was very active and participated

Fig. 3.1. "I still think [Bruce] Catton is [the] best narrative writer who's ever written about the Civil War," historian Gary Gallagher has said. *Quoted in Clayton Butler, "Understanding Our Past: An Interview with Historian Gary Gallagher," American Battlefield Trust, https://www.battlefields.org /learn/articles/interview -historian-gary-gallagher (accessed 1 October 2018). Library of Congress, Prints and Photographs Division, courtesy Katherine Young (LC-USZ62–132904).*

in all public occasions. Many of the veterans were still young enough to be vigorous and involved as civic leaders, politicians, and businessmen. Catton listened with rapt attention and hero worship to the stories the vets told of their war experiences and wrote about them in his memoir of a Michigan childhood, *Waiting for the Morning Train.* "We looked at these men in blue, existing in pensioned security, honored and respected by all . . . ," he later wrote, "and we were in awe of them."[3]

In 1916, Bruce Catton went to college at Oberlin, Ohio, but the call to arms for World War I intervened. Steeped in patriotism and tales of military glory, Catton joined the navy, but he saw no combat. Because of the drawdown of the navy after the armistice, he was one of thousands of volunteers who were allowed to leave the service before their tour of duty expired. He chose not to return to college and, instead, picked up freelance writing assignments for the *Cleveland News.* It turned out he was very good at reporting, and he enjoyed the freedom it gave him. Catton wrote for several other papers until finally he became a Washington, D.C., correspondent for the Scripps-Howard Newspaper Enterprise Association syndicate.[4]

When World War II began, Catton was too old for military service, but his work at the capital garnered him several government posts, among them director of information for the U.S. Department of Commerce in 1945–46 and special assistant to the secretary of commerce in 1948. When the war ended, his work in Washington done, he turned to the interest that would sustain him for the rest of his life: the American Civil War.[5]

By 1951, Catton had written and published his maiden historical offering. In *Mr. Lincoln's Army*, the first volume of what became a three-book series, Catton covers the Army of the Potomac from its inception until the publicly popular but pitifully ineffective General George McClellan is finally relieved of command. Beginning at the end, Catton's prose is masterful. He is fully in command of his subject:

> The rowboat slid out on the Potomac in the hazy light of a hot August morning, dropped down past the line of black ships near the Alexandria wharves, and bumped to a stop with its nose against the wooden side of a transport. Colonel Herman Haupt, superintendent of military railroads, a sheaf of telegrams crumpled in one hand, went up the Jacob's ladder to the deck—clumsily, as was to be expected of a landsman, but rapidly, for he was an active man—and disappeared into a cabin. A moment later he returned, and as he came down the ladder he was followed by a short, broad-shouldered, sandy-haired man, deeply tanned by the sun of the Virginia peninsula, with thin, faint lines of worry between his eyes: Major General George Brinton McClellan.[6]

Treason? Panic? Incompetence? Whatever happened to McClellan, it affected the Army of the Potomac for more than two years. In *Mr. Lincoln's Army*, Bruce Catton asks his readers to consider just exactly what buried sense of personal inadequacy gnawed at George McClellan, who saw himself through the eyes of those who looked at him as a hero.

Catton also follows McClellan's men from their anxious beginnings outside Washington, through the Peninsula Campaign, and into the bloody Battle of Antietam, a narrow Union tactical victory but a monumentally lost opportunity.[7] It seemed that bumblers and braggarts commanded the hard-luck soldiers in this hard-luck army, an immense and powerful juggernaut of Union industry. Told that they were constantly on the road to a "Grand Victory," they were time and again run off that road and into a ditch. Catton makes clear, in his lovely and evocative way, that by the end of the first year, the romance of war had been tarnished beyond any effort to restore its gloss.

Catton's writing is vividly detailed, re-creating the lives of the troops who fought under McClellan from letters, diaries, and press clippings, as well as official battle reports. He approaches his epic subject like a novelist, with attention to narrative. *Mr. Lincoln's Army* is well researched and copiously endnoted, although critics found Catton's academic qualifications lacking. He had never finished his degree from Oberlin. Additionally, Catton did not write for an academic audience, but for what was then called the "intelligent public." Then, as now, academe was suspicious of a readable writer without the abbreviation of an advanced degree behind his name.

Volume 2 of *The Army of the Potomac* is *Glory Road*. It contains one of the most moving accounts of the Battle of Gettysburg ever written. The empathy Catton created for the soldiers in McClellan's army carries over as it becomes, in succession, Pope's, Burnside's, Hooker's, and then Meade's army. Catton's words help the reader see the overall victory in Pennsylvania, although a narrow one at times, through the eyes of men who had endured Fredericksburg, the Mud March, and Chancellorsville. They cared more for each other than about who was in charge of the army, and Catton skillfully captures the shift within the ranks from the exuberant volunteers of 1861 to the battle-hardened veterans of 1863.

Several reviewers consider this volume to be the best of the series because it covers the three big eastern battles in the middle of the Civil War.[8] Another powerfully evocative part of *Glory Road* can be found in the last pages of the last chapter, "End and Beginning." The setting is the dedication of the battlefield of Gettysburg, and Catton alludes to the overpowering rhetoric of one of the most famous orators of the time, Edward Everett. But Everett was not the only speaker:

> Perhaps there was meaning to all of all somewhere. Perhaps everything that the nation was and meant to be had come into focus here, beyond the graves and the remembered echoes of the guns and the wreckage of lives that were gone forever. Perhaps the whole of it somehow was greater than the sum of its tragic parts, and perhaps here, on this wind-swept hill the thing could be said at last, so that the dry bones of the country's dreams could take on flesh.
>
> The orator finished, and after the applause had died away the tall man in the black frock coat got to his feet, with two little sheets of paper in his hand, and he looked out over the valley and began to speak.[9]

Volume 3 of Catton's series is *A Stillness at Appomattox*. This is the volume that won the Pulitzer Prize for History and the National Book Award in 1953 and established Bruce Catton as a historian. "By any measure, *Stillness* is a work of great war literature," historian David Blight assessed in 2011.[10] The book covers the last year of the war and the nation that had grown war-weary in the extreme. Grant and Lee finally take center stage, and their armies—the Army of the Potomac and the Army of Northern Virginia—make up the rest of the cast.

As the death toll for the Army of Northern Virginia continued to mount, the dwindling numbers of men fighting for the Confederacy became clear to Lee and his president, Jefferson Davis. Men had been lost who could not be replaced. They had not eaten regularly for months, and their clothing was in rags. Still, the Confederacy hung on, and so did the Union:

> So much of the killing these days seemed to be meaningless. In a great battle men died to take or defend some important point, and it could be seen that there was some reason for their deaths. But there were so many deaths that affected the outcome of the war not a particle—deaths that had nothing to do with the progress of the campaign or with the great struggle for union and freedom but that simply happened, doing no one any good.[11]

In the spring of 1865, when the end finally came, the prevailing mood of the army was relief and disbelief, not jubilation. Catton never takes us to Appomattox Court House. His last scene sends Grant, "a brown-bearded little man in a mud-spattered uniform," up the road to meet Lee there:

> All up and down the lines the men blinked at one another, unable to realize that the hour they had waited for so long was actually at hand. There was a truce, they could see that, and presently the word was passed that Grant and Lee were going to meet in the little village that lay now between the two lines, and no one could doubt that Lee was going to surrender. It was Palm Sunday, and they would all live to see Easter, and with the guns quieted it might be easier to comprehend the mystery and promise of that day. Yet the fact of peace and no more killing and an open road home seems to have been too big to grasp, right at the moment, and in the enormous silence that lay upon the field men remembered that they had marched far and were very tired, and they wondered when the wagon trains would come up with rations.[12]

Bruce Catton's writing career did not end with *The Army of the Potomac*. His *Centennial History of the Civil War* includes *The Coming Fury* (1961), *Terrible Swift Sword* (1963), and *Never Call Retreat* (1965). The *New York Times* again reviewed the series, calling it "a major work by a major writer, a superb recreation of the twelve crucial months that opened the Civil War."[13] Catton also wrote two volumes on Ulysses S. Grant, *Grant Moves South* (1960) and *Grant Takes Command* (1969), as well as book-length essays of both Antietam and Gettysburg—*Antietam* (1958) and *Gettysburg: The Final Fury* (1974)—and an overall history of the Civil War, *This Hallowed Ground* (1956).

That canon, said historian David Blight, made Catton "the most prolific and popular historian of the war" in the years leading up to and including the centennial—and throughout the politically tumultuous sixties beyond. "It is rare that a historian can capture the past with both accuracy and the skills of a dramatist," Blight said, but Catton recognized "a great story is a great story." The "Catton touch" succeeded because "Catton almost always wrote about the Civil War with a sense of the epic, and of romance and an appeal to the nostalgic, as well as his own brand of realism." That "appealed to [readers'] sense of awe, of horror and beauty, of human venality as well as heroism, and even of mystery." As a result, "legions of devotees who came of age reading his books or discovered them in their mature years experienced a vicarious, if ennobling pleasure—sometimes guilty and often not—in learning about the war. They came to 'love' the Civil War in an age when war, with its unfathomable destructiveness, was no longer lovable."[14]

Catton became an editor of *American Heritage* magazine in 1954, just after *A Stillness at Appomattox* was published. He saw this as a sort of calling, saying, "We intend to deal with that great, unfinished and illogically inspiring story of the American people doing, being and becoming. Our American heritage is greater than any one of us. It can express itself in very homely truths; in the end it can lift up our eyes beyond the glow in the sunset skies."[15] Catton remained an editor until 1959 and continued to write for the magazine for the rest of his life. All the while, he "rejected the label 'popular' historian, preferring to be accepted as a writer whose beat happened to be history . . . a simple journalist applying his trade on a broader canvas."[16]

Will there be another Bruce Catton? I think that for the last half of the twentieth century, it could possibly be PBS filmmaker Ken Burns. It is no accident that Burns's main scriptwriter and the author of the accompanying coffee table books to his epic documentary series, *The Civil War*, is Geoffrey Ward, a Catton disciple and one of his successors as *American Heritage* editor.

Ward even attended Oberlin College, although he graduated instead of leaving to fight a war. Although Ken Burns claimed to have been inspired primarily by another Pulitzer winner, Michael Shaara's *Killer Angels* (1974), he also admitted to having read Bruce Catton. In an interview with the *Boston Globe*, he compared Catton and Shelby Foote. Foote became much better known after Burns's *The Civil War* (1990), but by that time Bruce Catton had been dead for twelve years. Still, it is nice to think Ken Burns channeled Catton once in a while—or at least Burns's platoon of advisors and historians did. That might have helped with the funding as well.[17]

It is no accident that after the publication of *The Army of the Potomac*, Civil War studies almost immediately forgot the armies of the western theater. Nor was it an accident that Bruce Catton was the "go-to" author for the Civil War Centennial in all of its permutations. Ken Burns enjoyed the same sort of attention when PBS presented the nine-part series *The Civil War* in 1990. Many people who participated in the Civil War Sesquicentennial are "children" of Ken Burns and bear the imprint of his work in their notions of the war. Both productions are icons of their respective ages.

But . . . there is something about *those three books*, published in 1953 as a trilogy, that set the bar for readable, perhaps brilliant, Civil War histories. Thoroughly researched, very balanced, this is written history that aspires to, and easily reaches, the standards of literature. Catton's own words still stand. In an age of instant publication and an emphasis on *new*, it is good to remember that this series has stood the test of time and aged well. The volumes should be on every bookshelf, with pride of place.

Even better, they should have your father's signature or bookplates in them, from when they were new . . . maybe sitting next to an old record set and a book of photographs.

Notes

1. Patrick Murfin, "Before Ken Burns Bruce Catton Put the Civil War on the Coffee Table," *Heretic, Rebel, a Thing to Flout* (blog), 9 October 2016, http://patrickmurfin.blogspot.com/2016/10/before-ken-burns-bruce-catton-put-civil.html.
2. Bruce Catton, *Waiting for the Morning Train* (Michigan: Wayne State University Press, 1987), 41.
3. Ibid., 189–93.
4. "Bruce Catton, Civil War Historian, Dies at 78," 29 August 1978, http://www.nytimes.com/learning/general/onthisday/bday/1009.html.

5. Ibid.

6. Bruce Catton, *The Army of the Potomac: Mr. Lincoln's Army* (New York: Doubleday, 1951), 1.

7. Ibid., 324–25.

8. David Donald, review of *Glory Road*, by Bruce Catton, 16 March 1952, http:// www.nytimes.com/1952/03/16/archives/the-trail-of-defeat-that-ended-at -gettysburg-glory-road-the-bloody.html; Scribd reviews, https://www.scribd .com/book/281003282/Glory-Road; Amazon reviews, https://www.amazon .com/Army-Potomac-Glory-Road/dp/0385041675.

9. Bruce Catton, *The Army of the Potomac: Glory Road* (New York: Doubleday, 1952), 337.

10. David Blight, *American Oracle* (Cambridge, MA: Belknap Press, 2011), 94.

11. Bruce Catton, *The Army of the Potomac: A Stillness at Appomattox* (New York: Doubleday, 1953), 167.

12. Ibid., 379.

13. The quote is used on the publisher's webpage for the book: https://www. penguinrandomhouse.ca/books/25356/coming-fury-volume-1-by-bruce -catton/9780307833075, accessed 22 February 2017.

14. Blight, *American Oracle*, 81, 96, 111, 82, 96, 104.

15. Murfin, "Before Ken Burns."

16. Blight, *American Oracle*, 100.

17. "Filmmaker and History Fan: Ken Burns," 11 May 2013, https://www. bostonglobe.com/arts/books/2013/05/11/interview-with-bibliophile-ken -burns/GfEshMNYikLnYj19vYn8SO/story.html.

4. ❀ From the Pages to the Park: The Influence of Popular Literature on Andersonville National Historic Site

Chris Barr

"Excuse me, sir. There's a problem in the cemetery: somebody has stolen a headstone."

For a young park ranger in his first few months working at Andersonville National Historic Site, a visitor reporting a stolen headstone ranks quite high on the list of things that can induce a panic. Trying my best to remain professional, I inquired what made this visitor suspect that a headstone had been stolen.

"I watched the movie *Andersonville* before I came here and—"

Before the visitor could finish the sentence, I cracked a large smile and said that Martin Blackburn is buried in the back of Section H of Andersonville National Cemetery in grave number 10,674. In the 1996 film *Andersonville*, a fictionalized version of Martin Blackburn, 184th Pennsylvania Infantry, is one of the major characters. His horrific death from scurvy at the end of the movie is one of the emotional climaxes of the story. The closing shot of the film is a dramatic close-up of Blackburn's grave, and then the camera pulls back to reveal a sea of nearly 13,000 headstones. However, the real-life Blackburn's grave is in the back of the cemetery just a few rows from the brick wall that surrounds the property. To get the shot they wanted, the production team crafted a cloth replica of Martin Blackburn's grave and slipped it over the front-row headstone of Douglas Givin of the 8th Michigan Infantry. Even fifteen years after the movie came out, this visitor remembered the grave number from the shot and come to visit Martin Blackburn's grave, only to find it isn't there.

In many ways, this is not unlike how the movie *Gettysburg* and the novel *The Killer Angels* affected Gettysburg. Stories of visitors looking for Buster Kilrain's grave at Gettysburg are legendary among park staff. But the critical

Fig. 4.1. Fans of the film *Gettysburg* sometimes ask National Park Service personnel at the battlefield about the location of the grave of Buster Kilrain, a fictional character from the movie. At Andersonville, visitors ask about the grave of Martin Blackburn, a real soldier whose death was dramatized in the made-for-TV movie about the prison. Hollywood took creative license, however, with the location of Blackburn's grave. *Andersonville National Historic Site.*

difference between Gettysburg and Andersonville is that there is a vast array of quality scholarship on Gettysburg, and tens of thousands of visitors to the site use professional tour guides and park rangers to fill in the narrative. This is not the case at Andersonville, where the movies and novels retain a strong hold on popular understanding. Andersonville is a place that relatively few historians have written about.[1]

The site is well preserved, including the stockade line and surrounding earthworks and an active national cemetery. It is also home to the National Prisoner of War Museum. However, it is in a far-flung corner of rural southwest Georgia, surrounded by a sea of cotton and cornfields, pine trees, and Georgia peanuts. Most Civil War veterans never made the trek to the isolated prison camp, and its distance from the major cities and other major battlefields or parks precludes its inclusion as a stop on most modern visitors' Civil War road trips. Historians' and Civil War buffs' descriptions of Andersonville are almost always paired with a reference to a Northern prison camp in an effort to somehow explain that Andersonville wasn't that unique. In this environment, there is a vacuum of historical information and knowledge about Andersonville. Often filling that space are works of popular fiction, with little else to challenge those understandings.

When I first started working at Andersonville National Historic Site in the summer of 2011, my supervisor told me I would need to read one or two history books, but that I also needed to put MacKinlay Kantor's *Andersonville* and Saul Levitt's *The Andersonville Trial* on my reading list. Having grown up near the historic prison site, I was aware of these works and had even read them both when I was younger. However, I found it odd that works of historical fiction would be so high on my reading list as a park employee. After all, I had my doubts that rangers and guides at Gettysburg recommend *The Killer Angels* to new employees trying to learn about the battle, so why would this be the case here? My supervisor told me that I would be surprised at just how many people made the trek to the historic prison site simply because they had read that book or had seen the play fifty years ago.

Kantor and Levitt may be the most famous writers to shape the public's knowledge of Andersonville, but they were not the first. Examples of popular

Fig. 4.2. To commemorate the 150th anniversary of the trial of Henry Wirz, the Sumter Players of Americus, Georgia, staged a production of *The Andersonville Trial* in partnership with Andersonville National Historic Site. *Photograph by Patrick Peacock, courtesy of Andersonville National Historic Site.*

literature influencing perceptions of Andersonville came as early as 1865. Henry Wirz, the commandant of the prison, was on trial for the murder of thirteen prisoners and conspiring with the leaders of the Confederate government to intentionally kill and injure prisoners at Andersonville. He was the first major Confederate official to be prosecuted for his role in the war—something that attracted a good deal of attention from a public that felt treason could not go unpunished. Wirz's was to be the first of many trials, and his guilt would be evidence against Jefferson Davis and on through the Confederate government. The media swarmed to cover the trial, and reporters from competing newspapers clamored to get the best story, often at the expense of accuracy. What the public saw as its first glimpse of the famous prison camp came through the sensational lens of the trial of the century. The Wirz trial shaped public attitudes toward Andersonville in much the same way that modern Americans saw the O. J. Simpson trial 130 years later.[2]

Moving forward, the public would only accept an Andersonville that conformed to the sensationalized version they saw in the trial, and in the late nineteenth century, Andersonville survivors, eager to earn extra income, obliged. Dozens of prisoners published memoirs between 1865 and 1915. To sell more books, each prisoner-turned-author needed a more adventurous story than his competitors. Memoirs became filled with accounts of escaping prisoners chased by the dogs or a cartoonlike villain Wirz executing scores of prisoners in cold blood. Facts—such as that only around a dozen men successfully escaped from Andersonville, or that Wirz was charged only with thirteen counts of murder, and most of those by ordering others to do it—made little difference to the authors and a public eager for more. Even one of the prison's most famous episodes and locations, the "miraculous" Providence Spring, is a product entirely of the memoir era. No prison diaries, letters, or official records from 1864 describe a spring appearing during a storm, and no diaries even mention getting water from the famous spring. But the memoirs are filled with stories of praying prisoners blessed by God with a lightning strike opening up a spring that burst forth like a geyser.

Two prisoners' memoirs emerged as the most popular: John Ransom's *Andersonville Diary*, which was not a diary at all, but a memoir he wrote as a diary to make it more compelling and marketable, and John McElroy's *Andersonville.* McElroy's memoir became especially widespread, as he served as the editor of the *National Tribune*, a platform in which he could both advertise and serialize his work.[3] McElroy's and Ransom's memoirs both remain in print and are popular sellers in the park bookstore.

As the Civil War generation passed on, Andersonville ceased to be a major topic for writers, and the public largely began to ignore the site. Even the government seemed to forget the former prison. In 1933, when President Franklin Roosevelt issued an executive order transferring dozens of historic sites and memorials from the War Department to the Department of the Interior and the National Park Service, Andersonville was the only one omitted from the list. National Park Service director Horace Albright later recalled in 1971, "To my everlasting regret, I overlooked asking for the Andersonville, Georgia, concentration camp of the Civil War and the nearby cemetery."[4] Andersonville was so forgotten in the national conscience that the country simply forgot to turn it into a national park. This would soon change.

In 1955, MacKinlay Kantor published *Andersonville*. Drawing heavily on prisoner memoirs and accounts, the novel received widespread praise from critics and became a nationwide best seller. It not only garnered Kantor the Pulitzer Prize for Fiction in 1956 but also sparked interest in Andersonville and debate over Civil War prisons. However, the book was not simply an exercise in leisurely reading and writing for the novelist Kantor. Rather, *Andersonville* was a way for Kantor to explore his own experiences in Europe in April 1945, when he visited the recently liberated Buchenwald concentration camp. How could the Germans living near the camp be completely unaware of the atrocities occurring there? What responsibility do individuals have for systematic problems? With these questions in mind, Kantor found it impossible to separate Buchenwald from Andersonville. "I've researched Andersonville prison for years, and I smelled the stink of Buchenwald. . . . I know the things men do to men."[5]

Kantor's personal experiences at Buchenwald shaped his writing style and story arc in a way that gave *Andersonville* a raw emotion that made for an engrossing read. The American public could not get enough, and more than a hundred thousand copies sold in a matter of months. The same month *Andersonville* was published, *The Diary of Anne Frank* opened on Broadway. It was not difficult for the public to read *Andersonville* with images of Buchenwald, Auschwitz, Bergen-Belsen, and an innocent young victim in their minds. The problem with Kantor's analogy was that Andersonville was not the Holocaust. Open for fourteen months, Andersonville claimed thirteen thousand lives, nearly all of them soldiers taken prisoner in battle. The Nazi regime killed millions of people in concentration camps, nearly all of them civilians, including women and children.

Such a comparison may have helped sell books, but it also created the impression that Andersonville was a concentration camp. Even Albright had used the phrase to describe the camp. If Andersonville was a concentration camp, then Confederates must be Nazis, and Henry Wirz, the German-speaking commandant of Andersonville, was Heinrich Himmler. Understandably, white Southerners did not like such a comparison. They viewed the tragedy of Andersonville as the product of uncontrollable circumstances and Henry Wirz as a martyred victim of a vengeful and victorious enemy. Evocations of the Holocaust gave many Americans a lens through which to understand Andersonville. But it also hardened the resolve of many adherents of the Lost Cause to resist what they considered revisionism and a movement against Southern whiteness in the early throes of the civil rights movement. Not coincidentally, less than a year after Kantor published *Andersonville*, the Georgia Historical Commission erected a roadside marker to Henry Wirz just outside the prison site, absolving him of any wrongdoing and noting that "he gave his life for the South."[6]

Just four years after Kantor published *Andersonville*, the prison story once again received a pop culture overhaul, this time in the form of a play in New York City. Saul Levitt's *The Andersonville Trial* debuted in New York in December 1959. Based on the military tribunal of Henry Wirz, it initially evoked the memory of the Nuremburg Trials as it forced audiences to question the responsibility of soldiers in following orders. It even played in Berlin in 1960. But Levitt's work received widespread attention when PBS produced a television adaptation of *The Andersonville Trial*, starring William Shatner and directed by George C. Scott, which aired in May 1970 to a national audience. Coincidentally, the national broadcast occurred just months after news stories of the My Lai Massacre in Vietnam broke, and the play's questioning of the extent to which soldiers should follow orders struck a nerve with the public. The production won several Emmy Awards and a Peabody Award. *The Andersonville Trial* posed a challenge for production crews. In the traditional reading of the Andersonville story, Wirz was a villain and the prosecution team was supposed to be the heroes. But when put on stage, audiences sympathized with the ailing Wirz character, and the climactic guilty verdict at the end carried a tragic weight to it.

Many modern visitors to Andersonville National Historic Site continue to cite Kantor's and Levitt's works as having influenced them to visit the park. But those works also shaped the early interpretive direction of the staff.

Congress authorized the creation of Andersonville National Historic Site in 1970, and the site formally joined the National Park Service the next year. Faced with a shortage of published histories on the site, early park planners turned to Kantor's novel, which helped shape the interpretive direction of the park and the language used in exhibits. The best example of this influence is the word *shebang*. In Kantor's novel, the term is widely used to describe prisoners' shelters. Readers get the impression that *shebang* was unique to Andersonville and that it was the only term used by prisoners to describe their huts. However, the term was not used exclusively at Andersonville, and in fact, prisoners rarely used the word in their writings. Out of thousands of pages of congressional testimony and hundreds of published memoirs, only two prisoners used the term: Thomas O'Dea and Warren Lee Goss. Kantor cited both of these in his bibliographic essay and employed *shebang* liberally throughout the novel. Park staff adopted the phrase and used it extensively in published materials and exhibits, some of which still exist today. For example, an interpretive wayside exhibit in the park near a reconstructed section of the stockade is simply titled "Shebangs."[7]

Even Levitt's script still influences the park and its story around the nation. Influenced largely by the positive portrayal of the town in the play, local theatrical companies frequently produced *The Andersonville Trial* annually in an outdoor space near the prison site. Then, in the fall of 2015, during the 150th anniversary of the Wirz Trial, the community theater company in nearby Americus, Georgia, the Sumter Players, staged a full production of *The Andersonville Trial* in partnership with Andersonville National Historic Site as part of the park's sesquicentennial programming.

Both Kantor and Levitt based their writings on previous literary works—Levitt on the journalists who covered the Wirz Trial and the official transcript, and Kantor on a dizzying array of published memoirs by prison survivors. For the most part, they remained true to these memoirs. But Kantor and Levitt tapped into a reading public on a scale that memoirs never could.

In the mid-1990s, the film *Andersonville*, which came on the heels of Ken Burns's *The Civil War*, took up the mantle of conveying the story of captivity to the public. The specific details that it portrays may be mostly fictional, but it captures the emotional essence of what it felt like to be at Andersonville. And unlike many military activities, captivity was an experience to be felt.

In this light, my supervisor's advice that I read works of fiction makes sense. These works, more than any single memoir or testimony, not only inspired a generation of Americans to visit and study Andersonville and the Civil War prison experience, but also gave them a language by which to engage with park staff and each other on the difficult issues of responsibility, accountability, and memory of the Civil War.

Notes

1. William Marvel, *Andersonville: The Last Depot* (Chapel Hill: University of North Carolina Press, 1994) and Ovid Futch, *History of Andersonville Prison* (Gainesville: University of Florida Press, 1968) remain the two most prominent scholarly histories of Andersonville, along with Robert S. Davis, *Ghosts and Shadows Ghosts and Shadows of Andersonville: Essays on the Secret Social Histories of Andersonville* (Macon, GA: Mercer University Press, 2006).

2. See John Fabian Witt, *Lincoln's Code: The Laws of War in American History* (New York: Free Press, 2012) and William Hesseltine, *Civil War Prisons: A Study in War Psychology* (Columbus: Ohio State University Press, 1930).

3. Robert Doyle, *Voices from Captivity: Interpreting the American POW Narrative* (Lawrence: University Press of Kansas, 1994), 17–22; William B. Hesseltine, *Civil War Prisons: A Study in War Psychology* (Columbus: Ohio State University Press, 1930), 247–48.

4. Horace Albright, *Origins of National Park Service Administration of Historic Sites* (Philadelphia: Eastern National Parks & Monument Association, 1971), https://www.nps.gov/parkhistory/online_books/albright/origins.htm.

5. Jeffery Smithpeters, "'To the Latest Generation': Cold War and Post Cold War U.S. Civil War Novels in Their Social Contexts," (PhD diss., Louisiana State University, 2005), 36–64, http://etd.lsu.edu/docs/available/etd-04142005-121818/unrestricted/Smithpeters_dis.pdf. Also see Benjamin Cloyd, *Haunted by Atrocity: Civil War Prisons in American Memory* (Baton Rouge: Louisiana State University Press, 2010), 131–43.

6. The "Henry Wirz" historical marker was erected in 1956 along Georgia Highway 49 outside of the Andersonville prison site.

7. "Myth: Prisoners at Andersonville Called Their Shelters 'Shebangs,'" National Park Service, 14 April 2015, https://www.nps.gov/ande/learn/history culture/myth-shebang.htm.

5. ❀ History Meets Art Meets Television: Shelby Foote and *The Civil War*

Chris Mackowski

I first met Shelby Foote in my living room. He wasn't there in person, of course—although it felt like he was, sitting in my grandmother's favorite armchair, smoking a pipe and spinning Southern yarns as though it had been perfectly natural to call on me that September evening. Like 40 million other people, I was watching Ken Burns's monumental film *The Civil War*, and the Southern gentleman with the smooth-bourbon voice and basset eyes enthralled me as he did nearly everyone else. "His accent, his beard, and his hint of sadness incline us to think there must be profound depths to his tortured language," historian James Lundberg later testified.[1]

Within six months, some four hundred thousand of us went out and bought copies of Foote's even more monumental *The Civil War: A Narrative*. Coming in at 1.65 million words, filling 2,934 pages over three volumes, the books had "something of the look and heft of the Manhattan Telephone Directory," Foote once admitted.[2]

Foote's volumes proved daunting—not only in their physical size but also in their literary style. The sentences, long and labyrinthine, unwound across the pages like the endless earthworks that once surrounded Vicksburg. I knew Foote to be a literary disciple of William Faulkner, so Foote's maximalist bent did not surprise me. He jammed *so much* into each line, each sentence, each paragraph.

Consider this 120-word maze about Confederate general P. G. T. Beauregard, which appears at the beginning of Foote's chapter "Stars in Their Courses." It has as many tributaries as the Mississippi Delta:

> In mid-May with the laurels still green on his brow for the repulse of
> Samuel Du Pont's ironclad fleet the month before, he unfolded in a
> letter to the regional commander, Joseph E. Johnston—with whom

he had shared the triumph of Manassas, back in the first glad summer of the war, and to whom, under pressure from Richmond, he had just dispatched 8000 of his men—a plan so sweeping in its concept that the delivery of the Gibraltar of the West, whose plight had started him thinking along these lines, was finally no more than an incidental facet of a design for sudden and absolute victory over all the combinations whereby the North intended to subjugate the South.[3]

As a former journalist, I found that my own literary tastes gravitated less toward Faulknerish maximalism and more toward the Spartan style of Faulkner's contemporary, Ernest Hemingway—the very model of "less is more." Faulkner I could read, but Hemingway I loved. "You go back and read some Hemingway and you can learn how to write," Foote once said of him. "If any historian in this country wrote a single page of history that had the clarity of a single page of Hemingway, that page of history would live forever."[4]

Foote was someone I wanted to love, too, because of his subject matter, but instead his writing vexed me. What frustrated me even more is that *The Civil War: A Narrative* is one of those books widely considered a modern classic. The Modern Library ranked it at number fifteen on its list of the twentieth century's one hundred best works of English-language nonfiction. The *New York Times* praised it as "a remarkable achievement, prodigiously researched, vigorous, detailed, absorbing." The *New Republic* held it up as "a model of what military history can be."[5] Columnist George Will called it a "masterpiece of national memory."[6]

Yet I just could not access the writing in any kind of way that made it meaningful to me.

Then I found a Shelby Foote Rosetta Stone.

The explosive success of Foote's trilogy, sparked by Burns's documentary, prompted the Modern Library in 1994 to issue a hardcover excerpt, *Stars in Their Courses: The Gettysburg Campaign, June–July 1863*. Shortly thereafter, I picked up the audiobook version, which Foote himself read. Hearing Foote's voice capture the rhythm of his own words made the whole thing click into place for me. The *Washington Post* once described that cadence as having "a literate flair, a mournful lyricism that underscored the human agony of battle, defeat, and victory."[7] And finally, I could see that for myself. I finally got it.

In the freshman writing course I teach, I tell my students, "Punctuation serves as a guidepost to tell your readers how to read your writing." At the heart of it, that's the key to reading Foote. Take it slow and let the punctuation guide you. His sentences hold together like small, artfully crafted monographs, with the punctuation showing you the way. Everything unfolds—especially the story. It is writing meant to be savored.

* * *

Born in Greenville, Mississippi, on November 17, 1916, Shelby Foote grew up with the Civil War all around him, but his first professional foray into the war didn't come until 1949, when he began work on a novel titled *Shiloh*. Prescient of his later Civil War trilogy, *Shiloh* is "an affecting account of the famous Civil War battle through the monologues of soldiers in the blue and the gray," said the *New York Times*.[8]

"For me, something emanates from that ground, the way memory sometimes leaps up at you unexpectedly," Foote told journalist Tony Horwitz years later, explaining his attraction to that first narrative. "If you've drawn a picture or written about a particular historical incident in a particular place, the place belongs to you in a sense. I feel that way about Shiloh, a sense of proprietorship."[9]

Foote originally pitched *Shiloh* to his publisher as a follow-up to his first novel, *Tournament* (1949). "They liked it very much but said it wouldn't sell," Foote later recounted. "Did I have something else in mind?" After two more successes—*Follow Me Down* (1950) and *Love in a Dry Season* (1951)—*Shiloh* (1952) eventually "came crippling in."[10]

"This one does it," he trumpeted to his lifelong friend, the novelist Walker Percy. "I'm among the American writers of all time—got there on the fourth book, which surely is soon enough, and at the age of thirty-five, which surely is late enough. . . . Of course I'm perfectly prepared for its nonrecognition."[11]

However, *Shiloh* went into a second printing only a week after its release, burning through an initial print run of eight thousand copies fast enough to please Foote—but still not fast enough. "Shiloh has gotten good reviews but nothing like the prominent attention I thought it would," he wrote to Percy. "I should have known better. Who gives a damn about a battle in that war?"[12]

Well, Faulkner, for one, as it turned out. "This is twice the book that *The Red Badge of Courage* is," Faulkner told his stepson, Malcolm, praising Foote's realism. "He knows what he's talking about."[13]

"You can imagine how set-up I felt when I saw that," Foote admitted years later. "But almost at once a reaction set in. What compliment will I ever receive that will compare with it? It's all downhill from here on."[14]

Another person who cared was Random House publisher Bennett Cerf. So impressed was he by Foote's novel that he asked Foote to pen a two-hundred-thousand-word history of the Civil War. Foote quickly realized the war could not be written in so few words, so he countered with a much grander idea—one that ended up growing beyond even his own panoramic expectations.

"Foote's *Civil War* was not merely a work that took twenty years of his writing life," said biographer Stuart Chapman, "but one that determined the events of the rest of his life."[15]

* * *

Foote, who started *The Civil War* in 1954, expected the project to take nine years. He finished volume 1, *Fort Sumter to Perryville*, in 1958. Volume 2, *Fredericksburg to Meridian*, followed in 1963. The final volume, however, *Red River to Appomattox*, didn't come along until 1974. "Implicit in that forecast was that Foote's work on volume III would be steady and unrelenting . . . ," explained Chapman. "Foote assumed that in spite of any fatigue developed from writing two thousand-page tomes over the last decade, sheer momentum would bear him onward." Life got in the way, though—writing residencies, fellowships, family matters—and Foote found himself "tired and unexcited about putting pen to paper." His progress dragged.[16]

"Don't underrate it as a thing that can claim a man's whole waking mind for years on end," he once told Percy.[17]

In the beginning, that certainly seemed to be the case. "All I want is to work at my book, a great sea of words with a redoubled necessity for precision," he confided to his friend. "If I don't watch it every instant, it bolts off with me, degenerates into details, conversation and discussion. Every item is worth pages and pages."[18]

The ongoing correspondence between Foote and Percy over the twenty-year project provides fascinating insight into Foote's writing process. "I have been engaged in the hardest, or at least the most tedious, occupation of my writing life. That doesn't mean I don't enjoy it; I do indeed," Foote revealed.

> What I have to do is learn everything possible from all possible sources about a certain phase or campaign, then digest it so that it's clear in my own mind, then reproduce it even clearer than it has been to me until I actually began writing about it. (The right words will invariably do that,

if they're arranged so as to bring out the essential meaning and drama. Drama *is* meaning, just as character is action, provided it is clear.)[19]

Critics would later dismiss Foote for not being able to resist a good story, no matter how it strained credulity, and his lack of footnotes seemed all the evidence they needed to prove how unserious he was in his research. "Footnotes would have totally shattered what I was doing," Foote countered. "I didn't want people glancing down at the bottom of the page every other sentence."[20] Foote always maintained that he used sources of "absolute historical integrity."[21] "Sources come in different categories," he explained in a 1970 interview.

> There are the memoirs by the men who were there, there are the reports and *Official Records of the War of the Rebellion* which were written at the time. Then there are good studies. The work of Bruce Catton has been of great help to me. Douglas Southall Freeman's books, Stanley Horn's books, Robert S. Henry, a lot of good treatments, and they serve as a guide through the labyrinth of the material, to keep you from missing any of it and really show you the salient features of the source material. . . . Regimental histories are not much count. They're always interesting to read. You pick up good little features out of them. But they were written after the war, and the war took on a sheen when it was over.[22]

He also visited the landscapes. "When I write about a battle, I first go to the battlefield in the season of the year when the conflict occurred," he revealed. "I look at the foliage, smell the land, watch the sky. Then I go home and write it up. The revelation comes in going back to the battlefield afterwards."[23]

Foote wrote longhand, with a dip pen on sheets of notebook paper, averaging between five hundred and six hundred words a day. "I revise as I go along," he once explained in an interview. "Revision is heartbreaking. I just don't like it."[24]

As he wrote, he strove to balance action and analysis, with an ongoing focus on storytelling above all. "The idea is to strike fire, prodding the reader much as combat quickened the pulse of the people at the time. You'll see," he told Percy.[25]

"The battle scenes are lit by a strange, lurid light," Foote explained, and the long analytical sections (analytical in a new sense; not explanation, but demonstration—the problems are not so much analyzed as just shown, together with their effect on the men who tried to solve them, principally Lincoln and Davis). [*sic*] I have never enjoyed writing so much as I do this writing. It goes dreadful slow; sometimes I feel like I'm trying to bail out the Mississippi with a teacup; but I like it; I like it.[26]

The Civil War turned into Shelby Foote's rabbit hole. "The further I go in my studies, the more amazed I am," he admitted. "What war! Everything we are or will be goes right back to that period. It decided once and for all which way we were going, and we've gone." He marveled over all the things the war had to teach him. "For one thing, it teaches me to love my country—especially the South, but all the rest as well," he told Percy. "I never saw this country before now—the rivers and mountains, the watersheds and valleys." He also realized, "Through a study of one of the world's most horrible wars, I am coming to an understanding of the beauty of goodness . . . as a power in the world brought to bear by men."[27]

In 1957, he told Percy, "It's a long war, but enormously rewarding." By 1972—fifteen years later—he finally saw himself on "the swift downslope of [his] narrative." "I'm truly excited about this stage of the book, a gray ragged twilight shot through with lightning flashes," he said. Yet he admitted, too, "Ai! It scares me pissless; first, to finish it, be without it; second, to turn to new work and get my hand in, all over again."[28]

He was still a year and a half away from finishing, though. "Working tail off—some of the best writing I've ever done; all I'd hoped for when the end loomed," he said in January 1973. "If this part isn't copacetic, all the rest won't matter. But it is, man, it is!"[29]

A year later, in January 1974: "I'm midway through the final chapter, feeling as if I'm about to be orphaned or left childless; can't tell which."[30]

By April of that year, 109 years after Appomattox and Bennett Place, he was into his last ten-page stretch: "I'm feeling kind of spooky. . . . Twenty years!" He mused to Percy:

What could there be left worth writing about? What's a rape or a lynching or a kidnapping compared to Chancellorsville or Booth coming busting out of the smoke in Lincoln's box? Where am I going to find another hero to put alongside R. E. Lee or Bedford Forrest? . . . My life slips onto the downslope.[31]

"I knew the last line from the time I started the book," he told an interviewer years later. "'Tell the world that I only loved America,' he said." *He* was Jefferson Davis—but after all Foote had learned about the war and about America, he might just as well have been writing about himself.

* * *

Foote "had a dry season" after finishing *The Civil War.* "I was either in a stage of exasperation or I felt there was nothing left to write," he told an interviewer. "Those twenty years didn't exhaust me physically but they exhausted me from wanting to do another long work."[32] The project had been like "swallowing a cannonball."[33] He wrote one additional novel, *September, September* (1978), then poked impotently at an idea he'd toyed with his entire writing career, *Two Gates to the City.* Meanwhile, *The Civil War: A Narrative* sold roughly forty-five hundred copies a year.[34] Biographer Stuart Chapman said, "Foote was destined to be a footnote in American literary history, known for his trilogy and for his relationship with Walker Percy."[35]

And then came Ken Burns, and everything changed.

Noted Tony Horwitz with some irony: "A private, almost reclusive man who wrote with a dip-pen and distrusted modernity, Foote had gained his greatest fame appearing before millions of television viewers in the guise of a warm and folksy raconteur."[36]

Over the course of the film's eleven-hour span, Foote appears eighty-nine times, totaling almost an hour. "Foote is a font of anecdotes," noted journalist Alyssa Rosenberg when the remastered film reaired for its twenty-fifth anniversary. She contrasted his role against that of African-American historian Barbara Fields, who "provides a big intellectual framework the audience can use to understand the war."[37]

But Foote saw context as part of his job, too—at least in his writing, even if it wasn't captured in the documentary. "My job was to put it all in perspective, to give it shape," he once said.[38] As Burns observed, "He made the war real for us."[39]

When Faulkner won the 1950 Nobel Prize, he became "the expert on the South," said Foote's biographer, Chapman; now, because of his television renown, "Foote ascended to the position." Yet Foote grew "afraid that the focus on his Civil War expertise would lead people to forget that he identified himself, first and foremost, as a novelist."[40] As Foote told the *Paris Review* in 1999, "I think of myself as a novelist who wrote a three-volume history of the Civil War. I don't think it's a novel, but I think it's certainly *by* a novelist." The ancient Greeks "considered history a branch of literature," he said; "so do I."[41]

By that point, some twenty-five years after he'd finished *The Civil War*, Foote had come to terms with his magnum opus. "My book falls between two stools—academic historians are upset because there are no footnotes and novel readers don't want to study history," he said.[42] Yet as he wrote at the end of his volume, the two types of writers were after the very same thing:

> The novelist and the historian are seeking the same thing: the truth—not a different truth: the same truth—only they reach it, or try to reach it, by different routes. Whether the event took place in a world now gone to dust, preserved by documents and evaluated by scholarship, or in the imagination, preserved by memory and distilled by the creative process, they both want to tell us how it was: to recreate it, by their separate methods, and make it live again in the world around them.
>
> This has been my aim, as well, only I have combined the two. Accepting the historian's standards without his paraphernalia, I have employed the novelist's methods without his license. Instead of inventing characters and incidents, I searched them out—and having found them, I took them as they were.[43]

"Most historians are, I am afraid, so concerned with finding out what happened that they make the enormous mistake of equating facts with truth," he told an interviewer in 1978. "No great column of facts can ever pose as the truth. Truth is order imposed on those facts; truth is the breath of life breathed into facts. It is not the facts. You can't get the truth from facts. The truth is the way you feel about it."[44]

Foote believed that narrative history came closest to getting at that truth. "You can never get to the truth, but that's your goal," he said.[45] As a writer, he believed "the rhythm and the prose communicate the truth as much as the facts."[46] For that reason, he wished more historians paid closer attention to their writing. "Why should anyone pay any attention to prose rhythms, if what he wants to do is tell the facts?" he asked one interviewer rhetorically. To another, he said it was as if historians thought learning how to write was "an onerous waste of time. . . . I just wish more of them spent a bit more time learning how to write, learning how to develop a character, manage a plot."

He maintained that "anything you can learn by writing novels—by putting words together in a narrative form—is especially valuable to you when writing history."[47] However, much to his deep chagrin, he lamented that "historians—a lot of professional historians—have a profound distrust of good writing. . . . They mistrust anything that is well written."[48]

For me, this circles back to what is perhaps this story's *seventh* degree of Civil War separation: the quote by David McCullough, narrator of Ken Burns's *Civil War*, mentioned in this collection's introduction: "No harm's done to history by making it something someone would want to read."[49]

McCullough's comment perfectly reflects Foote's sentiment, and it has deeply influenced my own approach to history. If the history isn't written well, who aside from a specialized few will read it? What benefit does it have? How can we learn the lessons it offers? How can we appreciate it?

This is why I've come to love Foote's writing so much (and McCullough's and Bruce Catton's and Stephen Ambrose's, too). They care about the history, but they care, too, about the writing. They understood the epic scope and the human nature of what they wrote about, and they tried to do it justice not by picking it apart and navel-gazing it to death but by respecting it through their language.

Foote, as a role model, has stayed with me all these years to remind me that a historian must "bring [a] story alive—in other words, to bring it closer to the truth. I'm not talking about making it livelier than it was. I'm just talking about some attempt to make it as lively as it was."[50]

Notes

1. James M. Lundberg, "Thanks a Lot, Ken Burns," *Slate*, June 2011.
2. Douglas Martin, "Shelby Foote, Historian and Novelist, Dies at 88," *New York Times*, 29 June 2005; Jay Tolson, ed., *The Correspondence of Shelby Foote and Walker Percy* (New York: W. W Norton, 1997), 194.
3. Shelby Foote, *The Civil War: A Narrative*, vol. 2, *Fredericksburg to Meridian* (New York: Random House, 1963), 428.
4. James Newcomb, "WKNO Presents a Conversation with Shelby Foote," in *Conversations with Shelby Foote*, ed. William C. Carter (Jackson: University of Mississippi Press, 1989), 126.
5. Martin, "Shelby Foote."
6. Lundberg, "Thanks a Lot, Ken Burns."
7. Adam Bernstein, "Shelby Foote Dies; Novelist and Historian of Civil War," *Washington Post*, 29 June 2005.

8. Martin, "Shelby Foote."

9. Tony Horwitz, *Confederates in the Attic: Dispatches from the Unfinished Civil War* (New York: Vintage, 1998), 154.

10. Shelby Foote, "The Art of Fiction No. 158," interview by Carter Coleman, Donald Faulkner, and William Kennedy, *Paris Review*, no. 151 (Summer 1999), http://www.theparisreview.org/interviews/931/the-art-of-fiction-no -158-shelby-foote.

11. Tolson, *Correspondence*, 72.

12. Ibid., 89–90.

13. Ibid., 220.

14. Ibid., 200.

15. C. Stuart Chapman, *Shelby Foote: A Writer's Life* (Jackson: University Press of Mississippi, 2003), 272.

16. Ibid., 195–96.

17. Tolson, *Correspondence*, 101.

18. Ibid., 99.

19. Ibid., 111.

20. W. Hampton Sides, "Shelby Foote," in *Conversations*, 233.

21. John Griffin Jones, "Shelby Foote," in *Conversations*, 183.

22. John Carr, "It's Worth a Grown Man's Time," in *Conversations*, 30.

23. Bob Mottley, "Writer Critical of 'Tokenism' in the South," in *Conversations*, 19.

24. Foote, "Art of Fiction No. 158."

25. Tolson, *Correspondence*, 114.

26. Ibid., 109.

27. Ibid., 111, 101, 107.

28. Ibid., 115, 163, 168, 164.

29. Ibid., 169–70.

30. Ibid., 183.

31. Ibid., 184.

32. Foote, "Art of Fiction No. 158."

33. Bernstein, "Shelby Foote Dies."

34. Sides, "Shelby Foote," 233.

35. Chapman, *Shelby Foote*, 257.

36. Horwitz, *Confederates in the Attic*, 151.

37. Alyssa Rosenberg, "How Two Very Different Historians Defined Ken Burns' 'The Civil War,'" *Washington Post*, 11 September 2015.

38. Bernstein, "Shelby Foote Dies."

39. Martin, "Shelby Foote."

40. Chapman, *Shelby Foote*, 266–67.
41. Foote, "Art of Fiction No. 158."
42. Ibid.
43. Shelby Foote, *The Civil War: A Narrative*, vol. 1, *Fort Sumter to Perryville* (New York: Random House, 1958), 815.
44. Newcomb, "WKNO Presents," 124.
45. "Obituary: Shelby Foote, 88; Author of Civil War Tome," *New York Times*, 29 June 2005.
46. Newcomb, "WKNO Presents," 125.
47. Foote, "Art of Fiction No. 158."
48. Newcomb, "WKNO Presents," 125.
49. David McCullough, "The Course of Human Events," Jefferson Lecture in the Humanities, 2003, accessed 19 August 2012, https://www.neh.gov/about/awards/jefferson-lecture/david-mccullough-biography.
50. John Graham, "Talking with Shelby Foote," in *Conversations*, 70.

✳ "Rejoice. The Civil War Series for
All Time": Remembering Those
Silver Books from Time-Life

Meg Groeling

I began as a child with Bruce Catton, but by the time I was an adult, I was pretty sure that anything else I needed to know about the Civil War was contained in the magical book series published by Time-Life.[1] Those slim, silver volumes defined a Civil War buff in the 1980s. You subscribed to the series and then waited eagerly for the 8.5-by-14-inch metallic-pearl volumes to arrive in the mail, all snug in their corrugated cardboard wrappers. They were wonderful to the touch—hardbound in heavy, dull sterling leatherette. The covers were embossed, and each had, impressed in the middle, an oval image of what awaited inside. Every volume contained 176 pages and hundreds of illustrations from Time-Life's unparalleled collection of images of the Civil War period. The books felt substantial and held up well when carried to school, to reenactments, to the houses of friends, or into the bathtub for a long soak and an uninterrupted hour of reading. At least, mine did.

Published as *Time-Life: The Civil War*, the series began in 1983 and continued until 1987, following the Civil War from *Brother against Brother: The War Begins* to *The Nation Reunited: War's Aftermath*. A few titles focused on specific topics, such as the home front, soldier life, and irregular operations, but most volumes concentrated on battles and campaigns, presented in chronological order. When it was created, there was nothing like it on the market.

This series began as a spin-off of the series run in *Life* magazine to mark the 1961 Civil War Centennial. *Life* published a six-part series on the war, copiously illustrated by such artists as George Woodbridge (who also illustrated for *Mad* magazine), Isa Barnett, Louis Glanzman, and Tom Lovell. The company also reproduced a companion booklet in 1963 called *Great Battles of the Civil War*, which included most of the Woodbridge-Lovell work.[2] It was forty-eight pages long and sold for one dollar, including shipping. Both

Fig. 6.1. The Time-Life
Civil War series, while
now outdated, still looks
handsome on the shelf
of any Civil War library.
Chris Mackowski.

the magazines and the booklet are still considered to be excellent sources for
uniform information, but that hardly compares to the impact they had on
many impressionable young historians and war buffs alike when they first
came out. They are somewhat difficult to get now because most were read
cover to cover so many times that they simply disintegrated.

The positive reception to the magazine series lay fallow—but was not forgotten by the parent company. Harris Andrews, deputy editor for Time-Life
in Alexandria, talked about the genesis of the idea for the series in a C-SPAN
Book TV talk in 1998. He explained that Time-Life Books began to talk about
doing a series on the Civil War at about the same time that it issued a reprint
series of Civil War memoirs by the late Shelby Foote. The popularity of both
the earlier magazines and the memoirs encouraged the publishing company to
design its twenty-eight-volume narrative, complete with pictures. According
to Andrews, it was, and has continued to be, one of the better-selling publications ever released by Time-Life Books.[3]

Because the individual volumes were sold by direct contact subscription,
with the promise that a book would be delivered every two to three months,
the publishing schedule was tight. A staff of fifteen to twenty people did

the research in-house, and outside writers were hired to provide the text. Of special interest was the yearlong collecting of archival images. Twenty-five team members went to every major Civil War collection available, from the Library of Congress and the National Archives to small private collections in homes and local museums. This resulted in Time-Life then housing the largest collection of Civil War images and artifact resources anywhere in the world.[4]

The narrative style chosen for the original silver books did not allow for any sort of deep analysis of any one topic. Essays on specific topics were presented pictorially and were written by a diverse variety of authors. Once in a while, "Editors of Time-Life Books" would author a volume, but most were presented under the byline of a single author. Historian-writer-editor William C. "Jack" Davis credited much of the success of the series to the vision of editor Gerald Simons. Simons identified the Time-Life target buyer for the Civil War series as a parent, particularly a father, purchasing it for his teenage children—particularly a son. When asked how the series has held up, historiographically speaking, Davis said:

> If it were being done today perhaps/probably our current focus on diversity and minorities would result in more attention being paid to women's participation and that of blacks including slaves, freemen, and soldiers, probably separate volumes on women and blacks, and more on Indians, Hispanics, etc. And with the current interest in "memory studies," I suspect more attention would be paid to the postwar "Lost Cause myth," down to today's issues like the Confederate flag, etc.[5]

Writer Champ Clark's son responded to queries concerning the series by explaining that his father had been a huge Civil War buff, dragging his family all over eastern battlefields for summer vacations. Champ Clark Sr. had "loved working on those books" and would be pleased that there is still interest in them today.[6]

How has the series held up technically? In a C-SPAN Book TV talk in 1998, Kirk Denkler, another deputy editor for Time-Life in Alexandria, talked about the extensive use of images in a Shelby Foote–authored volume. Denkler discussed a couple of pictures taken by Timothy O'Sullivan in much detail, including one of General J. E. B. Stuart holding his plumed hat. There are two photographs, and the one that is a better image of the hat, which is the subject of Foote's writing, is not the better of General Stuart. Almost twenty years later, this subject might have been considered, but the solution would have been a simple digital tweak, not the elaborate reimaging that resulted from the editorial discussion. Ordering prints in huge formats would not have been necessary today, nor would cropping and editing be seen as a violation of someone's original work. And yet for many readers, the silver Civil War series was their first introduction to photographs on glass plates and to box cameras, ambrotypes, and dual images. Names like Timothy O'Sullivan and Alexander Gardner became better known, as did the pictures that were drawn by Alfred Waud, Edwin Forbes, and Winslow Homer, to be published in newspapers like *Harper's Weekly*. These images formed lasting impressions of the war for most readers. Additionally, this was the first time younger readers were exposed to pictures of dead people and of prison camp inmates. Today, if I were to ask readers to admit that these images still linger on, haunting our collective memories of the war we know only from books, I suspect many of us would nod in assent, and then we would all talk over each other trying to tell about our favorites.

The old silver series spawned a lot of other titles by Time-Life. In fact, it became a sort of industry for the publishing house. Time-Life used many of its in-house authors to create such series as *The Old West*, *World War II*, *Wings of War*, *The Third Reich*, and many, many other titles. Still, the company always managed to circle back to the original topic—the Civil War. From 1981 onward, it produced thirty volumes of a *Collector's Library of the Civil War*; *The Civil War: A Narrative*, a reprinted and illustrated version of Shelby Foote's original 1958 series; *Echoes of Glory* (1991), about Civil War military equipment and arms, along with a Civil War atlas; and *Voices of the Civil War* (1996–98), reproducing letters and diary entries from Civil War participants.[7]

According to Davis, the Time-Life company had a habit of assigning a few of their series titles to people with no special knowledge of the subject. These writers had been editors at the company but had other areas of historical expertise.[8] These "historians" learned on the job, and with the help of some heavy editing and the style model Time-Life insisted on for any individual series, the books developed into the familiar niche-oriented product available by mail subscription.

Neil Kagan, former publisher and managing editor of Time-Life Books, explained the differences and similarities between a reporter for *Life* magazine and a researcher for Time-Life: "If you work for a magazine, you are a reporter, and if you work for books, you do research." Nevertheless, the core culture of the organization stressed authentic research and authentic reporting—finding the stories, and then finding the stories behind the stories that are within the archives, the artifacts, and the photographs. In this way, *Time* magazine, *Life* magazine, and Time-Life books are entertaining and informative to readers. "Get it right, make it interesting," said Kagan.[9]

At the end of 2003, Time-Life was sold by Time Inc., the print division of Time-Warner, and now operates as Direct Holdings Americas Inc. while continuing to retain the Time Life brand.[10] The silver series (perhaps *platinum* would be a better adjective) can be bought for as little as a penny from online booksellers. And most current reviews for the books give them five stars. "Amazing pictures," "excellent and scholarly," "a great gift," "fabulous," "my husband loves them," "Civil War buff's delight" are only some of the phrases used in describing the series. The reaction people usually exhibit when the series is mentioned is one of misty reminiscence. Almost everyone seems to have either owned at least a few volumes or checked them out of the library. They sat on my bookshelf, no matter where I lived, with pride of place for many years. They are there now.

Whenever I need to find a quick piece of information, check a map, look for the provenance of an image, or research any of the other myriad things that come up when writing about something specific, they remain my go-to source. I use them much like a Civil War encyclopedia. The internet might be faster, but the silver books have the benefit of familiarity that comes with being old friends. I have also loaned them to the sons and daughters of friends who needed something to help them get a handle on a war long past. I have had them returned to me with pages bookmarked and an occasional note stuck here or there, and always with a heartfelt "Thank you."

If our personal interest in the Civil War were to be charted over a lifetime, there would be high points and low points for most of us. Interests ebb and flow as life hands out education, relationships, families, careers . . . but for most of us who remain at least moderately involved in American history, the thought of those books—those silver, leathery books with bright, glossy pages and memorable words, packaged in brown cardboard and addressed to our childhood homes or first apartments—still sparks a sweet, warm memory in our hearts.

Notes

1. The quotation used as the chapter's main title is from a book review by A. Smith on Amazon, 2 January 2017, https://www.amazon.com/Fight -Chattanooga-Chickamauga-Missionary-Ridge/dp/0809448165/ref=pd _sbs_14_2?_encoding=UTF8&psc=1&refRID=XNVAYZ478CHWE 59HYE2C.

2. roundshot, "Life Magazine Civil War Illustrations," Authentic Campaigner, 23 September 2007, http://www.authentic-campaigner.com/forum/archive /index.php/t-13071.html.

3. "Time-Life Civil War Books," C-SPAN Book TV, 15 December 1998, https://www.c-span.org/video/?117469-1/timelife-civil-war-books.

4. Ibid.

5. William C. Davis, email message to the author, 13 February 2017.

6. Champ Clark, email message to the author, 28 January 2017.

7. "About Us," Time Life, http://timelife.com/pages/about (accessed 18 February 2017).

8. Davis email.

9. "Time-Life Civil War Books."

10. "About Us," Time Life.

7. ❈ James McPherson's *Battle Cry*

Ryan Longfellow

It's a scene repeated innumerous times over the past fifteen years I've worked for the National Park Service: A visitor strolls through the doors of the Chancellorsville Battlefield Visitor Center.[1] He spends a few minutes talking to the seasonal interpreter or intern at the information desk, who highlights a few key exhibits in the museum, recommends the orientation film, and lets him know the walking tour schedule. The visitor browses through the exhibits and then stands awestruck by the more than seventeen thousand names in the Reflection Room, deciding whether he can express his emotions in the small black notebook meant for visitor comments. Starting to understand the gravity of the situation that transpired at the Battle of Chancellorsville, he postpones his driving tour to attend the park guide's presentation of the Jackson Wounding Walking Tour. The guide wows him with storytelling ability and insightful analysis. Captivated by his experience, the visitor returns to the bookstore and asks the manager, "What is the best book on the entire Civil War?" It is an easy question—one asked repeatedly. The answer is simple: James M. McPherson's *Battle Cry of Freedom: The Civil War Era*.

McPherson adroitly weaves the complex factors of America's antebellum economy, politics, and westward expansion into a cohesive and flowing narrative that culminates with the bloody conflict. Starting in the aftermath of the Mexican-American War, he convincingly establishes slavery as the principle cause of the Civil War. Chapters titled "Mexico Will Poison Us," "An Empire for Slavery," and "Slavery, Rum, and Romanism" leave little doubt about the fundamental source of sectional strife.[2] Once the war begins, McPherson brilliantly ties the battlefield to the political home front, while also recounting the gradual march toward emancipation and ultimately the Thirteenth Amendment. This artful telling of the complete story, centered on slavery, sets McPherson's work apart from other one-volume accounts of the Civil War.

Over the last thirty years, no other book on the American Civil War has met with such national approval as *Battle Cry of Freedom*. It satisfied the rigorous demands of academic historians and simultaneously captured the attention of the general readership of the United States. The book's popularity and success transformed McPherson into a nationally recognizable historian and presented him with opportunities to shape the country's understanding of the past, including the places where Americans experience their heritage in person—Civil War battlefields. Since its publication in 1988, *Battle Cry of Freedom* has become *the* book on the American Civil War.

Another historian's tragic misfortune catapulted McPherson to the national forefront of Civil War history. *Battle Cry of Freedom* is part of a larger series, the *Oxford History of the United States*, initially edited by C. Vann Woodward and Richard Hofstadter.[3] Woodward, McPherson's graduate advisor at Johns Hopkins University, first recruited the forty-year-old Princeton University professor to cover the period between 1865 and 1900. After all, McPherson's early career included *The Struggle for Equality: Abolitionists and the Negro in the Civil War and Reconstruction* and *The Abolitionist Legacy: From Reconstruction to the NAACP*, which made him an excellent candidate to cover the period from Reconstruction to the end of the Gilded Age. Meanwhile, Woodward selected Willie Lee Rose, author of *Rehearsal for Reconstruction: The Port Royal Experiment*, to complete the late antebellum and Civil War installment of the series. However, in the years after agreeing to write for the Oxford series, McPherson's interests shifted to the Civil War era. Then, in 1978, Rose suffered an incapacitating stroke and could no longer complete her task. McPherson asked to change his topic in the Oxford series.[4] The change transformed James McPherson, as well as America's understanding of the Civil War.

The task of writing a one-volume history of the Civil War era was immense. McPherson needed to condense the fifteen-year period from 1850 to 1865, which has tens of thousands of books written on it, into a single narrative. Complicating this undertaking, McPherson's contract for *Battle Cry of Freedom* was the second he'd signed in 1976. The first resulted in *Ordeal by Fire: The Civil War and Reconstruction*, published in 1982.

Once McPherson began work on *Battle Cry*, he did not focus on writing the whole book, but rather "one chapter, or section of a chapter, at a time." McPherson described his writing process: "I would sit down to read the sources, secondary and primary, for each part of a chapter, and then write that part before going on to repeat that process many times until I had a complete book."[5] Of all his published work, McPherson concluded, "It's the book that took the most effort to write."[6]

Once the book was complete, it needed a title. "The one that I liked best, but nobody else liked at all, was American Armageddon," he recalled. McPherson's wife, Patricia, suggested using the popular George Root song "Battle Cry of Freedom" as the title. After some initial skepticism that the title might appear biased, the editors relented. McPherson readily acknowledged that his wife "is entitled to the credit for the title."[7]

Twelve years after he signed the contract, Oxford University Press released the book. The academic community received it warmly. In a field rife with nit-picking criticism, most academic journals contained positive reviews. A review in the *Journal of American History* by Dudley T. Cornish of Pittsburg State University declared that McPherson's work is "a magisterial book unsurpassed in Civil War literature" and "sets new standards in historical writing." The book contains more than fifteen hundred footnotes, prompting Cornish to note that "McPherson's documentation is thorough, his bibliography excellent."[8] Rice

Fig. 7.1. This stylized lithograph of the Battle of Antietam by Kurz and Allison, published in 1888, became the cover artwork for *Battle Cry of Freedom*. *Library of Congress.*

University's Harold M. Hyman, writing for the *American Historical Review*, asserted, "This book is vigorous, engaging, informative and emphatic."[9] Michael P. Johnson, of the University of California, Irvine offered an extremely flattering review of McPherson's work in *Reviews in American History*. Johnson identified McPherson's central theme, "What unifies the Civil War era as defined in *Battle Cry of Freedom* is not war, but the politics of slavery," and he acknowledged the literary characteristics of McPherson's narrative: "The central plot—packed with dangerous reverses and close calls—is the political and military defeat of the defenders of slavery." Johnson continued, "*Battle Cry of Freedom* is no ordinary history book. Weeks on best-seller lists and a record-shattering auction for the paperback rights have already established *Battle Cry of Freedom* as America's choice for Civil War history"—a choice Americans eventually made by the hundreds of thousands.[10]

The acclaim McPherson's book garnered led Richard Slotkin of Wesleyan University to compare it to Bruce Catton's immensely popular series, *The Centennial History of the Civil War*. In *American Literary History*, Slotkin stated, "McPherson's account is less rich in anecdote, folklore, and apocalyptic poetics."[11] This is certainly true, as the pages dedicated to the clashes between armies are limited. The Battles of Fredericksburg, Chickamauga, and Wilderness combined for more than eighty thousand soldiers killed, wounded, or missing, yet for combat of those engagements, McPherson dedicates just two pages and a map. Only the fighting of Gettysburg receives extended attention, at eleven total pages.[12] Despite the brevity of battlefield drama, Slotkin conceded, "the loss of emotional power is more than compensated by greater clarity and depth of analysis."[13]

While academics lauded the book's magisterial research and the centering of slavery as the principle cause of the war, the public approved of its accessibility. Hugh Brogan of the *New York Times* proclaimed, "It is the best one-volume treatment of the subject that I have ever come across. It may actually be the best ever published." Brogan attributed this to one of "McPherson's many talents as a historian . . . his literary skill."[14] John F. Harris of the *Washington Post* called it "a blockbuster" and credited McPherson's success to "the collision of an academic passion he has followed for the past three decades and a public that . . . has turned a war that ended 123 years ago into a resurgent vogue."[15] According to the National Endowment for the Humanities, "*Battle Cry of Freedom* helped launch an unprecedented national renaissance of interest in the Civil War."[16] The book's popularity caused it to spend sixteen weeks of 1988 on the *New York Times* best seller list.

And that would prove to be only the beginning for *Battle Cry of Freedom.* The following year saw much higher accolades. With its release in paperback, the book returned to the *New York Times* best seller list for an additional twelve weeks. However, McPherson speculated that the book's immense commercial success was only the first part of a "one-two punch" that catapulted him "into a visibility beyond the normal academic world." The second part, and what McPherson described as "frosting on the cake," occurred when Columbia University awarded him the Pulitzer Prize for History.[17]

The Pulitzer Prize turned McPherson into a leader in the field of Civil War history for both academics and the mainstream America. During the 129th annual American Historical Association meeting, Clemson University's Vernon Butler described the transformative power of McPherson's work as it approached its twenty-fifth anniversary. "By the 1980s McPherson was a well-respected historian, influential in his field, but not widely known outside of the academic community," he stated. "This changed with the publication of *Battle Cry of Freedom: The Civil War Era.*" Butler continued, "He is, and has been, the face of the history profession to the general public for nearly three decades."[18] Dr. Judith Hunter, who was a teaching assistant for McPherson when *Battle Cry of Freedom* was released, observed that the "students had clued in" and that the class needed "to be moved to the largest lecture hall on campus." Speaking about the impact on McPherson, she noted, "It was a time of great transition for Jim, who had been working along very steadily, and all of a sudden the popularity, the *New York Times* best-selling stature of his book, revolutionized how he was regarded by the students and the university."[19] Between the book's time on the best seller list and "especially the Pulitzer," McPherson joked, the experience "taught me that I can't respond positively to every request for speaking engagement or public appearance. I've had to learn how to say no."[20]

The increased fame the Pulitzer Prize created propelled McPherson to an advisory role on Ken Burn's *The Civil War,* appearances in several *Civil War Journal* episodes, and many other Civil War programs that reached a broad audience. Furthermore, many of McPherson's post–*Battle Cry* books, including *For Cause and Comrades: Why Men Fought in the Civil War* (1997), *This Mighty Scourge: Perspectives on the Civil War* (2007), *Tried by War: Abraham Lincoln as Commander in Chief* (2008), and *The War That Forged a Nation: Why the Civil War Still Matters* (2015), acknowledge his Pulitzer on either the front or back cover.

The heightened renown also gave him access to alter the interpretation of the war on the battlefields themselves, where Americans, and others, most often experience their history. McPherson's popularity made him the ideal historian to join the preservationists' cause of protecting and expanding hallowed ground. McPherson served on the board of the Association for the Preservation of Civil War Sites. Then-president Gary Gallagher called him "the number-one Civil War historian in the country."[21] After the association merged with another preservation organization and became the Civil War Preservation Trust, McPherson continued to serve as a board member into the twenty-first century.[22] Additionally, in 1991, the U.S. Senate appointed him to the Civil War Sites Advisory Commission, which helped identify threatened battlefields and suggested strategies for their protection.[23] He aided the Conservation Fund in its efforts to purchase and preserve battlefield land by contributing to its fund-raising publications. In 1994, as president of Protect Historic America, he defended Manassas National Battlefield in front of Congress from the possibility of encroachment by the Walt Disney Corporation.[24] This effort helped thwart Disney's ambitions to build a history-themed amusement park and ultimately expanded the size of battlefield. In the first decade of the twenty-first century, he helped prevent Walmart from locating a store on what had been the "nerve center of the Union Army during the battle of the Wilderness."[25] McPherson joined other historians in petitioning Walmart to relocate, wrote at least one newspaper article, contributed comments for other articles, and was prepared to take the stand as an expert witness in court, before Walmart relented and moved its proposed building site.

Not only did McPherson help increase public landholdings of Civil War battlefields, he also contributed to the reinterpretation of those sites. In 1998, the National Park Service (NPS) held a conference in Nashville to discuss the state of Civil War landscapes and attempt to increase their inclusivity. The meeting concluded that NPS did an excellent job at interpreting the battles; however, its interpretation was "biased racially and socio-economically" by not including the larger context. To close the gap between expectations and implementation of a more inclusive narrative, the NPS proposed to "institute training and symposia to allow staff to address issues of causation and result with confidence."[26] It held its first symposium at Ford's Theatre in 2000. The NPS invited several key historians, including McPherson, and published the symposium commentary in *Rally on the High Ground: The National Park Service Symposium on the Civil War.* While McPherson's contribution focused on soldier motivation, which he had written about in his book *For Cause and Comrades*, it was his nationwide recognition for *Battle Cry of Freedom* that had led to his invitation in the first place. Despite the success of *For Cause and*

Comrades, including the Lincoln Prize, Robert K. Sutton, then-superintendent of Manassas National Battlefield, ignored the book and instead mentioned *Battle Cry of Freedom* in his introduction, acknowledging it as "the finest one-volume work on that war."[27]

McPherson's contribution to the NPS did not stop with his symposium appearance but continued through the sesquicentennial commemoration. He teamed up with historian Ed Bearss as the keynote speaker for Antietam's 150th anniversary. When Antietam National Battlefield chief historian Ted Alexander introduced McPherson, the first book he mentioned was *Battle Cry of Freedom*, and he described McPherson as "a Pulitzer Prize–winning author, beyond being a great historian."[28] McPherson also spoke at the commemoration of Lincoln's Gettysburg Address in 2013. Gettysburg College president Janet Morgan Riggs, in her introduction, described *Battle Cry of Freedom* as "a book that riveted its readers and put the Civil War back into the public's consciousness."[29]

More than three decades after Oxford University Press first published McPherson's work, it remains at the center of Civil War scholarship. The continued discussion of *Battle Cry of Freedom*'s significance speaks to McPherson's authoritative yet accessible narrative and its impact on the historical community and America's understanding of the pivotal event of its past. As the United States concluded the sesquicentennial remembrance of the Civil War, Gettysburg College invited McPherson to speak at the Civil War Institute's summer conference. Peter Carmichael, director of the institute, stated, "I believe the *Battle Cry of Freedom* stands as the single best volume on the Civil War."[30]

McPherson's *Battle Cry of Freedom* remains as relevant and important today as when it was published. As the country debates the symbolism of Confederate monuments and their place in modern America, it becomes more important to understand the root cause of the war and the story of how the nation survived. While there are better books on Civil War memory, McPherson's *Battle Cry of Freedom* is essential to gaining the necessary context of the era. So the next time you walk into a national park's bookstore, do not ask what the best book on the Civil War is—just imitate the seven hundred thousand people who have already purchased *Battle Cry of Freedom*.[31] It is *the* book on the Civil War era.

Notes

1. The Chancellorsville Battlefield Visitor Center is located at 9001 Plank Road, Spotsylvania, VA 22553. Renovated in 2014, it is a necessary visit

for anyone interested in the American Civil War. It is open from 9 A.M. to 5 P.M. daily, except Thanksgiving, Christmas, and New Year's Day.

2. James McPherson, *Battle Cry of Freedom: The Civil War Era* (New York: Oxford University Press, 1988), 47, 78, 117.

3. The contributions to the *Oxford History of the United States* have met with remarkable success. According to the Oxford University Press website, "The series includes three Pulitzer Prize winners, a New York Times bestseller, and winners of the Bancroft and Parkman Prizes."

4. James McPherson, interview by Susan Swain, C-SPAN2 Book TV, 10 July 2000, 9:35, https://www.c-span.org/video/?158168-1/battle-cry-freedom.

5. Rachel Toor, "Scholars Talk Writing: James M. McPherson," *Chronicle of Higher Education* 62, no. 24 (February 2016): 24.

6. McPherson, interview by Swain, 4:23.

7. James McPherson, interview by Peter Carmichael, C-SPAN3 American History TV, 15 June 2015, 13:38, 14:53, https://www.c-span.org/video/?326750-2/discussion-civil-wars-end-aftermath.

8. Dudley T. Cornish, review of *Battle Cry of Freedom: The Civil War Era*, by James McPherson, *Journal of American History* 75, no. 4 (March 1989): 1333–34.

9. Harold M. Hyman, review of *Battle Cry of Freedom: The Civil War Era*, by James McPherson, *American Historical Review* 95, no. 1 (February 1990): 261.

10. Michael P. Johnson, review of *Battle Cry of Freedom: The Civil War Era*, by James McPherson, *Reviews in American History* 17, no. 2 (June 1989): 215.

11. Richard Slotkin, "'What Shall Men Remember?': Recent Work on the Civil War," *American Literary History* 3, no. 1 (Spring 1991): 131, https://www.jstor.org/stable/489736.

12. McPherson, *Battle Cry of Freedom*, 571–73, 672–74, 724–26, 653–63.

13. Slotkin, "'What Shall Men Remember?'" 131.

14. Hugh Brogan, review of *Battle Cry of Freedom: The Civil War Era*, by James McPherson, *New York Times*, 14 February 1988.

15. John F. Harris, "Civil War Sensation: James McPherson and His Bestselling 'Battle Cry,'" *Washington Post*, 29 August 1988.

16. Amy Lifson, "Awards & Honors: 2000 Jefferson Lecturer, James McPherson Biography," National Endowment for the Humanities, accessed 28 January 2018, https://www.neh.gov/about/awards/jefferson-lecture/james-mcpherson-biography.

17. McPherson, interview by Swain, 5:50.

18. Vernon Butler, "Career of James McPherson," C-SPAN American History TV, 8 January 2012, 4:00, 5:40, https://www.c-span.org/video/?303793-1/career-historian-james-mcpherson.
19. Judith Hunter, "Career of James McPherson," ibid., 27:15, 27:32.
20. McPherson, interview by Swain, 7:00.
21. "Starting a National Movement from Scratch: An Interview with Historians Gary Gallagher and Bob Krick," American Battlefield Trust, 18 July 2017, https://www.battlefields.org/learn/articles/starting-national-movement-scratch.
22. McPherson, interview by Swain, 17:40.
23. Lifson, "Awards & Honors."
24. James McPherson, "Civil War Battle Sites and Disney Theme Park," C-SPAN2, 21 June 1994, 3:45:05, https://www.c-span.org/video/?58037-1/civil-war-battle-sites-disney-theme-park.
25. "Walmart Controversy Fully Resolved," American Battlefield Trust, 17 October 2018, https://www.battlefields.org/learn/articles/walmart-controversy-fully-resolved.
26. "Holding the High Ground: Principles and Strategies for Managing and Interpreting Civil War Battle Landscapes," *Proceedings of a Conference of Battlefield Managers*, Nashville, August 24–27, 1998, 9–10.
27. Robert K. Sutton, ed., *Rally on the High Ground: The National Park Service Symposium on the Civil War* (Washington, DC: Eastern National, 2001), https://www.nps.gov/parkhistory/online_books/rthg/chap4.htm. In 2000, Robert K. Sutton served as the superintendent of Manassas National Battlefield. In 2007, he became the chief historian of the National Park Service.
28. Ted Alexander, "150th Anniversary of the Battle of Antietam," C-SPAN3 American History TV, 16 September 2012, 1:55, https://www.c-span.org/video/?307917-113/150th-anniversary-battle-antietam.
29. Janet Morgan Riggs, "150th Anniversary of the Gettysburg Address," C-SPAN3 American History TV, 19 November 2013, 41:18, https://www.c-span.org/video/?316201-1/150th-anniversary-gettysburg-address.
30. McPherson, interview by Carmichael, 2:30.
31. Butler, "Career of James McPherson," 4:15.

8. ✤ There's More to Groom Than Gump: The Civil War Writings of Winston Groom

Richard G. Frederick

In the company of Civil War scholars, there's a heresy that goes like this: "After 150 years, everything's been written. Every battle has been described in minute detail; every general, colonel, and major has a biography; every diary by anyone living at the time has been published; every interpretation possible has been foisted on readers by some scholar somewhere. There is simply nothing left to write about the Civil War that hasn't already been minutely dissected and explained at length."

Or something like that.

The enterprising reader, however, even one steeped in the vast historiography of the thing, can easily fill a few shelves (or half a Kindle) with great books on the Civil War published in just the past few years. How is it possible to reconcile the "everything's been written" notion with the continuing flow of worthy tomes?

The best explanation for this seeming contradiction lies in the quality of the best work now published. The authors of these volumes are accomplished stylists, often novelists, whose talents reveal vivid descriptions of battles and strategies and in-depth characterizations of the principals involved. Couple that talent with modern research capabilities, which include access to a universe of official reports, memoirs, and other published and unpublished records, and out comes a library's worth of fabulous storytelling and often recast historiography. Foremost among these writers may be academic historians like James McPherson and Gary Gallagher, but also in the vanguard are talented amateurs. At the front rank of these is Winston Groom.

"Winston Groom attains the stratospheric narrative heights heretofore enjoyed by such popular-history masters as Bruce Catton, Shelby Foote and

James M. McPherson," the *Mobile Press-Register* once said. Maybe such praise is to be expected from Groom's hometown newspaper, but others have chimed in with similar comparisons, such as the *Minneapolis Star-Tribune*: "Groom has established himself unquestionably as heir to the late Shelby Foote with this commanding, thoroughly entertaining narrative account."[1]

I first encountered Groom when I was preparing a course on the United States in Vietnam and came across his excellent novel *Better Times Than These*, based on his personal experiences in the war. This led to an exploration of some of his other fiction, including a modestly received novel called *Forrest Gump*. After the movie came out, of course, everyone had heard of Winston Groom. I decided to inform my colleagues about his overall excellence in an informal lecture I called "There's More to Groom Than Gump." I didn't know the half of it!

In 1995, Groom published the first of what has become a trio of nonfiction books on the Civil War, *Shrouds of Glory: From Atlanta to Nashville; The Last Great Campaign of the Civil War. Vicksburg, 1863* followed in 2009, with *Shiloh, 1862* continuing the chronologically backward march in 2012. With the exception of one novel published in 1998, Groom eschewed fiction during this period to write about World Wars I and II, as well as an account of the Battle of New Orleans in the War of 1812.

Each of the Civil War books is meticulously researched, and it shows. But there are no stuffy moments or indications of pedantic renderings over historians' disagreements. Each book is replete with heroes and goats, searing descriptions of battle, and clear explanations of strategies and tactics, of what went right, what went wrong, and why.

My personal favorite in the Groom trilogy is the first, *Shrouds of Glory*. It is a story dominated by John Bell Hood, a character whose career course might well have been crafted by a novelist. A rising star in the Confederate army, he attained the rank of major general in his early thirties. He was engaged to be married to the most beautiful of Southern belles, Sally "Buck" Preston. But the personal loss that was so much of the story of the Civil War, for both individuals and families, hit Hood especially hard. He literally gave an arm and a leg for the Confederate cause. Shrapnel wounds at Gettysburg led to the nearly complete loss of movement in his left arm.

Shortly after recovery from this loss, he saw action at Chickamauga and was severely wounded by a bullet in the right thigh, resulting in the amputation of the leg. He would later be dumped by his fiancée. But the one-armed, one-legged soldier persevered. Just before the Battle of Atlanta, he replaced General Joseph E. Johnston as commander of the Army of Tennessee when the politicians in Richmond tired of Johnston's dithering before Sherman's Union forces.

After the fall of Atlanta in the fall of 1864, Hood devised a daring plan to advance his Confederate forces north of Sherman's main Union army into Tennessee. The ill-fated move received the approval of a desperate government in Richmond, but later commentators have almost universally assailed it as unrealistic and quixotic. In *Ordeal by Fire*, for example, James McPherson labels it a strategy "of boldness born of desperation," saying that Hood "intended to take his 39,000 men all the way through Tennessee and Kentucky to the Ohio River and then turn eastward to join Lee in Virginia. To achieve these goals, all he had to do was march 700 miles and defeat Thomas's 60,000 men in Tennessee, beginning with two veteran corps under John Schofield stationed near Pulaski."[2]

McPherson's skepticism is not entirely shared by Groom. He posits the endeavor through the mind of Hood, and the whole idea does not appear so ridiculous. Improbable, perhaps, but not absurdly so. Hood's men were veterans, and many were from Tennessee—they looked forward to fighting on and liberating their home soil. In addition, he expected large-scale reinforcements from regiments in Louisiana and Texas.

The march into Tennessee began auspiciously. While General George H. Thomas occupied Nashville, about half his army under John Schofield was encamped farther south in Tennessee. Hood's larger force managed to flank Schofield in late November and was emplaced between him and Nashville. As Schofield's troops began the short trek between the hamlet of Spring Hill and the town of Franklin, about thirty miles south of Nashville, Hood was poised to cut off the Union force along the pike and claim a decisive victory. Hood later averred he issued orders to accomplish this feat of military prowess.

"At least that's what he said he said," Groom tells us, then goes on in spirited fashion:

> What transpired from that moment through the next twelve hours—
> and a great deal did—became one of the great mysteries of the war,
> ranking right up there with Lee's infamous "lost orders" during the
> Antietam campaign. From that day until well into the next century
> when the last of the participants was dead and buried, what became

known as the Spring Hill affair prompted countless charges, counter-charges, rebuttals, speculations, rumors, analyses, and acrimonious debates. What is certain is that somewhere between "I told you to do it" and "No, you didn't," "I ordered it done" and "I never understood," the federal army managed to elude the lovely trap Hood had designed. As event piled upon event, a visible truth was put to the old adage, "For want of a nail the shoe was lost . . ." and so on.[3]

A short time later, Groom succinctly summarizes reasons for the failure of twenty-five thousand Confederates to crush Schofield's paltry advance party of fifty-five hundred troops. "As will be seen, that this was not accomplished remains one of the greatest might-have-beens of the Civil War, surrounded by dark accusations of drunkenness, cowardice, stupidity, debauchery, treachery, dereliction of duty, drug use, ennui, lying, failure to follow instructions, and failure to give them—characteristics thus far so foreign to Confederate armies as to inspire disbelief."[4] Groom goes on to discuss the circumstances surrounding each of these accusations and to whom they applied in an entertaining explication of foolhardiness bordering on tragedy.

The brilliant center of the book lies in a chapter titled "An Indescribable Fury," describing the Battle of Franklin on November 1864. Following units and individuals on both sides into battle, as well as including the observations of townspeople, Groom captures the sights, sounds, smells, and feelings of a furious onslaught in a way few other writers have. In twenty-five pages, he manages to pile up such horrors and carnage that by the end of the chapter the reader can hardly believe anyone survived the battle on either side. In fact, Hood had the dubious distinction of losing the most men (and the most generals) on the Confederate side in any single-day battle of the Civil War.

Schofield hastened to Nashville to join Thomas, and at this point, any realistic element of Hood's plan began to dissolve in wispy hopefulness. Pressing forward to meet Thomas at Nashville appears a suicidal strategy, but as Groom points out, Hood had no real choice. The battle was delayed by Thomas's temerity based on faulty reports of Hood's strength, but after persistent goading from Ulysses S. Grant, Thomas moved, the battle was fought, and the outcome was a foregone conclusion. Hood's shattered remnants reeled back into Mississippi, and the Army of Tennessee dissolved.

Fittingly, Groom gives Hood the last word on throwing his men against an overwhelming enemy force: "It was more judicious that the men should face a decisive issue, rather than retreat—in other words, rather than renounce the honor of their cause, without having made a last and manful effort to lift up the sinking fortunes of the Confederacy." This existential-sounding observation goes along nicely with the quote from Jean-Paul Sartre from which the book derives its title: "I buried death in the shroud of glory."[5]

Groom's other two Civil War books, on Shiloh and Vicksburg, are similarly filled with the observations of a masterful writer. The literary qualities we usually associate with fiction are all there—pithy characterization, attention to detail, irony, pathos, wit, and a tendency to see how a pattern of mundane events fits into a larger landscape of meaning. And there's more!

A terrific bonus from reading the three books in tandem, in the reverse order of publication, is that they constitute a nearly complete history of the western theater of operations during the war. *Shiloh, 1862* does not begin at Pittsburg Landing in April 1862, but rather with a consideration of earlier events of the year in places like Forts Henry and Donelson and the conflicting strategic plans of Generals Halleck and Grant concerning western operations. In establishing the context for the battle, Groom also writes the early history of the war in Tennessee.

Similarly, the volume on Vicksburg, the longest and thickest in detail, covers not only the siege but also major events from Shiloh in April 1862 to the fall of Vicksburg in July 1863. Along the way is a good deal of naval history, including the victory at New Orleans, followed by naval strategies on the Mississippi, successes and failures (mostly the latter) around Vicksburg, and personal imbroglios, such as the one involving Admiral David Farragut and his meretricious foster brother, David Dixon Porter. Again, Groom provides a fine mix of battle writing; information about weapons and tactics; biographies of interesting individuals such as the Philadelphian John Pemberton, who commanded the Confederate troops at Vicksburg; and personal observations from contemporaries, both military and civilian.

In two of Groom's three Civil War books, the author tells the story of a young boy visiting a Civil War cemetery with his grandmother whose father fought at Vicksburg. "Why did they do it?" the kid asks. "Why did they die?"

The old lady's rather prosaic response: "Oh, I don't know, son. I suppose they'd all be dead by now anyhow." They might all be dead, but their stories are as alive as ever when retold by writers like Winston Groom, who, by the way, has a much more eloquent answer to the kid's question. The final words of *Shiloh, 1862* (and of this essay) seem most fitting: "When they [Civil War veterans] were gone, the trust they passed along remained exceptional in the

American character, a willingness to fight, and to die if necessary, for ideas instead of conquest and territory, and for ideals rather than plunder and pillage—an exalted distinction by any measure."[6]

Notes

1. Both review blurbs can be found on the publisher's promotional page for the book: http://www.penguinrandomhouse.com/books/72311/vicksburg-1863-by-winston-groom/9780307276773/.
2. James M. McPherson, *Ordeal by Fire: The Civil War and Reconstruction*, 2nd ed. (New York: McGraw-Hill, 1992), 463.
3. Winston Groom, *Shrouds of Glory: From Atlanta to Nashville; The Last Great Campaign of the Civil War* (New York: Grove Press, 1995), 137.
4. Ibid., 138.
5. Ibid., 278, ii.
6. Winston Groom, *Shiloh, 1862* (Washington, DC: National Geographic, 2012), 402.

9. ❊ A Conversation with Jeff Shaara

H. R. Gordon

N ovelist Jeff Shaara talks about the process of writing historical fiction, his responsibility as the writer, and the impact the genre has had on pop culture and battlefield preservation.[1] A *New York Times* best-selling author, Shaara has written seven books related to the American Civil War—*Gods and Generals* (1996) and *The Last Full Measure* (1998), which bookend his father's Pulitzer Prize–winning *The Killer Angels* (1974), and a tetralogy on the western theater, *A Blaze of Glory* (2012), *A Chain of Thunder* (2013), *The Smoke at Dawn* (2014), and *The Fateful Lightning* (2015)—as well as a novel of the Mexican-American War, *Gone for Soldiers* (2000).

Fig. 9.1. "My goal is not to offer a complete detailed history of the event," Jeff Shaara said in the introduction to his novel *A Blaze of Glory*. "I hope that when all is said and done, you will accept that what I am trying to offer you is a good story." *Quoted from Jeff Shaara,* A Blaze of Glory: A Novel of the Battle of Shiloh *(New York: Ballantine Books, 2012), xi–xii; photo by Olivia Cowden, courtesy of Jeff Shaara.*

GORDON: How do you see the role of historical fiction as it relates to pop culture?

SHAARA: Well, I think historical fiction can have a much broader appeal to a much wider audience than a typical history book. So often, history books, which are naturally enough written by academic historians, are written in a way that might appeal to a professor or a classroom, but when you bombard a reader with names, dates, places, facts, and figures, sometimes you just lose people. And I think the nature of historical fiction—what I interpret it to be—is good storytelling. If you can tell a good story with good characters, you can capture an audience in a way that a simple history book can't.

GORDON: So, do you meet a lot of people who aren't necessarily historians but simply history lovers who have come into a Civil War fascination because of your books or other historical fiction?

SHAARA: Most definitely. A bunch of people have said this to me, they'll say: "I hated history in school. I left school and never wanted to touch a history book again, but somebody handed me a copy of one of your books and I sort of said, 'Oh, I don't know if I want to read this.' I reluctantly read it. Now I'm bringing the kids to Gettysburg." I've heard that a lot.

To me, it's an enormous compliment that someone would gain an interest in the subject matter by reading something I wrote. I mean, that's wonderful right off the bat. But I think it goes back to what I said before: it's about storytelling. You can appeal to people who think they have no interest—people who are reluctant to even look at the subject matter—and suddenly they're caught up in it. I have heard that a great deal.

GORDON: I think it's interesting with kids even, with books like the "Magic Tree House" series [by Mary Pope Osborne]. It's historical fiction and it brings children into an interest in history. Your books are geared toward adults, obviously, but do you see a need to bring children into this fascination with history beyond just what they're learning in school?

SHAARA: Oh, absolutely. But I'll correct one thing you said. I started out naturally assuming that my books would be for an adult audience, and then I began to hear from parents and a whole range of different kinds of people—homeschool parents, for example, who are using my books to teach history to their kids in their home. Then I began to hear from high school teachers who were using the books in their literature and history classes as a way of teaching the subject by getting away from the normal, typical history book. I've heard of this a lot, and I was really surprised by it. I had no expectation of it. I hear from teachers and their students who will write my website and . . . I've heard from a lot of college students that say, "I'm majoring in history because I read your books." I mean, that's an amazing thing to hear! I didn't set out to write books for the "tween" audience—not kids, not grown-ups—but they found the books. I didn't find them. They found me. Again, it's a huge compliment. And really—I'll be redundant here—I think it goes right back to the theme of storytelling.

GORDON: Walk me through your process as a writer. On your website, you said it takes a year of research and six months of dedicated writing to crank out a book. So what's the process for you to get into the characters and place? Where do you begin with that?

SHAARA: The research is the larger part of it, because I am dealing with real events, real people. Typically, historical fiction will take you to a real place with fictitious characters. What I do is take you to the real place with mostly real characters, and that's a very risky thing to do, because some of these are some of the most significant figures in our history, and people have very definite ideas about who these people are, and it's up to me to make sure I get that right.

And also I'm putting words in the mouths of these people, so they had better be the right words. And by that I mean they had better be true to the character—to who that person was. You can't have Robert E. Lee using some kind of modern slang. The whole story would fall apart, and it should.

So part of the research is to get to know these people on a personal level, and the only way to do that is by hearing their voices—and by that I mean reading their diaries, memoirs, collections of letters. Most of the research I do is personal. Right now, I'm working on a story about Korea. The advantage for that is that I have living veterans to talk to, so I can get their points of view firsthand, which is a huge advantage. But when you're going back to the Civil War or even earlier, obviously you don't have that advantage, and so I do a tremendous amount of searching for this kind of original material. Today a lot of it is available that wasn't available in my father's day. Because of the internet [and] because of so much renewed interest in the Civil War, a lot of these old, rare, out-of-print sources have been reprinted, and it makes it much easier to find things.

But that's the first thing. Do the research. Get to know the characters. I don't always know who the voices in my books are going to be. I'll have some kind of an idea. I'll guess who the characters might be. Then in the process of the research, I might stumble upon somebody else. That's happened a bunch of times. It's a process of discovery for me when I'm doing the research for just who the voices are going to be in the story.

After that, another part of the research is to walk the ground. Go to these places. See them. I don't mean to sound mystical, but walking in the footsteps of these characters makes a huge difference. The illustration that I use is if I'm going to describe a hill to you that the character is walking up with a musket in his hands, walking into the guns of the enemy, it's really better if I've walked that hill rather than just seen a picture of it in a book. I put myself there when I'm writing, and it really is important to me to see the ground. To walk to ground and get a feel of what it's like. And not just the battlefields—the homes, the houses where these people lived. All of that is a big part of the research.

Once that's done—and *all* done, because one thing I don't do is research, write, research, write; that won't work for me at all—once all the research is done, only then will I feel comfortable sitting down and telling the story. In every book I've done, the same thing happens: I stare at the blank computer screen of page one, chapter one, and I just stare at the blank screen, and I'll start to write a couple words. [I write] a few more words, and then it's like the faucet turns on. And it just comes.

I know—because I've talked to a lot of writers—I know how fortunate I am. I feel like I'm in the story. I'm just telling you what I see and what I hear. That process—I hate to use the word *magic*—but that's what it feels like. And sometimes that faucet turns off, and I'm done. You can't force it; you can't make it happen. It's time to get up and walk away.

I will write things that I'll go back and read tomorrow and don't remember writing. That's part of how I edit myself. I'll read tomorrow what I wrote today. Clean it up, fix it, make it a little bit better if I can. Sometimes I'll read things and think, "Wow, this is pretty good. I wonder who wrote that." And realize it's me!

It's a strange process, and I certainly don't expect a lot of people to understand that. But a lot of writers I've talked to absolutely understand it. That flow—if you can get into that flow and that rhythm—it's a wonderful thing.

GORDON: You said you never really do this "research, write, research, write" kind of thing, but do you ever find yourself staring at that blank page and you think, "I don't know what to put here"? And you find yourself needing to go back and do more research or needing to go visit a place that you didn't during your initial research period?

SHAARA: Once in a while, but mostly, going back to the research is for fact-checking. I want to make sure I get the date right. I want to make sure I spell something right. What river were they crossing on a certain day? I have an enormous advantage because I am writing about real events.

People ask me a lot if I make an outline before I write, and the answer is no, because the history is my outline. I'm working within actual events and a real timeline and a real calendar, so that's my outline. So I will sometimes go back and do some fact-checking, but for the most part, once I've done the research, the story is there. And because the history is real, it's not like I have to make up a bunch of stuff or that I get stumped by suddenly having a blank in my head because I don't know what's going to happen next. What happened next is already well documented.

GORDON: So, in the same vein, do you find yourself when you're doing the research—walking up that hill, looking at a particular museum, working on a particular project—saying, "Oh! I'd like to go here next!" or "I'd like to work on this!" and seeing things that spark your interest for the projects you'll do next?

SHAARA: Oh yeah, that's happened to me! I'll give you the perfect example, talking about the Civil War. I was going to do a trilogy set on the war in the West, and I wrote the first two of those, which are *Blaze of Glory*, which is about Shiloh, and the second, *A Chain of Thunder*, which is [about] Vicksburg. I intended to do the third book dealing with Sherman's march from Atlanta to the end of the war in the Carolinas. Well, that ended up being the fourth book. As I joke to a lot of audiences, I ended up writing a four-book trilogy because I suddenly realized that the third book of that set needed to focus on Chattanooga and Lookout Mountain. I didn't know this going in. I didn't realize just how much history there was that was so important, not just to the Civil War but to the characters I was dealing with, mainly Sherman. Sherman was the principal character all through the series, and I realized I couldn't skip that area. So I stopped after the Vicksburg book and went to Chattanooga, to Lookout Mountain and Chickamauga—that whole area. And I added that book in the middle of the whole process, which was a surprise. I had to convince my publisher that we needed to expand this to four books instead of three, and that's not always an easy thing to do.

GORDON: So, something you just said echoes what you said in the American Battlefield Trust's In4 video you did on historical fiction.[2] You said that your job isn't necessarily just about the history. It's about storytelling. What do you see as your responsibility as the storyteller to the reader, the history, and the historians who work with this material daily?

SHAARA: Well, that's a really good question. I've actually discussed this with a lot of academic historians. I've talked to them about the history when I'm doing my research—the minutiae to make sure I'm getting all the little details right. And I've had these guys say to me, "Why are you doing this? You don't have to do this. You're writing fiction. You can do anything you want. You don't have to dot the i's and cross the t's and get everything exactly correct."

My father, with *The Killer Angels*, he fudged the timeline a little bit here and there. He sort of shaped the history to fit the story he wanted to tell. Because nobody was looking over his shoulder fifty years ago, it didn't really matter—but there's a whole bunch of people looking over my shoulder now. And I've found two things. First of all, I've found something I said before about getting the characters right: people care. People have actually said to me, "How dare you put words in the mouth of Robert E. Lee." Well, OK. I have to accept that challenge. If I dare to do that, they'd better be the right words. I can't play games with history or just make up so much stuff that the character loses his credibility. Because people care about that.

Well, that's one part of it. The second part of it is when I talk about the schools. When I began to hear from teachers that are using my books in their classroom, I realized if they're going to use a novel to teach history, they have to have confidence that the facts are straight; they're counting on teaching an accurate history. That adds to the responsibility immediately when I hear that. I think, "OK, get it right. Don't make dumb mistakes." And I do occasionally, but I correct them, and readers will catch little things, and I fix them because I feel a real strong responsibility, because if kids, particularly, are reading this stuff and learning about the history by reading my novels, they need to be accurate.

So that I think makes me different from a lot of people writing historical fiction, because I really do feel that obligation to get it right.

GORDON: I think that's a good obligation for you to feel, especially for someone of your prominence in the Civil War community. So, you said you feel these people are looking over your shoulder. You mentioned the teachers. Who is fact-checking you and making sure that you're doing justice to the history?

SHAARA: Well, the best way I can answer that is to compare what I'm doing with what my father did. In my father's day, there was no internet. He did not have a website, so he had no idea who was reading his books. Once in a while, he'd get a letter that someone would send to his publisher, and they would forward it to him. So once a month he may hear from somebody. I'm getting fifteen or twenty emails *a day* through my website from people who are reading my books, and many times they're just very complimentary, which is a very nice thing. But every now and then, somebody takes me to task, or they want to argue a point that I'm making, or they're simply pointing out a mistake, which I deeply appreciate because then we fix it. We correct the mistakes in the subsequent printings of the books or for the paperback.

But something my father never knew was how many people were reading his work or paying attention—but I hear from those people on a daily basis. I have to be careful here because I'm not just writing to please everybody else, but at the same time, those people are out there, and because I hear from them on a regular basis, that automatically just pumps me up. [I think,] "Let's make them happy." Instead of making them mad at me, let's tell the right story. I like getting compliments! I like when someone sends me an email and tells me they really liked my book. So let's have more of that!

GORDON: What do you see as coming first: pop culture turning people on to historical fiction, and that getting people turned on to a love of history? Or do you see the historical fiction coming up from a small group of people who have a love of history and love of the written word, and that inspires things like movies and TV shows and other pop culture things?

SHAARA: That's a tough question. I think it's the latter, and I'll tell you why. I can name three people who are primarily responsible for the resurgence of interest over the last twenty-five years in the Civil War. Those three people are Ted Turner, Ken Burns, and my father. My father wrote *The Killer Angels*. It was Ken Burns who read it, and he's told me and is quoted on the cover of *The Killer Angels* that reading that book inspired him to do his Civil War series that brought a huge number of people into the subject. And then it was Ted Turner who was approached by Ken Burns, who said, "You have to read this book." Ted Turner read *The Killer Angels* and put up twenty-two million dollars of his own money to make the film *Gettysburg*.

[It was] that combination of those three people. My father was gone; he died in 1988. The stars lined up in about 1990. And all you have to do is ask the tourism people in Gettysburg how their numbers jumped after that two-to-three-year period in the early nineties. All three of these things came together and caused a huge uptick of interest in the Civil War.

Now, I came later. And I'm not comfortable taking credit for being part of that group; I think other people would tell you I probably am. But that's how it started. So I think the answer to your question is the second part. It's a small group of people and a particular time and place, and for whatever reason it worked, and boy, did it work. I've talked to so many writers who never would have been writers—if it wouldn't have been for that period of time, they would have never been drawn into writing about the Civil War.

GORDON: It makes sense that writers have said, "This is why I'm doing this," because you've even said people have approached you and said they are majoring in history because of your books. Do you see the genre of historical fiction itself playing a role in people visiting the battlegrounds or other important sites? Does the genre and its readers have a responsibility to battlefield preservation?

SHAARA: Absolutely. It goes right back to the people I meet all the time—and sometimes it's on a battlefield or sometimes it's in a bookstore in Cincinnati or something. The people will tell me that because they read *Blaze of Glory*, they go to Shiloh; they want to see it. I tell people to go to Shiloh because it's one of those magical places that's almost completely in its original state of preservation. And the other two places that are closest to that are probably Gettysburg and Antietam.

And I think my books and other novels in historical fiction have definitely brought a whole group of people into the battlefield preservation world that might never have understood that value. They might never have understood just how important this ground is.

GORDON: So, do you see responsibility on the writers and readers of the genre to help preserve these sites and fight for them?

SHAARA: Certainly. There's another way of looking at it. I'm the writer sitting at the visitor center at Gettysburg doing a book signing. Somebody wanders in there who's never heard of me or any of my books. Never heard of Ken Burns. Never heard of any of that. Walks in there. Takes a look at my book. Well, why is this person there in the first place? He's there because maybe he happened to drive past a sign that says, "Gettysburg National Military Park." And he thinks, "Well, maybe I should take a look at this thing." Well, if there's nothing for him to look at, or if there's a Taco Bell in the middle of a cow pasture, he's probably not going to stick around.

And I keep saying "him." Please forgive me for that, but it's a family. I love the expression about "the back-seat people." The front-seat people are looking at all the cannons and the monuments, and you got the people in the back seat going, "Ugh, can we go to McDonald's now?" If you can get those people to start paying attention and start looking around, you've just doubled your audience. The way you do that is by having a cool place for them to see and go to. Not by reading it to them from a book, not by showing them a map. It's got to be something tangible—a place where they can walk the ground.

To me, there's definitely a connection between that storytelling, which might attract somebody who may or may not have any interest in the subject matter, and very often, they take that next step, but the next step has to be there. There has to be something appealing for them to take that next step.

GORDON: I remember going to Gettysburg as a child with my parents and thinking how cool it was to walk on that same ground.

SHAARA: There are tons of places like that, but it goes right back to preservation. If you want the place to be there, it has to be protected.

GORDON: Absolutely. So, as a closing question, where do you see the future of the genre and the interest in the Civil War heading? Has it had this big spark and it's just going to draw back now, or is it igniting and it's going to just fly forward? How do you envision that?

SHAARA: That's a tough question. Certainly, the 150th was sort of a peak time. I was in Gettysburg for a week during that time doing book signings, and I met people who said, "Well, I've never been here before." And they picked the 150th anniversary to come to the battlefield! People said the same thing: "I'll be back." How many more of those kinds of events can gather up people with a collective enthusiasm? A lot of it might depend on a film. . . . Beyond that, it's very cyclical.

I did a four-book series on World War II because, a few years ago, World War II was hot, and maybe I contributed to that. I don't know. Maybe it's the other way around. Now World War I is getting a little hot. I wrote a book on World War I about ten years ago, but I've noticed it's getting an uptick now because of the 100th anniversary of World War I. So sometimes things come up because of the calendar. Sometimes there are things you can't predict. I mean, look at *Saving Private Ryan*. When that movie came out, it inspired a huge interest in World War II just like *Titanic* inspired a huge burst of interest in the *Titanic*. Sometimes it will be totally unpredictable.

But I look at the Civil War . . . and especially with the kids. I actually said to a bunch of kids during my book signing in Gettysburg, "You will be back here for the 200th. I will not be. But you will be, and you'll remember this, and you'll bring your grandkids back to the 200th." That gives me goose bumps thinking about that. It's not that far away; it's not eternity. Those kids—that's who will keep it alive. So I think as long as we can *keep* appealing to the younger audience. The younger audience will not be younger eventually. They'll have kids of their own, and that just keeps it going.

Notes

1. Jeff Shaara, interview by the author, 11 November 2016.
2. Jeff Shaara, "The Civil War in Four Minutes: Historical Fiction," American Battlefield Trust (ABT), https://www.battlefields.org/learn/videos/historical -fiction. At the time the video was produced, ABT operated under its former name, the Civil War Trust, which is now a subsidiary under ABT's larger umbrella.

10. ❦ *Cold Mountain* and the Itch of Interest

Paul Ashdown

I'm sure my friend David Madden, novelist and founding director of the United States Civil War Center, was right when he claimed "interest in the Civil War has been monumentally stimulated by popular culture events and works far more than by academic history books."[1]

Notice he said *academic* history, leaving plenty of room for Bruce Catton, Shelby Foote, Carl Sandburg, and the other old book club favorites whose multivolume tomes, a bit musty now, still have their place of honor on many home library shelves even when they are brushed aside by the professional historians. And when he said *events*, he included just about anything that makes news, from battlefield reenactments to flag controversies and maybe a political convention or two. *Works*, as well, leaves space for *Birth of a Nation*, *Gone with the Wind*, and even *Abraham Lincoln: Vampire Hunter*.

In a recent book, *The Tangled Web of the Civil War and Reconstruction*, Madden listed those things he believed have reinvigorated the public history of the war over time, including eight popular novels, one of which, *Cold Mountain*, is my personal favorite. He didn't include *Cold Mountain* among his personal choices for the twelve *best* Civil War fiction works, but I will leave it to the literary scholars to debate the merits of *Cold Mountain* against novels by Mark Twain, William Faulkner, and Robert Penn Warren. Even what constitutes Civil War fiction is part of that debate. Madden, for example, would include *Huckleberry Finn* and *All the King's Men* as anticipating the war or shaping its legacy.[2]

My interest in *Cold Mountain* as a popular work contributing to public history, myth, and memory began in the summer of 1997 after a friend with no interest in the Civil War extravagantly praised the novel and insisted I read it. I'm told Civil War fiction usually doesn't attract many readers, so when I get an endorsement from someone who doesn't frequent roundtables or military parks, I take notice. A map on the inside cover shows Cold Mountain in North Carolina to be about seventy-five air miles from Knoxville, where I live. Knoxville and the surrounding area has quite a lot of Civil War history. General James Longstreet marched an army into the outskirts of town from Chattanooga and attacked a Knoxville fort defended by General Ambrose Burnside on November 29, 1863, sustaining 813 casualties in twenty minutes. A Civil War novel set in the western North Carolina mountains, by contrast, didn't sound promising to one who also had prowled the battlefields at Chattanooga, Shiloh, and Stones River. The ostensible obscurity of Cold Mountain turned out to be what drew many readers to the book, however.

Any reservations I might have had about the book quickly were disabused when I read Charles Frazier's magnificent first chapter. A badly wounded Confederate soldier, known only as Inman, languishes in a Raleigh hospital, contemplating desertion. He steps through a window (the word appears seventeen times in the first five pages, so we know the novel will have something to do with perception) and starts walking west toward his home below Cold Mountain, where he hopes to find Ada Monroe, the preacher's daughter he left behind when he marched off to war several years earlier.

The laconic Inman doesn't say too much about the fighting he's seen at Malvern Hill, Sharpsburg, Fredericksburg, Petersburg, and other slaughter-houses, nor does he have much regard for the generals, politicians, and planters who shaped the course of the war. It's not that kind of book. What we do learn is that Inman is done with fighting, but fighting is not done with him until he finally is shot down in an encounter with the Carolina Home Guard on Cold Mountain just months before the war ends.

Cold Mountain is a historical novel with not much history-book history even though the story is based on a real character, the author's distant ancestor William P. Inman. Frazier told journalist Tony Horwitz that all he knew about Inman could have been written on the back of a postcard. That's a lot more than most Americans know about any of their progenitors, and what cannot be known must be imagined. As Inman's mythic quest developed, Frazier thought of the *Odyssey* as the book's "literary ancestor." A journey narrative put the author in good company with writers from James Joyce to John Cheever to Cormac McCarthy. Jack Kerouac, Gary Snyder, and the Beats surely would have appreciated some of the *Dharma Bums* mysticism announced in an epigraph attributed to the Tang Dynasty poet Han-shan, whose name means Cold Mountain: *Men ask the way to Cold Mountain. Cold Mountain:*

there's no through trail. A second epigraph, by Darwin, is just as unlikely in a Civil War novel: *It is difficult to believe in the dreadful but quiet war of organic beings, going on in the peaceful woods, & smiling fields.*[3]

Inman's journey is, like Odysseus's, a transformative trek away from war and toward an inward grace. To help him get there, Inman, a reflective high-country farm boy, has only a battered copy of William Bartram's *Travels* through the Carolinas, some Cherokee myths picked up from his friend Swimmer, snatches of scripture and hymnody learned in Cold Mountain meetinghouses, and a fragment from Heraclitus as translated by Inman's hospital roommate Balis, a former University of North Carolina student, before he died. Just what Frazier is up to by outfitting Inman with such an odd collection of literary and philosophical fragments is not initially clear. Perhaps Inman's struggle reflects the general incoherence of the war, which possesses meaning in spite of itself if only we could divine a pattern from the shards of experience.

All very literary, indeed, but what about Civil War history? To satisfy my curiosity about the largely implied historical backstory, I wrote a short book with a map that roughly follows Inman's meandering journey back home and lots of footnotes. With some digging, I learned much more about the Civil War by coming at it from Frazier's less traveled direction in western North Carolina. After *Cold Mountain* won the National Book Award, eventually selling some 4 million copies, the book was made into an Oscar-winning eponymous film (mostly shot in Romania!) written and directed by Anthony Minghella, and then an opera composed by Jennifer Higdon, a Pulitzer Prize winner who grew up near Knoxville. This quixotic epic made its own peculiar journey through large and, more important, diverse audiences. Each medium brought something and someone new to the story.[4]

At one level, *Cold Mountain* is a traditional star-crossed wartime romance, but it beckons us to step through one of those first-chapter perceptual windows into a deeper, richer story. It goes against the grain of Civil War fiction in a number of striking ways. For one thing, the hero, Inman, is a Confederate deserter, although no coward. Before the war, we learn, "he had never been much of a one for strife. But once enlisted, fighting had come easy to him." Armed with his shotgun-barreled LeMat revolver, Inman kills at least ten men on his circuitous five-hundred-mile journey home, feeling like "God's most marauded bantling" long before he gets there. He might have had a lot in common with Wild Bill Hickok, Matt Dillon, Lucas McCain, Paladin, Johnny Yuma, and all the other troubled gunfighters who tried to put the war behind them in popular TV western series a century after the Civil War. Strife is hard to avoid when you have a talent for killing.[5]

That trope is encompassed by the more important matter of Confederate desertion and the struggle for survival on the home front, however. By the end of the war, more than a hundred thousand soldiers had deserted from Confederate armies. Almost 23 percent of that number deserted from North Carolina. As early as May 1863, General Robert E. Lee had warned that the departure of North Carolina soldiers was so "serious an evil" that unless it could be stopped, the Confederate cause would be in jeopardy. The North Carolinians were missed because the state had sent a disproportionately large contingent of soldiers into the war, and they accounted for about a fourth of all Confederate deaths. Like Inman, the North Carolinians gave their all for the cause, and many survivors, when they had had enough, just walked away. What motivated this "farewell to arms" is a principal theme of the story and is not something taken up by many Civil War novelists.[6]

Ada Monroe's struggle to survive on a farm below Cold Mountain is another principal theme. She is on her own after the death of her father and must rely on others until she gains the knowledge and confidence to live independently as the war closes in. Charleston born and bred, the cultured Ada is nearly helpless until she is rescued by Ruby Thewes, an uneducated waif with an abundance of common sense. Their bond transcends class as they learn from one another. I came to see Ada's story, told in alternate chapters, as a kind of counternarrative to Inman's journey. Ada's education in self-sufficiency reminded me of the old *Foxfire* magazine articles and books I started reading in the 1960s. Ada is, in a way, a surrogate for the modern urban reader learning about lost ways of life. She gets stronger throughout the novel, while the doomed Inman, who seeks escape from discord, wanes. Their reunion is brief and happy but not destined to last. She deals with war. He leaves it. Ironically, she survives, the unwed mother of Inman's child, and Inman dies, shot down by the inchoate albino religious fanatic Birch, who looked to be "some inbred product of Cornwall . . . American all through, white skin, white hair, and a killer." Death himself by the look of him.[7]

The focus on the home front in the novel is enhanced by Frazier's attentiveness to the idioms, diction, and folklore-drenched superstitions of the place and time. "Always in my mind this was a book about language," Frazier says. "What I was interested in was the old lost culture of the southern Appalachians." Readers will not find in the novel the contrived clodhopper lingo that too often dooms Civil War fiction, but it does plenty of damage to the movie. When Frazier occasionally slips into his Faulkner voice, however, he can be a little showy: "Their horses were foul spine-sprung things, malandered about the necks, beshat greenly across the hind-quarters, and trailing ropy harls of yellow snot blown from all the orifices of their heads." But I think it works beautifully in the novel. We're a long way from *Gone with the Wind* here.[8]

As Ada masters the language of nature and craft, she becomes increasingly skeptical of the rhetoric that fuels the war. She finds newspaper accounts of battles "preposterous," full of weak details not to be trusted, and never "glorious." Inman assures her, "You could tell such things on and on and yet no more get to the full truth of the war than you could get to the full truth of an old sow bear's life by following her sign through the woods." Walt Whitman said it best: "The real war will never get in the books." Especially this part of the war, in the mountain shadows.[9]

Anything that increases public understanding of the war as a national upheaval, not just a series of pitched battles fought around Washington, brings us a little closer to the evasive "full truth of the war." The novel takes us away from the rhetoric and puts us on remote ground facing ultimate questions. If not quite an American *War and Peace*, *Cold Mountain* is at least something worthy of its subject. The film, too, at least hints at these questions and quickens perception of what the war really entailed and why it has never left us.

And the opera? A friend saw *Cold Mountain* at its world premiere in Santa Fe, New Mexico, in 2015. In the lobby gift shop, he spotted, and bought, a copy of my *A Cold Mountain Companion*. I had no idea the book was being marketed to the opera crowd. The opera was performed the next year in Philadelphia, and other performances are scheduled. Maybe a few more copies will be sold. Previously, I had heard only from college and high school students reading the novel in classes, so I was especially pleased to know another audience, albeit perhaps small, was being reached.

And to what end? What reason have we to assume that opera and movie goers, novel readers, television viewers, and students will develop an "itch of interest" in Civil War history? How does that interest become "monumentally stimulated," as Madden suggests? I like what John Dean, a cultural historian at the University of Versailles, France, has to say about "acorn knowledge": "Popular culture for a vast amount of people is a seed. It is germination and first step in growth along a root of knowledge. Acorn knowledge can lead to talking about or watching the show—the subject—again. It can lead to reading its book, to researching the subject, to thinking. It is the itch of interest."[10]

Notes

1. David Madden, *The Tangled Web of the Civil War and Reconstruction: Readings and Writings from a Novelist's Perspective* (Lanham, MD: Rowman and Littlefield, 2015), 110.

2. Ibid., 110–12.

3. Charles Frazier, *Cold Mountain* (New York: Atlantic Monthly Press, 1997); Tony Horwitz, "Celebrated in Fiction, Real Cold Mountain Is a Far Different Place," *Wall Street Journal*, 16 July 1998; Charles Frazier, interview by Elizabeth Farnsworth, *PBS Newshour*, 20 November 1997. See also Emily A. McDermo, "Frazier Polymetis: Cold Mountain and the Odyssey," *Classical and Modern Literature* 24, no. 2 (2004): 101–24.

4. Paul Ashdown, *A Cold Mountain Companion* (Gettysburg, PA: Thomas Publications, 2004).

5. Frazier, *Cold Mountain*, 96, 51.

6. Ella Lonn, *Desertion during the Civil War* (1928; repr., Lincoln: University of Nebraska Press, 1998), 231; Richard Bardolph, "Inconsistent Rebels: Desertion of North Carolina Troops in the Civil War," *North Carolina Historical Review* 41 (April 1964): 165, 168; John G. Barrett, *The Civil War in North Carolina* (Chapel Hill: University of North Carolina Press), 28–29. See also Mark A. Weitz, *More Damning Than Slaughter: Desertion in the Confederate Army* (Lincoln: University of Nebraska Press, 2005). Just how many Confederates deserted, and when, why, and to what effect, remains in dispute, along with a satisfactory comprehensive definition of desertion.

7. Frazier, *Cold Mountain*, 351.

8. Maile Carpenter, "Hot Mountain," *Raleigh News and Observer*, 10 July 1997; Mel Gassow, "How a Family Tale Became a Word-of-Mouth Phenomenon," *New York Times*, 27 August 1997; Frazier, *Cold Mountain*, 143.

9. Frazier, *Cold Mountain*, 140–41, 342; Walt Whitman, *Specimen Days in America* (London: Scott, 1887), 125.

10. John Dean, "The Social and Cultural Construction of Abraham Lincoln in U.S. Movies and on U.S. TV," *American Studies Journal* 53 (2009), https://doi.org/10.18422/53-06.

11. ❀ Revisiting *Confederates in the Attic*: An Interview with Tony Horwitz

H. R. Gordon

Editor's note: On May 27, 2019—between H. R. Gordon's work on this essay and its publication—Tony Horwitz died unexpectedly. His most recent book, Spying on the South: An Odyssey across the American Divide, *which examined some of the same issues he explored in his landmark* Confederates in the Attic: Dispatches from the Unfinished Civil War, *had just been released weeks earlier.*

America's fascination with the Civil War may not have changed much since Tony Horwitz explored the South in *Confederates in the Attic*, but Horwitz said the way people are invested in the history has shifted.

Published in 1999, *Confederates in the Attic* was Horwitz's answer to his boyhood passion for the Civil War. The book features Horwitz, a Pulitzer Prize–winning journalist, as the protagonist, navigating the South and meeting a plethora of characters along the way who nearly all share a vibrant passion for the Civil War, history, and Confederate culture. Juggling the opinions of Confederate descendants and their opponents, as well as his own perspective, Horwitz produced a journalistic story with humor and thought-provoking commentary.

Though the book is a seamless recollection of his travels weaved with the history of the sites, his research process for the book was to not have much of a process at all, he said. "I set off with the general idea of exploring the contemporary landscape of the Civil War and then pretty much went where my encounters led me. I tried to hit certain historic landmarks, like Fort Sumter and Richmond and Vicksburg, but wasn't rigid about this and spent a considerable amount of time in small communities I'd never heard of."[1]

After his approximately eighteen-month excursion, he spent what he called a "difficult year" deciphering his notes, reading, and conducting archival research. Most of the book was firsthand reporting, and Horwitz said he didn't

Fig. 11.1. A decade after the publication of *Confederates in the Attic*, Tony Horwitz admitted, "No matter how much I learn about other eras and events, [the Civil War is] still the one I'm most passionate about." More than a decade after that, he still finds the war endlessly fascinating. *Quoted in Kim A. O'Connell, "Tony Horwitz and Confederates in the Attic: Ten Years Later," America's Civil War 21 (March 2008): 16; photo by Randi Baird, courtesy of Tony Horwitz.*

have a well-defined process while writing his material—though it was more defined than his travels because his notes guided his writing.

"I just dove in and let the material lead me through the narrative," Horwitz said. "As much as possible, I recounted my travels in the order they occurred, so that the reader experienced the South as I had. I tried to find the right balance of history, humor, and hard-nosed reporting, so that one element didn't overwhelm the others. Also, of course, I threw away 75 percent of my reporting and focused on the best material."

Horwitz said he was pleasantly surprised when the book debuted. He didn't expect the wide acceptance and positive reviews so quickly.

"I knew there were plenty of people riveted by the Civil War but had no idea if my rather quirky approach would find a readership," he said. "I was also gratified that so many Southerners responded, mostly positively, though a vocal minority took issue with me, mostly conservative neo-Confederates who claimed I'd misrepresented and defamed the Cause."

The book's initial success hasn't diminished. Horwitz still receives emails every week from readers, some of whom are high school and college students assigned the book in class. And he said when topical debates surface periodically—noting the rebel flag or related issues—he typically sees a spike in emails and media interview requests.

What Horwitz said in those interviews, though, has likely changed, as he noted the people of the South have changed much since he wrote the book, so the South he presented in *Confederates in the Attic* isn't necessarily the case anymore.

"Watching cable TV or reading the news, it's easy to imagine that America is hopelessly divided and on the brink of another civil war," Horwitz said. "The biggest change is demographic, due to the influx of Hispanics, Asians, African Americans from the North, and others. A diminishing percentage of people living in the South have a blood tie to the Confederacy or a passion for honoring it. This is particularly so among the young and in fast-growing urban centers."

Those changes in demographics represent a change in attitudes. For instance, in *Confederates in the Attic*, Horwitz described an instance when AT&T supported removing the rebel flag. Horwitz quoted a man as saying, "We won't spend any of our money on a phone company that likes queers!" and then wrote, "What exactly this had to do with the rebel flag isn't clear." Later in the book, he recounted a conversation with Frances Chapman, who said, "Blacks just need to get over slavery. You can't live in the past. . . . Don't put us where *they* used to be." But Horwitz contends that those incidents don't define current Confederate culture.[2]

"Those incidents were true to the world I explored in the 1990s and spoke to the way in which, for some white Southerners, the Confederacy and its symbols had floated free from historical context, becoming fodder for a contemporary culture war," Horwitz explained. "A sector of white Southern society that feels discomfort with the rapid change in America—regarding race, immigration, gender—chooses to use the flag and other emblems as a rallying point and bludgeon. But I don't think this amounts to a 'defining rhetoric' for any but an aging minority."

With a turn from the commitment to the Confederate cause came a shift in the way the Civil War—and the South's history in general—is presented in the South, Horwitz says. With fewer people dedicated to preserving the memory of their ancestors' hard-fought battles, a more open approach to historical events and challenges has taken hold. The difference in interpretation of plantations, museums, and other sites in the present day compared with the 1990s is striking, he says.

"Slavery is presented much more fully and honestly than before, as a central part of the history of that era," he said. "You see many more African Americans at these sites, as employees and as visitors. We still have a long way to go in confronting all the ghosts of our past, but a lot of progress has been made in just the last twenty years." Of course, as Horwitz noted, there are still some who want to defend the rebel flag and emblems of the Confederacy. But to him, "they're fighting a rearguard action."

And as for the Confederate heritage groups Horwitz describes in *Confederates in the Attic*? "[They] used to operate a bit like the NRA, threatening to dislodge any legislator who didn't fully embrace their agenda," Horwitz said. "That power is gone, as we saw most vividly with the lowering of the flag at the South Carolina statehouse."

But the rebel flag has crept out of the Confederate museums and into the hands—and wardrobes—of many. Plastered on belt buckles and car decals, and flown off the back of pickup trucks in even the northernmost parts of the United States, the flag has a legacy of its own.

"During the Civil War, it was a battle standard, not a political emblem, and for many Southern veterans in the decades that followed, it was a symbol of their combat service and sacrifice," Horwitz explained.

> But over time, the flag took on other connotations, including its appropriation by the Ku Klux Klan as a symbol of white supremacy and resistance to civil rights. In the twentieth century, the flag was also commercialized, plastered on beach towels and bikinis and license plates, not only as an emblem of Southernness but as a more generalized expression of rebel-dom, a raised middle finger.

That raised middle finger may represent the original intent of the flag best, though. The antiestablishment ideas push against the politicians who, as Horwitz observed, tend to "draw on history in ways that suit their aims and ambitions."

"As a result, knotty issues with complex historical roots—for instance, the Founders' intent when they crafted the Second Amendment—get reduced to a sound bite," Horwitz lamented. "But the responsibility for this rests as much on the public as it does on politicians. We need to be better educated about our history and ask hard questions when we hear politicians claim the mantle of Thomas Jefferson or Abe Lincoln or some other icon."

That responsibility to be historically vigilant is something Horwitz explored in *Confederates in the Attic* along with his own fascination with the Civil

War, which he passed on to his reluctant wife, novelist Geraldine Brooks. Initially, she called him a "Civil War bore," but she was drawn in just the same.

"It wasn't the battlefields that truly stirred her interest; it was the human and family drama of what happens to both men and women during war," Horwitz said. "I think this speaks to the breadth of the subject. While many Civil War buffs are drawn in their youth to the great leaders and battles, there's so much more to the story, including the home front. So for all the tens of thousands of books that have been written, there's always new territory to explore."

Brooks's experience of the Civil War alongside Horwitz led her to write *March*, which won the 2006 Pulitzer Prize for fiction. *March* retells Louisa May Alcott's story *Little Women* from the perspective of the father's experience as a Union chaplain in the Civil War.

"I retract unreservedly my former characterization of my husband . . . as a Civil War bore," Brooks wrote in *March*'s afterword.

> I would like to apologize for all the times I refused to get out of the car at Antietam or whined about the heat at Gettysburg; for all the complaints about too many shelves colonized by his Civil War tomes and all the moaning over weekend expeditions devoted to events such as the interment of Stonewall Jackson's horse. I'm not sure quite when or where it happened, but on a sunken road somewhere, I finally saw the light.[3]

But Horwitz and Brooks certainly weren't the first nor the last to discover a fascination with the war. The cover of *Confederates in the Attic* boasts a large black-and-white photo of a burly man in a plaid shirt holding a dagger of sorts. His stone face holds a glare—his furrowed brow highlighted by dirt. To someone who doesn't know better, it seems to be a Civil War–era photograph. But a couple of chapters into the book, the reader finds out it is Robert Lee Hodge—a "hardcore" reenactor. Horwitz noted in *Confederates* that Hodge is known for his bloating—the act of lying stiffly on the ground and bloating one's body out to appear as the dead in the war would look.

In an article for *America's Civil War* in March 2008, Hodge wrote that he felt naïve. When Horwitz asked to join their reenactment to do a story for the *Wall Street Journal*, Hodge invited him. "Initially, I thought the article would be positive, but when I read the piece I was disappointed," Hodge said. "I never wanted any popularity for mimicking a bloated corpse or urinating on buttons." Hodge went on to say he didn't want to be the poster child for reenactment because he felt many others had a lot to offer as well.[4]

After *Confederates in the Attic* gained popularity, though, Hodge became a center for media attention because, as he said, "there I was, on the cover of the book." Despite this, he said his experience with Horwitz was positive and that the fifteen minutes of fame that came with it was both humbling and amusing—sentiments that some reenactors feel simply by donning the garb of the era.[5]

Horwitz revisited a Civil War–related topic in his 2011 book, *Midnight Rising: John Brown and the Raid That Sparked the Civil War.* He said his interest in telling the story sparked from a want to understand the beginnings of the war, as well as to explore the Northern side of the conflict more. He also wanted to experiment with writing traditional historical narrative in contrast to his work in *Confederate in the Attic* and other books, which weave together the past and present narratives.

"Like most Civil War buffs, I'd always focused on the 1861–65 period, and I wanted to get a better understanding of how Americans came to this bloody crisis in the first place," Horwitz explained. "John Brown seemed a good way to get into all that, and I was also struck by how dramatic and misunderstood the story of Brown and the raid were."

After moving to New England from Virginia a dozen years ago, Horwitz no longer purposely visits battlefields and other sites, though he often returns to the South for research, and because of the pervasive history of the Civil War, sites are inescapable, he said. "While looking for something else, I often stumbled on intriguing, little-known sites. But I'm more focused these days on the antebellum South or contemporary issues—not the Civil War years, per se."

Even without constant immersion in Civil War–specific history and sites, Horwitz still has a deep appreciation for the stories the era holds.

"Simply put, the Civil War is the most engaging, dramatic, and consequential episode in U.S. history, and its echoes can be heard in the present day," said Horwitz. "In so many ways, studying that era provides a window into our history and character as a nation." Gertrude Stein put it best: 'There never will be anything more interesting in America than that Civil War[,] never.'"

Notes

1. Unless otherwise noted, this and other direct and indirect quotes from Tony Horwitz come from two email interviews with the author, on 19 October 2016 and 15 January 2018.

2. Tony Horwitz, *Confederates in the Attic: Dispatches from the Unfinished Civil War* (New York: Vintage Departures, 1999), 79, 99.

3. Geraldine Brooks, *March* (New York: Penguin, 2005), 280.

4. Robert Lee Hodge, "My 15 Minutes Out of the Attic," *America's Civil War* 21, no. 1 (March 2008): 26–27.

5. Ibid.

12. ❈ The Civil War Periodically

Mary Koik

I had just turned thirteen years old the first time I picked up a Civil War–themed magazine—the June 1995 *Civil War Times*, with a dashing J. E. B. Stuart on the cover. I was always a compulsive reader but still haven't pinpointed what about the Civil War had captured the imagination of this New England middle schooler and prompted me to pick up the issue. Perhaps it was no single influence. It was the early 1990s, and the air was thick with Ken Burns, Ron Maxwell's *Gettysburg*, and *Civil War Journal* airing Saturday mornings on A&E.

From this youthful subscription, I learned plenty of history but also, somewhat unexpectedly, became aware of the broader Civil War community. The idea that there was an active population of people who did more than just read history books (plus those lofty few who wrote them) took me by surprise. From living historians to amateur and professional archaeologists to tour guides to preservationists, people across the country and around the world found their own meaningful ways to connect to the past.

I quickly learned that for such a seemingly small universe, there is a tremendous diversity within the Civil War magazine community. Titles vary in frequency, length, audience, and mission; from the general-interest glossy to the deeply academic journal, there truly is something (or a half dozen somethings!) for everyone with an interest in the topic. Moreover, these periodicals are highly digestible, offering a gateway for those who are first entering into the fold. And given the flexibility of the medium, even with hundreds of articles published each year—and in some instances, a catalog of past issues stretching back decades available online—there's little danger of authors, editors, and publishers running out of new avenues to explore this history.

Despite my early exposure, I was still taken by surprise a decade later when the opportunity arose to apply for a job at the Civil War Preservation Trust, now the American Battlefield Trust. Through high school and college, I'd been preparing for a career in journalism, racking up internships and editorships along the way. Finding a job where I could put my communications skills to use working to protect American history was the opportunity of a lifetime. When the organization asked me to take over its membership magazine, *Hallowed Ground*, I was both flattered and overwhelmed. The sixty-thousand-piece circulation was more than fivefold larger than anything I'd previously held any direct authority over, and the scope of responsibilities was daunting—decisions on theme, scheduling, content across all departments, and scheduling all fell primarily to me, as did a significant amount of writing.

Hallowed Ground is the trust's primary membership benefit and a key means of communications to donors, advocates, and partners across the nation. Unlike most other history-focused magazines, it is not available at newsstands or under a traditional subscription model, instead mailed directly only to those who contribute to the cause of battlefield preservation. All this adds up to a very different editorial mission and content mix than those of other publications within the genre. My early experiences at the trust advocating on

Fig. 12.1. Civil War magazines have been geared toward several audiences over the years: general readership, serious buffs, and scholars. *Hallowed Ground*, produced by the American Battlefield Trust, aims at preservation-minded readers. *American Battlefield Trust.*

behalf of threatened battlefields, writing for policy and public communications efforts, and getting to know the membership proved critical to adapting to this unique editorial mission.

The first magazines focusing their content on historical topics related to the Civil War appeared in the late nineteenth century and commonly featured personal reminiscences by prominent officers. In the Reconstruction era, many of these publications displayed an obvious preference for one side of the war's narrative, the allegiance often betrayed with a title like *Southern Bivouac* or *Confederate Veteran*. Most of these early magazines died out with the old soldiers themselves, although *Confederate Veteran* was revived in 1984 as the membership publication of the Sons of Confederate Veterans and Military Order of the Stars and Bars following a fifty-year hiatus. The *Banner*, a national publication of the Sons of Union Veterans (successor to the Grand Army of the Republic), completed its 123rd volume of issues in 2019, and the *Loyal Legion Historical Journal*, published by the Military Order of the Loyal Legion of the United States, its 76th.

A renaissance in the genre began amid the Civil War Centennial with the founding of the now-venerable *Civil War Times* in 1962. Other titles still available on newsstands appeared steadily in the decades that followed—*Military Images* in 1979, *America's Civil War* in 1988, *Gettysburg Magazine* in 1989, and most recently, the *Civil War Monitor* in 2011—while others, including the once-beloved *North and South* (1997–2013) and *Blue and Gray* (1984–2017), have come and gone.

With so many Civil War magazines currently available (more than a dozen, depending on the specificity of your definition;[1] far more if you count more broadly focused history periodicals that feature Civil War content multiple times each year), each must find an internal manifesto or editorial vision to distinguish itself in what is inherently a niche field. This is a matter of not just what topics are selected for exploration but also how those stories are approached and presented. Some distinguish themselves by examining a narrow slice of the topic, like *Civil War Navy: The Magazine* or *Military Images* (detailed biographies of the often-anonymous faces in period portraits) or *North South Trader's Civil War* (focused on physical artifacts and relics). *Blue and Gray*'s format was unique, tackling a single battle in exceptional depth each issue, while *Civil War Times* and *America's Civil War* cover much more figurative ground, with several disparate features in each edition. New journals with subscription options published by the University of North Carolina, Shenandoah University, and Kent State offer an academic approach.

Despite these differences, all Civil War magazines face challenges universal to the periodical industry—struggles that in some cases have already proven fatal. Industry-wide—according to *Folio*, a magazine for publishing professions—in an effort to remain financially stable, titles are transferring to publishing conglomerates (witness the transformation of the nine-title Weider History Group into the World History Group, now owned by Los Angeles investment group Regent, which purchased West Coast lifestyle magazine *Sunset* last year), reducing frequency (in 2012, the National Trust for Historic Preservation took its membership magazine from six issues per year to four), reducing page counts, or going digital-only (a transition that military history, strategy, and gaming magazine *Armchair General* made in 2015).[2]

As in all aspects of the journalism and publishing world, the proliferation of online content and other market forces have eroded circulation numbers. For instance, in 2016, *Civil War Times* reported a paid circulation of 39,000 compared with a historical figure of 145,000 in 1988.[3] Although other titles have not seen so precipitous a drop, circulation numbers at the sesquicentennial are almost universally more modest than in previous decades. Following its nonprofit parent's membership, *Hallowed Ground*'s print run has been more sheltered from this trend. In the same period as the *Civil War Times* example, readership has risen from virtually zero (the Association for the Preservation of Civil War Sites, the current group's origination, was founded in 1987) to approximately 55,000, although this has fallen perhaps 15 percent from its all-time high. We aren't alone; *Preservation*, the National Trust membership publication, self-reported that its "subscriber" base has dropped from 155,000 to 135,000 in the last two years.[4]

Simultaneously, editors and publishers have been faced with the rising costs of paper and postage, even as their traditional advertisers have been able to experiment with dynamic hypertargeted and pay-per-click online formats. Still, we needn't write a eulogy for print yet, according to Jeanne Spooner Carr of the Sheridan Group, a press specializing in modest print runs that produces *Hallowed Ground*. "It amazes me how many startup publications keep springing up. They are niche, typically small runs, published by people with passion about a certain subject and if created properly—excellent content with dramatic design—can stimulate more interest and develop followers."[5]

And yet, as all historians know, nothing can stop the passage of time, and generational shifts in attitude are not to be underestimated among either content consumers or producers. Amid all these other pressures, it was the decision to retire by longtime editors that finally shuttered *Blue and Gray* and triggered the sale, leading to a major overhaul, of *Civil War News*.[6]

More philosophically, whereas book authors customize their storytelling for a desired audience, magazine editors must ask contributors to conform their narrative to an existing subscriber base and voice.

As a membership magazine—though it is not the only one in the Civil War sphere, joined by the Sons of Union Veterans, Sons of Confederate Veterans, and United Daughters of the Confederacy on the national level, and others more regionally—*Hallowed Ground* is unique in many ways. In simple and obvious terms, the news section is confined to organizational achievements and challenges or those of partner groups; paid advertising and book reviews, nearly universal elements in such periodicals, are both eschewed in its pages. In a broader sense, without the need to attract new subscribers or prevent membership attrition based solely on the strengths of the magazine, it is free to explore the stories of preservation and interpretation across time that might not find homes in other publications and to seek out fresh new voices in the field.

I am deeply grateful to the authors who have contributed—virtually all as outright donations to the American Battlefield Trust—to *Hallowed Ground* in the dozen years that I've been its editor. Together, we've experimented and refined and, ultimately, solidified a formula that furthers the trust's mission and meets the expectations of its members. This has evolved to include focusing issues around a theme, perhaps looking at history and preservation stories related to a single battle or several engagements that are tied together by common elements.

Where do these overarching themes come from? Sometimes they come from a glance at a calendar—a focus on wherever this year's annual conference will be held, for example. Knowing that during the sesquicentennial I wanted to focus each quarterly issue on battles that occurred during the corresponding period 150 years ago, I mapped out themes for the entire anniversary ahead of time, determining what battles and events every issue from mid-2010 through mid-2015 would focus on.

Other ideas stem from a desire to bolster the trust's educational mission, creating high-quality, long-form content to augment the efforts of the history and education department. Early in my tenure with *Hallowed Ground*, I was helping a colleague look in the organization's archives to see what we might have about the Battle of Chickamauga. Finding nothing more than a short summary, we felt the choice to devote an issue to the war's second-bloodiest battle was obvious. Similarly, the spring 2017 issue played a role in the broader effort to increase our offerings related to naval warfare. Since the creation of the American Battlefield Trust umbrella structure in 2018, I typically seek to include battles from the three conflicts now under our banner—the Revolutionary War, the War of 1812, and the Civil War—that all relate to a unifying theme. These may be engagements where a future president was the field commander (Washington at Princeton, Jackson at New Orleans, and Grant at Cold Harbor in the fall 2018 edition) or battles fought in especially oppressive heat (Monmouth in 1778 and Cedar Mountain in 1862 for the summer 2019 issue).

However, even if a single edition can function as a self-contained unit, I've also found a need to be mindful of how it fits into the broader sweep of issues around it. Gettysburg issues may be perpetually popular, but you can only do them every so often! And in a general-interest magazine, I need to bear in mind that readers have a variety of specific interests—eastern versus western theater, infantry versus cavalry and the like—that need to be recognized and balanced.

With the germ of a fully suitable thematic idea in hand, I begin by reaching out to one or more historians who I know have an interest in that particular topic. The trust is lucky to have existing relationships with a tremendous number of outstanding historians who are perpetually receptive to opportunities to work with the organization, whether writing for the magazine, leading tours, filming short videos, or assisting by other means.

Of course, some historians politely decline to contribute because they don't feel able to fit their work into the length of articles we typically publish or to the level of assumed knowledge of our readers. Writing for a weighty, peer-reviewed, and thoroughly footnoted academic journal is vastly different from writing for a membership magazine used as an outreach vehicle for a charity. Thank heavens for those who are comfortable producing quality work in both categories, but I cannot fault those who strongly prefer one or the other.

When we first begin discussing an article with the author—usually at least nine months before it will arrive in any mailboxes—there are three major points to consider, beyond the obvious parameters of word count and deadline.

First, the ultimate goal is finding a storyline that will be both interesting to old hands and also accessible to government partners or those coming to the cause of battlefield preservation from a different perspective, such as environmental concerns and green space protection. Miscalculating the assumed knowledge of the audience is perhaps the most profound way an article can misfire. In the case of features for *Hallowed Ground*, we aim for an interested but nonexpert audience—college students who signed up for an elective course, not PhD candidates.

Second, pieces strive to reflect the organization's devotion to the physical landscape of battle, focusing when possible on actions that occurred on preserved land. And third, authors should be mindful of the need to illustrate their story. While a book may have a smattering of period pictures, a well-designed magazine also integrates maps and modern photography.

Given its focus on physical battlefields, *Hallowed Ground* places tremendous emphasis on modern landscape photography. The talented artists who donate their work in this capacity are doing much more than snapping shots along the park tour road. Our photographers may spend hours before their visit reading about the battle—and not just the article they're shooting to accompany. They will haul ladders through fields to painstakingly re-create images taken by Alexander Gardner. They will drive through the wee hours to catch the light of dawn on a battlefield landmark and sometimes return multiple times if the weather doesn't cooperate. And in one memorable instance, they have slept overnight in a swamp to capture the feeling of desolation and loneliness experienced by the fugitive John Wilkes Booth.

For all this guidance I do offer, I have learned to steadfastly refrain from placing too explicit an order for any article. I've done my fair share of reading and I've visited plenty of battlefields, but I would never consider myself more qualified than an expert historian to determine what the most compelling line of narrative regarding a particular topic might be. I've learned to inherently trust the instincts of those who have spent months or years researching a topic, sharing their discoveries with friends, and gauging reactions along the way. The story they enjoy telling is almost certainly one that trust members will enjoy reading.

There's no absolute recipe for a successful potential feature. What makes a good book doesn't always translate into a compelling magazine article, in part because you don't have the length available to do a dense topic justice. In three thousand words, you may be able to give an overview treatment to an entire battle. But devoting the same space to exploring the experience of one unit during the same engagement—as the winter 2016 issue did for the 14th New Jersey at Monocacy—can result in a fast-paced and detailed account that still conveys the outcome of the fighting elsewhere on the field. Conversely, this same space limitation can work in favor of an author who wants to try a novel approach that might not stand up to a much longer format, as was the case with a 2012 piece that covered the entire Battle of Shiloh by looking at the experiences only of those soldiers who had signed the Mississippi Ordinance of Secession the previous year.

Theoretically, there is great appeal in the idea of excerpting a longer work for a magazine feature, but I've found that it's far more difficult than simply cutting and pasting. Even if a book is organized so that each chapter is a stand-alone essay with appropriate introduction and conclusion, those may still be too long and in need of truncation or significant editing. More often, however, an excerpt will rely on arguments made elsewhere in the longer text, potentially creating the impression that the author is making unsupported assumptions and undermining the quality of the full work. In extreme instances, this can make the article feel more like a promotional effort on the part of the publisher than a sincere educational offering from the magazine.

The most successful and well-received features and issues give readers some kind of exclusive access or perspective that they can't get elsewhere. The sesquicentennial provided many such opportunities. For example, at the anniversary of John Brown's raid, we looked at how the National Park Service had marked the 100th anniversary shortly after the establishment of Harpers Ferry National Park as the country stood poised on the cusp of the civil rights movement. For Gettysburg, we explored the history of preservation at the battlefield instead of the well-trodden narrative of the actual battle. More recently, an issue on "lost" battlefields where little land remains available for interpretation created a visceral and highly visual case for the ongoing importance of the trust's work.

Ideally, each issue, whether an edition of *Hallowed Ground* or any other magazine within the genre, will reveal something new to its readers. This may come from an essay about a relatively obscure battle or a new interpretation of a well known personality. It could be a foray into previously unexplored academic territory—social history for those of a purely military mindset or photographic examinations for those whose work has focused solely on the textual. It could be an exciting archaeological or archival discovery, perhaps even a major achievement in preservation. Regardless, for a month or a quarter year, it provides readers and the broader Civil War community with a shared experience of discovery—and, given that some of these titles have been publishing steadily for more than fifty years, a tangible connection to past generations of history lovers.

Notes

1. As of mid-2019, regularly published Civil War magazines included *America's Civil War*, *Civil War Times*, *Civil War Monitor*, *Civil War Navy: The Magazine*, *Confederate Veteran* (Sons of Confederate Veterans membership), *CVBT: On the Front Line* (Central Virginia Battlefields Trust membership), *Gettysburg Magazine*, *Hallowed Ground* (American Battlefield Trust membership), *Journal of Civil War History*, *Journal of the Shenandoah Valley during the Civil War Era*, *Military Images*, *North South Trader's Civil War*, *Shenandoah at War* (Shenandoah Valley Battlefields Historic District publication), *UDC Magazine* (United Daughters of the Confederacy membership), the *Banner* (Sons of Union Veterans membership), and *Virginia's Civil War*.

2. Caysey Welton, "Three Predictions for Magazine Media in the Year Ahead," *Folio*, 11 January 2018, http://www.foliomag.com/3-predictions-year-ahead -magazine-media/#.Wlf0Gyd701g.email.

3. William H. Honan, "The Media Business: The Lessons of War Sell in Peacetime," *New York Times*, 19 December 1988, http://www.nytimes. com/1988/12/19/business/the-media-business-the-lessons-of-war-sell-in -peacetime.html

4. "2018 Media Kit," National Trust for Historic Preservation, https://nthp-saving places.s3.amazonaws.com/2017/09/12/08/45/41/854/2018Preservation_Media %20Kit%20for%20download.pdf.

5. Jeanne Spooner Carr, email message to the author, 11 January 2018.

6. Dave Roth, "*Blue and Gray Magazine* Ceases Publication," *Blue and Gray*, 31 May 2017, https://blueandgraymagazine.com/2017/05/31/blue-gray -magazine-ceases-publication/.

Part Two

SEEING IS BELIEVING: THE CIVIL WAR ON FILM

The biggest event in our history belongs on the biggest canvas humans can devise.

—William C. Davis, "The Civil War and the
Confederacy in Cinema," *The Cause Lost*

Scan to see exclusive online material related to this part of the book.

13. The War Laid in Our Dooryards: Civil War Photography

Kevin Pawlak

Barely before the smoke released its haunting grasp of the heavily trodden ground, and while the explosions of distant cannons filled the air like approaching claps of thunder, a wagon rolled down the macadamized highway leading from the agricultural crossroads town of Sharpsburg, Maryland, to points north. The driver swatted through clouds of flies to get a clear view of the recently destroyed landscape around him. Perhaps feeling the same as another witness to this charnel house, that "words are inadequate to portray the scene," he yanked on the reins, slowing the horses to a standstill. Fascination was perhaps not exactly what the driver felt—more of a shock to pull oneself away from such gruesome images—but the dreadful scenes laid out in front of him and his partner drew his attention. The driver removed his cumbersome baggage from the wagon, plopped it on the ground, awkwardly unloaded the contents, and began to record history, photographing these scenes too horrible to describe by text.[1]

The first photographs that Alexander Gardner and his assistant James Gibson likely captured on the Antietam battlefield consisted of a series of five images: dead Confederate soldiers lay grotesquely frozen in death, bloating and blackening along the fence rails of the Hagerstown Turnpike.[2] These images have been widely dispersed and repeatedly used in various media since their creation. The unnamed Southern soldiers are perhaps some of the most easily recognized soldiers from the Civil War, even though their stories and identities remain an eternal mystery.

A Wisconsin major that traversed this same ground as Gardner and Gibson thought that the scenes on either side of this roadway "surpassed all in manifest evidence of slaughter." "The scene was indescribably horrible," he continued. "Great numbers of dead, swollen and black under the hot sun, lay upon the field." The major felt the sweat running off his nerve-racked mount as it "trembled in every limb" while attempting to push through the mass of humanity.[3]

Folks far away from battlefields such as Antietam could never truly experience the uneasiness—no, abhorrence—at witnessing scenes like this. Yet soldiers on the frontlines still acknowledged that dead men on the battlefield meant vacant chairs around the dinner table back home. "Thus it is that a sad calamity has befallen us," wrote one Union soldier after reflecting for a month on the scenes of Antietam's killing fields. "It has left many a void in a once happy household, a vacancy around the hearthstone that the world cannot fill. How long must our country suffer?"[4] Words were unable at the time to answer such a question, but Gardner's images surely did nothing to lessen the suffering. These images brought—and still bring—the Antietam battlefield and countless other battlefields from the Civil War to the very parlors of civilians who likewise could not pull their curious glances away from such destructive views.

It only took a couple of weeks for Gardner to transfer his images from the hot rear of the accompanying photographic darkroom to the second story of Mathew Brady's photographic gallery at the corner of Tenth Street and Broadway in New York City. (Gardner worked for Brady at the time.) Even though not everyone who passed by Brady's gallery entered the exhibit—it is unclear how many people actually did—its location on Broadway and the sign perched above the front door with the simple words "The Dead of Antietam" written on it ensured that many people at least knew of the horrors shown in Gardner's photographs.[5]

Two advertisements appeared in the *New York Times* alerting readers to the exhibit's existence and contents. An October 3, 1862, piece stated that the images "comprise pictures of the field of battle, the position of the several corps, and many thrilling incidents." The write-up three days later focused more on the human side of the images: "If our readers wish to know the horrors of the battle-field, let them go to Brady's Gallery, and see the fearful reproductions which he has on exhibition, and for sale." The October 6 article continued, "In all the literal repulsiveness of nature, lie the naked corpses of our dead soldiers side by side in the quiet impassiveness of rest. Blackened faces, distorted features, expressions most agonizing, and details of absolute verity, teach us a lesson which it is well for us to learn."[6]

These notices no doubt drew people into Brady's gallery. After entering the exhibit, crowds pressed up the staircase to the second floor, where Gardner's photographs awaited their curious eyes. "There is a terrible fascination

Fig. 13.1. Mathew Brady's studio at 359 Broadway, between Leonard and Franklin Streets in lower Manhattan, was named a New York City landmark in 1990. In 1860, he moved his gallery to 785 Broadway (Tenth Street and Broadway); there, he displayed his Antietam photos. *Chris Mackowski.*

about [the photos] that draws one near these pictures, and makes him loth to leave them," the *New York Times* reported. Audiences drew closer and closer to these novel photographs, "chained by the strange spell that dwells in dead men's eyes."[7]

The popular culture of the 1860s did not restrict portrayals of Antietam's dead to one medium. Indeed, while Brady's gallery displayed the original glass negatives, the October 18, 1862, *Harper's Weekly* reproduced sketches based on the photographs with an accompanying article captioning the prints. Perhaps in an effort not to overwhelm readers who ventured into the descriptive text for each sketch, the article first focused on a view of the Burnside Bridge. The article explained that the sketch—and the photo it emulated—"exhibits little or no traces of the conflict." Surrounding this peaceful scene, which appeared largest on the page, were the ghastly likenesses of dead Rebels bleaching in the sun along the Hagerstown Turnpike, silent horses struck down next to a limber chest, federal burial parties, Confederates lined up for burial, and more. "Here and there are beautiful stretches of pastoral scenery, disfigured by the evidences of strife," the article summarized.[8]

The oft-quoted *New York Times* article reviewing Mathew Brady's exhibit noted how these pictures brought war as close to the home front as one could get it: "Mr. Brady has done something to bring home to us the terrible reality and earnestness of war. If he has not brought bodies and laid them in our dooryards and along the streets, he has done something very like it." Usually, the reviewer said, Northerners (and Southerners) read the list of dead in the morning's paper "but dismiss its recollection with the coffee." But even if only a small number of people ascended the steps leading to Brady's exhibit on Broadway to get a close and personal look at Antietam's victims, the *Harper's Weekly*'s reproduction of the images did not make the whisking away of thoughts of the dead as easy as sipping on a hot cup of coffee. More Americans read *Harper's Weekly* than any other newspaper during the Civil War, and it seems likely that few escaped catching at least some glimpse of the sketches inspired by Gardner's photography.[9]

Images, or sketched reproductions of the negatives, reached the home front not just in the wake of Antietam, but throughout the war. They were not all of dead soldiers, either. Yet any image produced on the frontlines took on an increasing role in preserving the story of the war. The month before Antietam, Brady's crews photographed portions of the Cedar Mountain battlefield, though they did not capture images of slain soldiers. Regardless, these images held immense importance. "Over this common-place corner of the Old Dominion then, as over historic Yorktown, and Williamsburgh [*sic*], and Richmond, the red light of battle has fallen. Never again shall the new glow depart from the scene."[10]

The images of Antietam by Gardner and Gibson still evoke feelings of awe and shock today and can bring the Civil War home to roost for many people who believe the war is so distant from us over 150 years later. But these images were far from the only photographs captured during the four-year conflict, and Gardner and Gibson were far from the only artists striving to immortalize such grisly scenes, as well as those of lesser brutality. These photographic records have become a mainstay of Civil War historiography—images that continue to draw audiences to this American epic. A list could easily be prepared ad nauseam of all the books (chief among them William Frassanito's *Antietam: The Photographic Legacy of America's Bloodiest Day*) and—especially—documentaries that have used these still-frame images to bring a more personal touch to the Civil War. Likely none is more moving or recognizable than Ken Burns's nine-part epic widely broadcast on PBS in 1990, *The Civil War*. Burns's overlay of scores upon scores of Civil War–era photographs with heart-wrenching music and the slow magnification and reduction of the images seemed to bring the orphans, widows, and soldiers of the war out of the television set and into our living rooms, making them come alive. Burns's masterpiece, like Brady's exhibit, brought "home to us the terrible reality and earnestness of war."[11]

Of course, thanks to advances since Brady's time, Burns reached a much wider audience with reproductions of Gardner's photos than Brady did with the originals. "He turns dull black and white photos into haunting images full of life. They hold us captive. They make us choke up," one reviewer noted.[12]

The countless documentaries that grace our screens today with the still images from the war have helped preserve our battlefields by bringing folks to them. One *New York Times* author believed Brady did the same in his time:

> In the case of our American battle-fields, the debt we owe to the art which seizes their main features before decay, or (more formidable still,) improvement's "effacing fingers" have begun to sweep their lineaments, is peculiarly heavy. So frail is our domestic architecture, and so uncertain the tenure of the picturesque even in the most deserted and lonely regions of the land, that five years might well suffice to obliterate all the leading accidental characteristics of any one of the scenes which our children will care to revisit, and desire to see, in imagination at least, as their fighting fathers saw them. Let us, then, heartily acknowledge our obligations to such an "abstract and brief chronicle of the times" as this which Mr. Brady has been so earnestly and unobtrusively making up for us.[13]

If Mathew Brady, Alexander Gardner, and the scores of photographers across the United and Confederate States of America could have seen how widespread and recognizable their images have become in today's culture, they surely would have been humbled. While some can recite the Gettysburg Address or their favorite accounts of the Civil War from memory, none who have seen a black-and-white image of a Civil War battlefield can ever forget that scene. Such images not only heighten the senses of the eye but touch the nose and the ear, too. What must that place have smelled and sounded like while the men behind the camera quietly went about their business?

In 1866, Alexander Gardner published some of his best photographs from the war in a single volume called *Gardner's Photographic Sketch Book of the War*. In his preface to the picture book, Gardner expressed the earnest hope that the images contained therein "will possess an enduring interest." He continued, "Verbal representations of such places, or scenes, may not have the merit of accuracy; but photographic presentments of them will be accepted by posterity with an undoubting faith."[14] To a certain extent, he was correct. Posterity has continued to view his photographs, and those of others, with an immense "enduring interest."

Notes

1. Charles Carleton Coffin, "Antietam Scenes," in *Battles and Leaders of the Civil War* (Secaucus, NJ: Castle, n.d.), 2:684.
2. William A. Frassanito makes the argument that Gardner's photographs of Confederate dead along the Hagerstown Turnpike were the first images of battlefield dead that Gardner recorded at Antietam. William A. Frassanito, *Antietam: The Photographic Legacy of America's Bloodiest Day* (Gettysburg, PA: Thomas Publications, 1978), 126.
3. Rufus R. Dawes, *Service with the Sixth Wisconsin Volunteers*, ed. Alan T. Nolan (Madison: State Historical Society of Wisconsin, 1962), 95.
4. George Stockton Graham to Mary Margaret Graham, 16 October 1862, Graham Family Papers, Civil War Document Collection, U.S. Army War College Library and Archives, Carlisle, PA.
5. "Antietam Reproduced," *New York Times*, 6 October 1862; "Brady's Photographs: Pictures of the Dead at Antietam," *New York Times*, 20 October 1862.
6. "Antietam Reproduced," *New York Times*, 3 October, 6 October 1862.
7. "Brady's Photographs," *New York Times*, 20 October 1862.
8. "The Battle of Antietam," *Harper's Weekly*, 18 October 1862.
9. "Brady's Photographs," *New York Times*, 20 October 1862; David S. Heidler and Jeanne T. Heidler, eds., *Encyclopedia of the American Civil War: A Political, Social, and Military History* (New York: W. W. Norton & Company, 2000), s.v. "Harper's Weekly," 931.
10. "Brady's Photographs of the War," *New York Times*, 26 September 1862.
11. "Brady's Photographs," *New York Times*, 20 October 1862.
12. Gabor S. Boritt, "Ken Burns' Civil War," *Pennsylvania History: A Journal of Mid-Atlantic Studies* 58, no. 3 (July 1991): 215.
13. "Brady's Photographs of the War," *New York Times*, 26 September 1862.
14. Alexander Gardner, *Gardner's Photographic Sketch Book of the War* (Washington, DC: Philp & Solomons, 1866), text preceding contents page of vol. 1.

14. ❋ The Gettysburg Cyclorama: Entertainment of the Past, Present, and Future

Chris Brenneman

The Battle of Gettysburg Cyclorama on display at the Gettysburg National Military Park is an amazing piece of art and history.[1] The cyclorama is a giant circular painting that depicts "The High Water Mark of the Confederacy" at the height of Pickett's Charge on the third and final day of the Battle of Gettysburg. The cyclorama teaches us not only about the battle of 1863 but also about the history of entertainment. When French artist Paul Philippoteaux painted the cyclorama in 1884, it was at the start of a craze that was sweeping the country. Cycloramas were one of the first forms of mass entertainment, like the movies of today. With their giant circular canvases and unique method of displaying the paintings in specially built buildings, the cycloramas created an illusion of depth comparable to today's 3-D and IMAX movies. Furthermore, by giving viewers a feeling of being immersed in the scene around them, the cyclorama offers an experience that the entertainment of the future (virtual reality) will seek to replicate and improve on.

The first large round paintings, or panoramas, were painted in the eighteenth century, and by the late 1800s, they had become a popular form of entertainment in Europe. In the mid-nineteenth century, artists also began incorporating a foreground of real objects to obscure the boundary between reality and the painting. This foreground of real terrain prevents the viewer from seeing the bottom of the canvas, while an overhead canopy prevents the viewer from seeing the very top of the canvas. By displaying these paintings in large buildings that included a raised viewing platform and an overhead canopy, artists were able to perfect the illusion and make the viewer feel immersed in the scene as if it were real.

The Gettysburg Cyclorama is 42 feet high and 377 feet in circumference. Viewers stand on a raised observation deck that places them at eye level with the middle of the canvas. Real objects, such as dirt and grass and the debris of battle, lead from the edge of the viewing platform down to the edge of the painting. These illusions are very similar to the effects of our modern 3-D and IMAX movies. When viewers are looking at the center of the screen in an IMAX theater, they cannot see the edges of the screen. By taking away the boundaries, it tricks viewers' minds into thinking that they are part of the movie. When you watch a movie wearing 3-D glasses, it appears as though objects are coming out of the screen toward you. The real objects in the artificial foreground of the painting use a similar trick to make you feel as if everything around you is real. Viewers in the nineteenth century said that the cycloramas were so realistic that they could be confused with reality.

One of the most respected teams of cyclorama artists was led by the French artist Paul Philippoteaux and his father, Felix Henri Philippoteaux. In 1881, a Chicago businessman hired Paul Philippoteaux to paint the first American cyclorama, *The Battle of Gettysburg*. In 1882, the artist traveled to the United States and did about six months of study in order to plan the massive painting. The first version opened in Chicago in 1883; it was such a big hit that the artist was commissioned to paint three more copies of the painting. The second copy opened in Boston in 1884. It is this copy that still survives and is on display in Gettysburg. The artist also painted copies for Philadelphia in 1885 and New York in 1886.

The Gettysburg Cyclorama was a huge success, and it created a craze in the United States. In addition to the four original versions, as many as two dozen more copies of the Gettysburg Cyclorama may have been painted by other artists. Cyclorama studios were built in several other towns, and artists created cycloramas of many other Civil War battles, such as Shiloh, Second Manassas, Vicksburg, Atlanta, and Missionary Ridge. Before long, every major city had one or more cyclorama buildings that could display these giant round paintings.

If cycloramas were the movies of their day, then *The Battle of Gettysburg* was the *Star Wars* of cycloramas on two different levels. First, both were huge commercial successes. The promoters estimated that two million people saw the Chicago version of the painting during the first ten years it was on display. All the other versions were also commercial successes. Investors in the companies that built the cyclorama buildings received good returns on their investments. Copies of *The Battle of Gettysburg* made it as far away as Australia and New Zealand. Second, both were on the cutting edge of technology in the entertainment industry. These giant paintings were a spectacle beyond any other form of entertainment viewers had ever seen before. In the same way, the special effects of *Star Wars* were years ahead of their time. It took years until other moviemakers could create special effects as good as those in *Star Wars*. Many of the special effects–driven movies of today rely on techniques pioneered by George Lucas and his team.

I recently discovered that the Gettysburg Cyclorama painting was modified in 1889. The promoters closed the painting and added more troops, flags, generals, and cannons to the canvas. These changes were based on suggestions from the audience, which included actual veterans of the battle. In this way, the cyclorama now on display in Gettysburg is the "director's cut" of the painting. It is very much like George Lucas's special edition of *Star Wars* with improved special effects.

Cycloramas were extremely popular in the late nineteenth century. Unfortunately, when motion pictures became popular in the early twentieth century, the cycloramas were no longer profitable, and most were neglected and abandoned. The Boston version of the cyclorama traveled to several different cities before it was brought to Gettysburg in 1913 for the fiftieth anniversary of the battle and reunion of the veterans. By this point, the painting was in bad condition, with visible seams and tears. The diorama of real objects had been lost, and some of the sky had been cut off the top of the painting. Since the top and bottom of the painting were now visible, it ruined any illusion of depth that the painting was meant to create. Even though the cyclorama had deteriorated, it was still a popular attraction. As the years went by, the condition of the painting worsened. By the end of the twentieth century, the painting was badly in need of repair.

Fortunately, the National Park Service and the Gettysburg Foundation worked together to fund a complete restoration of the painting. The cyclorama opened in its current location in 2008, after years of extensive restoration. All the elements that are necessary to create a cyclorama are now in place, including the raised viewing platform, diorama, and overhead canopy. In its newly restored condition, the cyclorama is one of the most magnificent works of art in the United States. Now that it is displayed properly, it has the same effect on viewers as it did back in the late nineteenth century. Modern viewers cannot believe how realistic the cyclorama appears, especially for a painting. Viewers again feel completely immersed in the scene, as it is difficult to tell where the real objects end and the painting starts. We can be thankful that this amazing painting has survived and is viewed by hundreds of thousands of visitors every year. Newspaper articles in the 1880s said that the painting brought tears to the eyes of some of the old veterans who saw it. The painting still brings tears to the eyes of modern viewers.

Today only two of these massive paintings have survived in the United States, *The Battle of Gettysburg* and *The Battle of Atlanta*, slated for a summer 2017 opening. It is unfortunate that more of these wonderful artworks have not survived. But in Gettysburg and Atlanta, the Civil War enthusiast can still become immersed in this lost form of art and entertainment.

The cyclorama is important today for other reasons. By studying the cyclorama, we can learn about the contrasts in how the battle was interpreted in 1884 and the way it is interpreted today. We can also learn about the terrain of the battlefield and the way it has changed over the years. Paul Philippoteaux did months of extensive research before the creation of the painting. You could say that the cyclorama was the first documentary of the Battle of Gettysburg, the equivalent of Ken Burns's *The Civil War*. As part of his research, the artist interviewed several participants in the battle, including Generals Hancock, Doubleday, and Webb. Philippoteaux toured the battlefield with a guide and went to the War Department to study the records and maps of the battle. Finally, he hired a local photographer to take terrain photographs of the area of the High Water Mark. Using all these sources, the artist and his team were able to make the painting highly accurate. Even though the cyclorama is the product of the artist's imagination, it can still teach us about the actual battle.

Fig. 14.1. Chris Brenneman (*second from right*) orients visitors to the Gettysburg Cyclorama from the observation platform at the center of the painting. *Ray Matlock.*

I've compared the cyclorama to a documentary, but that might not be the best comparison. The cyclorama is actually more like historical fiction. A better comparison would be the 1974 book *The Killer Angels*, by Michael Shaara, or Ron Maxwell's 1993 movie *Gettysburg*, which was based on the book. Considering the fact that the cyclorama was a moneymaking entertainment venture, this is not surprising. Creators of historical fiction typically seek to be as accurate and authentic as possible. However, sometimes a good story eclipses the truth. Not everything in the painting is 100 percent accurate; we can see some cases of artistic license. Some of the liberties taken by the artist were done to help tell the story and make every part of the painting as entertaining as possible. For example, in the later versions of the painting, the artist moved General Meade's Headquarters closer to the viewer, into an area where there was not much action in the first version. Also, some of the scenes depicted in the painting may not have happened at the exact same moment in time. In the painting, both Confederate general Lewis Armistead and Union lieutenant Alonzo Cushing are being killed at the same moment in time. In reality, however, Cushing was killed as Armistead and his men overran Cushing's artillery battery. Armistead was mortally wounded in the fighting that ensued inside the Union lines, past Cushing's position, several minutes later. The artist clearly had heard both stories and wanted to include as many interesting vignettes as possible on the canvas, even if they happened a few minutes apart. In a similar artistic choice, in the book *The Killer Angels* and the movie *Gettysburg*, we see Colonel Chamberlain taking part in the final fight at the end of Pickett's Charge. In real life, Chamberlain was not in that area at the end of the battle. However, it only made sense to keep the main character of the book (and movie) involved in the climactic ending of the story.

During his research in 1882, Philippoteaux hired a local photographer named William H. Tipton to take terrain photographs of the area where Pickett's Charge ended. These photographs were some of the first pictures taken of the area that is now known as the High Water Mark of the Confederacy. In the days after the battle, teams of photographers arrived with the goal of documenting the battle. The photographers wanted to show the effects of a battle in terms of human suffering, so most of the pictures focus on bodies, not the terrain itself. By the time the photographers arrived, the bodies in the area of the High Water Mark had already been buried, so they moved on to other areas. As a result, the Tipton photographs are still some of our best views of the way the terrain looked during the battle and are important for this reason alone. By comparing the painting with the terrain photographs that the artists used, we can see that the landscape in the cyclorama is extremely accurate. The artist and his assistants, particularly the landscape specialists on his team, were highly skilled, and they missed few details. Historic maps help us fill in the gaps in time between 1863 and when the Tipton photographs were taken in 1882. For example, a few farms that were built after the war can be seen in the painting (and the 1882 photographs). The evergreen trees that line the border of the National Cemetery are also visible in the painting but were not present in 1863.

The cyclorama also helps us see some of the ways the battlefield has changed over the years. By comparing the battlefield today with the painting and the historic pictures, we can see that the tree cover has changed. Historic maps show more trees and woodlots than are visible in the painting. However, we know that many trees were cut down after the battle to replace damaged fences and as a source of income for farmers who had lost their crops. Today there are also more trees than can be seen in the cyclorama. The National Park Service tries to keep the tree lines on the battlefield as close to their 1863 locations as possible. However, in many areas, the trees are larger and the woods are thicker than they were in 1863. With only a little bit of imagination, the painting becomes a great tool to help us visualize the way the landscape looked in 1863.

One of the most frequently heard comments among modern visitors to the cyclorama is that they cannot believe a painting from the nineteenth century could have such a convincing effect on the viewer.[2] The cyclorama makes you feel as if you are outside and could walk into the scene. The modern sound and light presentation also helps draw the viewer into the action. Sound effects mimic the sounds of battle as a narrator reads dramatic quotes from Civil War soldiers. Lighting effects create the illusion of smoke and the flash of cannons and muskets. The result is quite dramatic, and the cyclorama serves as a great educational tool for hundreds of thousands of visitors each year. The current cyclorama presentation is truly a piece of modern entertainment.

One might even postulate that the cyclorama is a good example of what the future of entertainment may look like. The biggest trends in entertainment today all involve making viewers feel more and more immersed in the scene around them. As discussed earlier, 3-D and IMAX movies use optical illusions similar to those of the cycloramas. Virtual reality goggles are becoming the video gaming trend of the future. These goggles, along with the sounds and images of the game, remove as much of reality as possible and make the gamer feel immersed in the scene. Even science fiction includes virtual reality spaces similar to the cyclorama. Fans of *Star Trek: The Next Generation* are familiar with the holodeck, a giant virtual reality recreation room. The holodeck can project moving images and objects to make viewers feel as if they are in almost any location or situation, such as horseback riding, skiing, or at a historic event. This concept of a holodeck is like a cyclorama where the people in the scene move. We don't know what the entertainment of the future will look like, but it likely will include some of the immersive illusions that the cycloramas used so effectively.

The cycloramas of the nineteenth century were the movies of their day. Like *Star Wars*, the Gettysburg Cyclorama was the biggest commercial success of the genre. Over the years, millions and millions of visitors have viewed this artistic masterpiece. Today, after years of restoration, the cyclorama has been returned to its original glory. With the addition of modern lights and sound effects, the cyclorama is just as impressive as some of our modern entertainment venues. With its immersive illusions, it also points the way to the virtual reality entertainment of the future.

Notes

1. For a full treatment of this topic, and for source material on some of the information cited in this essay, see Chris Brenneman's book, coauthored with Susan Boardman, *The Gettysburg Cyclorama: The Turning Point of the Civil War on Canvas* (El Dorado Hills, CA: Savas Beatie, 2017).
2. For historical and modern first-person testimonials about the painting from visitors, see Susan Boardman and Kathryn Porch, *The Battle of Gettysburg Cyclorama: A History and Guide* (Gettysburg: Thomas Publications, 2008).

15. ❧ Marching against Dixie: The Creation of *Gone with the Wind* as an American Icon

Sarah Kay Bierle

"War, war, war! There isn't going to be any war," Scarlett O'Hara boldly proclaimed, completely unprepared for life, love, or a coming world where she'd lie, steal, and cheat to survive. Seated on the veranda of her beloved Tara, the fictional Southern darling could hardly imagine what tomorrow would bring. Flirtation, rejection, and heartbreak loomed large in her centered little world at the next day's barbecue. In a superb cinema moment, the news of Fort Sumter's fall echoed into the Twelve Oaks plantation hall, and the beaux and other belles rushed toward the door, eager for the fray, while the movie soundtrack played "Dixie." Scarlett resolutely marched up the stairs, against the tide of swirling, flowing skirts. Dixie had no appeal to her.

It's strange how a girl who had no patience with war or the Lost Cause has become the figurehead of pop culture views of the Civil War South. The absorbing popularity of Margaret Mitchell's novel, fascinating beauty of the Hollywood film, relatable aspects of the characters and conflicts, and all the glorious, impractical, pretty dresses have factored into the foundation, growth, and endurance of *Gone with the Wind* in American and international societies.

Margaret Mitchell, author of *Gone with the Wind*, modestly downplayed her intentions for the novel in public, but some of her letters reveal her hopes for the best seller. As one critic has observed, "She sought to correct northern stereotypes of the South and to replace them with her own 'truth.'"[1] Mitchell successfully followed the adage for authors: write what you know.

Born on November 8, 1900, Margaret Mitchell was a Southern girl, and more important, she was an Atlanta girl; from her birth to her death, she lived in her favorite busy city—leaving only for a year at college and short business trips. In her childhood, she listened to Confederate veterans as they "refought the old campaigns, and argued about the tangled, bewildering muddle of politics in the Reconstruction days." Mitchell explained, "So how could I help knowing about the Civil War and the hard times that came after it? I was raised on it. I thought it all happened just a few years before I was born."[2]

Fascinated and influenced by the history and people around her, she enjoyed writing and studying history. By age twenty-one, Mitchell had read all the books on Southern history in the Atlanta Public Library, imbibing a very Southern view of her local history.[3] Returning from a year at school in the North, Mitchell shocked the Atlanta matrons with "scandalous" actions during her debutante year and eventually married a charming rogue, Red Upshaw. Her first marriage collapsed, and Mitchell took a job at the local newspaper to support herself. In 1925, she married John Marsh. Laid up at home with troublesome health, Mitchell read voraciously until Marsh exclaimed she would have to write her own book. Years of secretive writing and stashed manila envelopes later, Mitchell summoned her courage and allowed Henry Latham, an editor from Macmillan, to see her manuscript. Latham was highly impressed with the draft. Contracts and months of feverish editing, proofreading, and historical fact-checking followed.

The first edition of *Gone with the Wind* was bound in "Confederate gray" cloth with blue lettering and a small pictorial scene of two men and a Southern belle; the volume weighed almost three pounds and was 1,037 pages in length. Review copies created a buzzy grassroots campaign among literary critics, reviewers, booksellers, and a few literary figures, while the Macmillan publicity department barraged and besieged the newspapers and other advertising outlets with flashy and exciting ads and news releases in one of the best publicity campaigns up to that time, helping establish instant popularity.[4] By June 30, 1936—the official release date—America was anxious for the new novel, and the Book of the Month Club quickly gave its stamp of approval. Readers flocked to the bookstores, and retailers couldn't keep the book on the shelves.[5] Margaret Mitchell received the millionth copy as a Christmas gift in 1936, just six short months after the book's release.[6] The following year on May 3, 1937, she received a telegram announcing *Gone with the Wind*'s Pulitzer Prize.[7] Each milestone and positive review for the book was celebrated and broadcast by the publicity department, and the books continued to sell to waiting readers, most eager to embrace the story and "history" Mitchell presented.

The novel's popularity created a large fan base, but those fans didn't always appreciate the historical context Margaret Mitchell had spent hours researching. In 1936, the author complained about reviewers, "I wish some of them would actually read the book . . . I wrote—not the book they imagine I've written or the book they think I should have written." Reviewers and readers have interpreted *Gone with the Wind* in ways that suit themselves, often taking Mitchell's ideas and morphing them into a new perception. Mitchell shared her frustration:

> Since my novel was published, I have been embarrassed on many occasions by finding myself included among the writers who pictured the Old South as a land of white-columned mansions whose wealthy owners had thousands of slaves and drank thousands of juleps. I have been surprised, too, for North Georgia certainly was no such country—if it ever existed anywhere—and I took great pains to describe North Georgia as it was. But people like to believe what they like to believe and the mythical Old South has too strong a hold on their imaginations to be altered by the mere reading of a 1,037-page book.[8]

Imagination would receive additional fuel from the 1939 Hollywood epic *Gone with the Wind*. Acknowledged as a best film from Hollywood's studio days, and with a title that is "synonymous with Hollywood itself," *Gone with the Wind* was one of the most anticipated movies in its day and remains a classic for many.[9] Producer David O. Selznick paid $50,000 for the movie rights to the best seller, and by the end of 1936, he had received seventy-five thousand letters from fans across the nation regarding the adaptation.[10] Margaret Mitchell insisted that she wanted nothing to do with filmmaking and positively refused to work on the script, declaring that she did not want blame for Hollywood's version of history.[11] As one researcher has pointed out, "The film Selznick made was his own creation, not Mitchell's."[12]

Selznick launched a fantastic publicity campaign long before filming began. The search for an actress to play Scarlett O'Hara took two years and $92,000, involving fourteen thousand candidates and ninety screen tests.[13] In the end, British actress Vivien Leigh was cast as Scarlett O'Hara, joining Clark Gable (Rhett Butler), Leslie Howard (Ashley Wilkes), Olivia de Havilland (Melanie Wilkes), and Hattie McDaniel (Mammy). Filming began on December 10, 1938, with the burning of Atlanta scenes.[14] Five months and one day later, 449,512 feet of film had been shot, about twelve scriptwriters had worked on the project, and three directors rotated through the sets with plenty of off-screen cast drama. When the final film cut was complete, it was 160,000 feet of classic cinema, costing $4,085,790.[15]

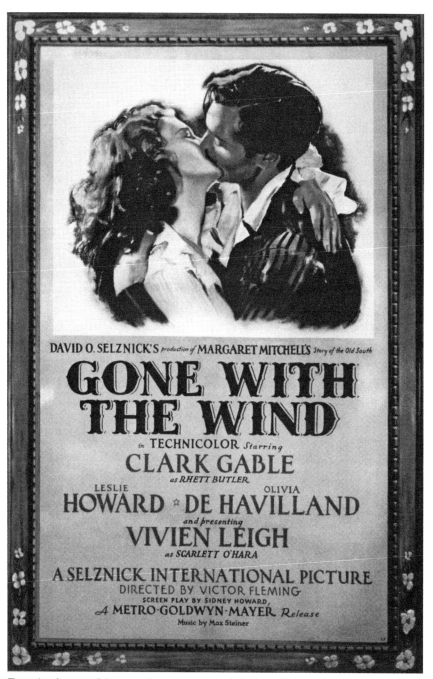

Fig. 15.1. As one of the most famous movies of all time, *Gone with the Wind* overshadows the Pulitzer Prize–winning novel that inspired it. *Library of Congress.*

For three years, America had been waiting for the movie, following the "search for Scarlett" and other fan magazine stories. In Atlanta, advance ticket sales reached $47,000 by December 11, 1939.[16] The film premiere held in Atlanta celebrated the idealized Old South and the Lost Cause and was attended by the film's stars and celebrities, while three hundred thousand people lined the streets. Margaret Mitchell, usually publicly shy of her adoring fans, attended the movie's opening night in her home city. By the following June—after winning ten Academy Awards—*Gone with the Wind* had been viewed by 25 million people at advance ticket prices.[17]

The movie's popularity continued in the theaters, and with the eventual advent of television, new profits became available. On November 7, 1976, the first television broadcast of *Gone with the Wind* aired to 33,750,000 viewers.[18] A researcher has suggested, "The simplicity of Selznick's presentation allowed Southerners and Northerners alike to enjoy his portrait of the Old South with little hesitation or much consciousness of the divided and irresolvable realities Mitchell sought to reveal."[19] Despite the differences between Selznick's movie and Mitchell's novel, the film has more powerfully captured and shaped the American imagination. However, the movie's simplicity was misleading, sweeping unsuspecting viewers deep into the myths of happy plantations, rebellious belles, and shallow gentlemen.

From the beginning of *Gone with the Wind*'s saga in culture, it faced criticism. Literary critics weren't always quite sure what to do with or where to place a novel written by an Atlanta housewife who claimed she had written it in her spare time.[20] Additionally, both book and movie faced heavy criticism from the African American community through all decades. Selznick made a sincere effort to remove (or cover up) most of the eyebrow-raising language in the script but kept (and exaggerated) some 1930s stereotypical roles, like Prissy portrayed by Butterfly McQueen. With passing decades and increasing ethnic and gender sensitivity, other objections have been raised. Some have called for a ban on *Gone with the Wind* for its cringe-worthy or slanted paragraphs and moments; others defend the publication and production as art forms, historical pieces from the 1930s, or "classics." The debates over *Gone with the Wind* have sometimes created a warlike frenzy, almost as hostile and exciting as the naïve mad dash to war during the Twelve Oaks barbecue. Nonetheless, fans' devotion to *Gone with the Wind* remains as unswerving as Scarlett's love for Ashley, despite changes, challenges, and debates involving sensitive scholars and citizens.

Why has *Gone with the Wind* remained an enduring and (to some extent) enjoyed tradition? Certainly, some love the book for its literary qualities, and the movie is considered an old Hollywood masterpiece. But why has it lasted? Film actress Olivia de Havilland believed the universal themes of conflict, defeat, and renaissance have made it successful and popular.[21] Whether viewed as a survival story, feminist declaration, or piece of nostalgia, *Gone with the Wind* is a powerhouse of inspiration for many.

The book and film were released during the Great Depression, when many families were struggling financially. They identified with the survival themes in the story: if Scarlett survived, they could too.[22] Similarly, *Gone with the Wind* gained popularity as a resilience tale in Nazi-occupied Europe during World War II and in postwar Japan; recognizing the power of the "underdog wins" story, the Soviet Union refused to allow publication in that country because it might provide hope for the citizens in the Eastern Bloc.[23] In the modern era, *Gone with the Wind* is often the imagery that foreigners and immigrants find as their introduction (or "complete" education) to Civil War history.[24] Right or wrong, it continues to shape ideals of a past era in U.S. history.

At the center of that "history lesson" is a controversial Southern belle. Scarlett is bold. She knows what she wants, or at least thinks she does. Reflecting ideas from her author's earlier life and the flapper image of the Roaring Twenties—though gracefully disguised in hoops and bustles—Scarlett O'Hara Hamilton Kennedy Butler was a "modern woman" cavorting in an old period. Eventually shunned by "good" Southern society (more vivid in the book than the movie), Scarlett frequently tossed 1860s propriety, manners, and morals to the wind, eager to pursue any course that would bring her a good time, security, money, or idealized love. She's a flawed heroine who literally controls her own story—this is no damsel in distress waiting for a rescuer. Aspects of this attitude have appalled and appealed to women, the most avid readers and viewers of the epic over the decades.[25] Through the lens of literature and imagined history, generations of women have identified with Scarlett's struggles and—perhaps subconsciously—adopted some of her gumption, ambition, and goals as they press against their own glass ceilings.

While the modern female audience draws lessons from Scarlett's "success," some express a nostalgic longing. Scarlett's mantra (particularly in the book) relates to tomorrow: "I'll think about that tomorrow" or "tomorrow is another day." She resolves not to look back, but her fictional story and movie invite readers to do that. Many women (and some men) find solace in picturing "the good old days"—including the antebellum period in the South. They imagine "a land of Cavaliers and Cotton Fields" where "Gallantry took its last bow," with "Knights and their Ladies Fair . . . A Civilization gone with the wind."[26] They create a world of white-pillared mansions, ruffled hoop-skirted dresses, a bevy of beaux, and swirling dancing. "Oh, what marvelous days, what lovely dresses," they sigh, forgetting—at least momentarily—that slaves worked the plantations, propriety was required to be "a lady," marriage held limited rights for the wife, and those were starving times in the Civil War South. Rose-colored spectacles provide alluring images of the past and prompt feelings of wistful longing for a different era and place—a unique setting existing almost entirely in the mind's eye.

"He never really existed at all, except in my imagination," Scarlett finally realizes, on Melanie's dying day. "I loved something I made up. . . . I made a pretty suit of clothes and fell in love with it. . . . I kept on loving the pretty clothes—and not him at all."[27] Her epiphany reveals the shallowness of her love for Ashley Wilkes—and, it may be, for the larger South.

Perhaps it also sheds light on an aspect where *Gone with the Wind* reigns supreme, and almost unquestioned, in pop culture: clothes! Dresses, gowns, corsets, hoops, hats, bonnets—Scarlett O'Hara, or more correctly, Vivien Leigh—had it all, as well as the right figure to look charming in silk or calico. With a wardrobe (costumer's rack) to make many women jealous and a physical appearance appealing to male viewers, Scarlett O'Hara has epitomized the image of the Southern belle. She has become the figurehead for the South. The poster child for the Civil War lady. And there the fateful reality begins.

Scarlett O'Hara may have looked the part, but she was "no lady," to quote Rhett Butler. Additionally, she was no Confederate supporter. The war held no charms for her. She did not align with the postwar Lost Causers, siding instead with scalawags and carpetbaggers to make money. And yet—somehow—she is the beloved image of the Old South views of Civil War and Reconstruction, the ideal of a hoopskirted belle reigning on a throne of pop plantations, surrounded by chivalric gray-clad officers. It's an image that, unlike Scarlett O'Hara, constantly needs rescuing when assaulted by historical facts but still, remarkably, rises again to announce that "tomorrow is another day."

Whether Margaret Mitchell realized it or not, she crafted, nurtured, and revised an American legend of the antebellum period, Civil War, and Reconstruction; David Selznick expanded and capitalized on the imagery, creating a motion picture that has influenced generations of viewers and will continue to do so. The wars regarding the political correctness and societal appropriateness of *Gone with the Wind* will rage on while the fan base adores the inspiration for survival, feminine achievement, and bygone dreams. At the core of the public image floats Scarlett O'Hara, supposedly epitomizing Southern grace, dedication, and success.

Historical research and long-winded lecturing do not uproot the lovely myth of happy Tara with contented slaves and charming belles. Somehow, the darker images in *Gone with the Wind* are obscured or ignored. Scarlett, Rhett, Ashley, and Melanie repeat their colorful drama again and again in theaters, on television, and as home entertainment. For many, they are the Civil War; their story exemplifies the divisive conflict. Though "tomorrow is another day," it seems that the book's and movie's influence on pop culture will continue strong for a while yet. Scarlett O'Hara was not a loyal Confederate or Southern lady, but society has said, "Frankly, my dear, I don't give a damn," determined to keep her as the iconic Southern darling . . . even if she marched against "Dixie" as others charged naïvely toward the excitement of the conflict on that fateful, fictional day at the Twelve Oaks plantation barbecue.

Notes

1. Elizabeth I. Hanson, *Margaret Mitchell* (Chapel Hill: University of North Carolina, 1991), 58.
2. Finis Farr, *Margaret Mitchell of Atlanta: The Author of* Gone with the Wind; *Her Story* (New York: William Morrow, 1965), 15.
3. Marianne Walker, *Margaret Mitchell and John Marsh: The Love Story behind* Gone with the Wind (Atlanta, GA: Peachtree, 1993), 71.
4. Ellen F. Brown and John Wiley Jr., *Margaret Mitchell's* Gone with the Wind: *A Bestseller's Odyssey from Atlanta to Hollywood* (Lanham, MD: Taylor Trade, 2011), 59–60, 117.
5. Walker, *Margaret Mitchell and John Marsh*, 275.
6. Brown and Wiley, *Margaret Mitchell's* Gone with the Wind, 133.
7. Walker, *Margaret Mitchell and John Marsh*, 359.
8. Ibid., 275, vii.
9. Jeremy Arnold, *Turner Classic Movies: The Essentials; 52 Must-See Movies and Why They Matter* (Philadelphia: Running Press, 2016), 68.
10. Brown and Wiley, *Margaret Mitchell's* Gone with the Wind, 111.
11. Farr, *Margaret Mitchell of Atlanta*, 169.
12. Hanson, *Margaret Mitchell*, 94.
13. Molly Haskell, *Frankly, My Dear:* Gone with the Wind *Revisited* (New Haven, CT: Yale University Press, 2009), 69.
14. Brown and Wiley, *Margaret Mitchell's* Gone with the Wind, 185.
15. Walker, *Margaret Mitchell and John Marsh*, 418.

16. Ibid., 420.

17. Farr, *Margaret Mitchell of Atlanta*, 198.

18. Brown and Wiley, *Margaret Mitchell's* Gone with the Wind, 299.

19. Hanson, *Margaret Mitchell*, 95.

20. Darden Asbury Pyron, ed., *Recasting:* Gone with the Wind *in American Culture* (Miami: University Press of Florida, 1983).

21. Missy Schwartz, ed., Gone with the Wind: *The Great American Movie 75 Years Later* (New York: Life Books, 2014), 18.

22. Helen Taylor, *Scarlett's Women:* Gone with the Wind *and Its Female Fans* (New Brunswick, NJ: Rutgers University Press, 1989), 98–99.

23. Farr, *Margaret Mitchell of Atlanta*, 214–19; Brown and Wiley, *Margaret Mitchell's* Gone with the Wind, 293.

24. Taylor, *Scarlett's Women*, 105.

25. Ibid., 94, 22–23.

26. Ben Hecht, opening text of *Gone with the Wind*, 1939.

27. Margaret Mitchell, *Gone with the Wind* (1936; repr., New York: Pocket Books, 2008), 1418–19.

16. ✻ "The Elephant in the Room": Slavery in Cinema from *Gone with the Wind* to *12 Years a Slave*

Kevin Pawlak

Adorned in an aqua blue dress with gardenia flowers affixed to her hair, gripping a purse bumped with rhinestones, Hattie McDaniel sat in the back of the packed room. It was not for her lack of importance that she was relegated far from the stage: her director had said that without her, the movie never would have happened. In the front of the room, a woman approached the microphone, holding a golden man on a pedestal. "I'm really especially happy that I am chosen to present this particular plaque. To me it seems more than just a plaque of gold," she began. It exposed "the whole of America; an America that pays tribute to those who give their best, regardless of creed, race, or color."

Finally, the announcement came, and McDaniel rose from her seat in the back of the room and dashed to the stage. Cameras flashed as she accepted the award and took her place at the podium. Her ovation "will go down in history as one of the greatest ever accorded," remembered one witness. But it was not the ovation that went down in history—that constituted only a piece of the evening. Here at the 1940 Academy Awards, Hattie McDaniel became the first black actress to win an Oscar. Most people knew McDaniel simply by her character in the silver screen epic *Gone with the Wind*, Mammy.[1]

Seventy-four years later, another woman, similarly adorned in a light-blue dress, sat among the awards show crowd, waiting for her name to be called. It was. With tears in her eyes, she stepped onto the stage and took the golden man in her hands. Lupita Nyong'o, too, received an outstanding ovation for her role in the successful adaptation of Solomon Northup's memoir *Twelve Years a Slave*. Other black women had won Oscars for their roles in movies since McDaniel became the first, but this time, in 2014, it was different.

Fig. 16.1. Hattie McDaniel (*left*) and Vivien Leigh (*right*) both won Academy Awards for their roles in *Gone with the Wind*; Olivia de Havilland (*center*) was also nominated but lost to McDaniel. The movie has painted our perception of the Civil War era—and the relationships and characteristics of black and white people—since its release in 1939. *MGM Studios/Wikimedia Commons.*

The next day, I sat in my African American history class during my last semester of college, waiting for class to begin. Without warning, my professor burst through the door and yelled something to the effect that it was about time Hollywood granted an Academy Award to an African American for their role in a film that attempted—and came closer than any previous film had—to portray the true character of slavery, America's peculiar institution. His meaning was not lost on me. Both Hattie McDaniel and Lupita Nyong'o portrayed female slaves in their respective films; both of their films proved to be successful, but one—*Gone with the Wind*—has been labeled a justification of the Lost Cause mentality, while *12 Years a Slave* has been lauded for its more critical view of American slavery.

Slavery has never been an easy issue to depict for Hollywood. Yet that does not preclude one from jotting down a lengthy list of films that, either directly or indirectly, deal with slavery and race, from the 1915 *Birth of a Nation* to the 2016 *Birth of a Nation*. To keep this essay within the confines of its limits, it will not give an exhaustive rundown of how scores of films have interpreted slavery. While films such as *Mandingo, Song of the South,* and a host of others have molded popular culture's depictions over many decades, this chapter, while sporadically drawing from some of these films, will focus much of its attention on two films: David Selznick's 1939 *Gone with the Wind* and Steve McQueen's 2013 *12 Years a Slave.* This is not to say that the story begins and ends with these motion pictures, but when the two are examined by their popularity, success, and laurels (most notably, two black women receiving the same award for two very different roles), they serve as wonderful bookends from which we can truly measure the changes in the silver screen's rendering of that peculiar institution.

* * *

Since its initial release, *Gone with the Wind* has remained one of the highest-grossing and most-watched films of all time, not to mention one of the most prominent Civil War–era films, if not *the* most prominent. Its role in shaping the public's perception of the antebellum, Civil War, and postbellum South has diminished little in the nearly eight decades since its release. In the movie's first six years making the rounds, approximately 120 million Americans saw the film (and there were about that many adults living in the country at that time).[2]

Filmgoers were engrossed from the start, drawn away into "a land of Cavaliers and Cotton Fields," as the movie's prologue states. And how could one not be transfixed by the stunning views of Southern plantations—plantations too large for that part of Georgia—and by characters like the shrewd and beautiful Scarlett O'Hara?

Margaret Mitchell's novel and David Selznick's adaptation of *Gone with the Wind* clearly portray the mid-nineteenth century from a Southern white perspective (the story was a product of its time). To be more precise, it is the aristocrats of the antebellum South who string the story along behind them, while slaves predominantly occupy the background, serving as simplistic and, in some cases, comical characters in an otherwise complex and serious story.

Slavery is dismissed entirely as a cause for the war. "Land is the only thing worth fighting for," explains Mr. O'Hara. When Southerners like the renegade blockade runner Rhett Butler and Scarlett's love, Ashley Wilkes, say things such as "The cause of living in the past is dying right in front of us" and describe a postwar South as a world "worse than death," they are not lamenting over the loss of their servants, but over the loss of the chivalric land "of Knights and their Ladies Fair" known to them before the war. In fact, in the film, it does not even appear they had lost their slaves at all.

Benign and *caring* are words that come to mind—and are often used—to describe *Gone with the Wind*'s version of slavery. Slaves are pictured as content, perhaps even pleased, with their situation in bondage, and the affection they display toward their masters seems mutual. "I don't like the way you're treating Prissy and Mammy," Mr. O'Hara says, scolding Scarlett for her treatment of two of the film's most memorable servants. "You must be firm with inferiors, but gentle with them. Especially darkies," he continues. Another scene, this time from the postwar portions of the movie, includes a dialogue between Ashley Wilkes and Scarlett that perfectly plays into the theme of white owners' feelings toward their slaves. When Ashley implores Scarlett to let him hire "free darkies" rather than convicts for their lumber mill, Scarlett shoots back that hiring free black people would break their enterprise financially. "Scarlett, I will not make money out of the enforced labor and misery of others," he says, though he had no qualms owning slaves, as Scarlett notes. "That was different," says Ashley. "We didn't treat them that way. Besides, I'd have freed them all when father died if the war hadn't already freed them," he concludes in a repetition of an oft-quoted postwar defense of slave owners.

Other portions of the film demonstrate the seemingly inseparable bond between slave and master and white benevolence toward blacks. While Scarlett spends time in Atlanta during the 1864 siege of that city, she comes upon a column of marching black men the Confederate army had impressed to dig fortifications. Immediately, she sees several slaves she knows, including one who portrays the stereotypical faithful slave in the film, Big Sam. Scarlett and Big Sam talk of Tara and of Scarlett's family before the slave segues into why he and the others are in Atlanta. With a grin on his face, Big Sam exclaims they had been taken from Tara "to dig ditches fo' de white sojers to hide in." As he marches away, Sam reassures Scarlett, "Don't worry—we'll stop dem Yankees." Scarlett, being the compassionate owner, in a moment demonstrating the paternalistic views of slave owners toward their slaves, promises to care for any of the slaves if they become sick or injured, demonstrating a sense of devotion that her loyal slaves return in kind.[3]

The most significant instance of slave loyalty in the film plays out not just in one scene but throughout the entire movie. Despite the destruction to Tara, despite the fact that all of Southern society was swept away with the wind, the O'Haras' servants—first enslaved and later free—remain a constant. Pork,

Prissy, and Mammy never leave Tara when it nearly falls to pieces during the war. Even after Scarlett returns to her war-ravaged home, the three servants remain steadfast by her side. Incredibly, it seems that their roles hardly change from the prewar and war scenes to the postwar.

Hattie McDaniel's Mammy, whether as a slave or a free black, is the most prominent black character in the film, and certainly its most memorable. She defined a mammy for film "once and for all," said one student of Civil War reels.[4] In the ever-changing society of the South that serves as the tracks along which *Gone with the Wind* moves, Mammy is always there, particularly for Scarlett. Mammy's appearance, even so small as her wardrobe, barely changes, blurring, in the viewer's mind, her status—slave or free? And Mammy, like the other slaves in the film, is never the rebellious character. In fact, Scarlett fills most of that characteristic, while Mammy, constantly sniffing out Scarlett's plots and schemes, is the more traditional of the two. Mammy even openly confronts Scarlett about going to Atlanta, knowing that Scarlett wants to go only so she can be nearer to Ashley Wilkes when he comes home from the war.

This theme of slave loyalty to their white masters has reverberated through-out reels of film over the decades since *Gone with the Wind*'s big-screen debut. In fact, in the 1965 film *Shenandoah*, the main black character of the film is a young slave named Gabriel, who befriends the youngest son of the film's protagonist, Charlie Anderson. Gabriel (a slave from another farm) and Boy (Anderson's youngest) remain close throughout the movie. When a patrol of biracial federal soldiers confronts Boy and Gabriel—historically inaccurate because the army did not have mixed-race regiments—Boy is taken prisoner as a Confederate, while a black soldier tells Gabriel he is free and can do as he pleases. Armed with his freedom, the ever-loyal Gabriel hurriedly races back to the Anderson homestead to inform the family about Boy's fate.

Gabriel's controversial place in the movie does not end there, however. In an unspecified (and probably not real) battle in the Shenandoah Valley be-tween the two opposing armies—where Boy is compelled (by his unfortunate circumstances) to fight for the Confederacy after he escapes from the hands of the federals—Boy is wounded during the collapse of the Rebel line. As he helplessly lies there with enemy troops streaming around him, the cold steel of a Yankee bayonet enters the picture. It appears to be the end for the young Anderson. That is, before the camera reveals who the bearer of Boy's near ruin is: his friend Gabriel, who, though not a slave of the Andersons, remains loyal to his white Southern friend, picks him up, and carries him to safety before rushing back to partake in the fight.

The theme of slave loyalty to white people is one that has even made its way into twenty-first-century motion pictures. Ted Turner and Ron Maxwell's 2003 *Gods and Generals*—a film looking at the first two years of the Civil War, much of it through the eyes of Stonewall Jackson, Robert E. Lee, and Southerners on the Virginia home front—was said by one critic to be "the most pro-Confederate film since *Birth of a Nation*." The reviewer continued, "The film depicts slaves as generally happy, vaguely desiring freedom at some future date, but faithful and supportive of their beloved masters and the cause of the Confederacy."[5] Does this sound like an echo back to *Gone with the Wind*?

Fortunately, director Ron Maxwell cut from the theatrical version of the film one of the most pro–Lost Cause scenes, although it appeared in a director's cut of the film Turner Pictures later released. In a cold, wintry Confederate camp, as black laborers for the Confederate army huddle around a fire singing "Steal Away to Jesus," a song about dying and going to heaven but also about slaves running to freedom, Stonewall Jackson's black cook, Jim Lewis, slowly approaches another set of slaves placing a body in a pine coffin before shutting it. "What you gonna do now your massa dead?" Lewis asks his black kitchen assistant, who appears in the script as Helper. "He my boss, not my massa," Helper replies. What is Helper going to do now? Lewis wonders. Go north and join his brother in free Pennsylvania? No, says Helper, he will get his "boss's" body home. Then, tearing up at his loss, Helper explains why this Confederate is different from the rest: "This here rebel give me my freedom papers." This scene is a blatant showing of the Lost Cause legend and promulgates that belief among Civil War enthusiasts and moviegoers across the country.[6]

* * *

Lupita Nyong'o's role in *12 Years a Slave*—the true story of free black Solomon Northup's kidnapping and subsequent experiences as a slave—sheds light on the changing nature of Hollywood's depictions of slavery. Both McDaniel and Nyong'o were the main female characters of their film, but their lots were wholly dissimilar from one another. Nyong'o's character Patsey sits at the forefront of some of the film's most distressing and squeamishly uncomfortable scenes. In his memoir, Solomon called Patsey "queen of the field" but sorrowfully noted, "Patsey wept oftener, and suffered more, than any of her companions. She had been literally excoriated." Northup was quick to place her pain on the shoulders "of a licentious master and a jealous mistress."[7] The film does not shy away from portraying Patsey's suffering. Edwin Epps rapes

Patsey, and during two dance scenes in Epps's home, Patsey receives a blow from a decanter thrown by Epps's wife, who also pricks Patsey in the head with a sharp object at the second social. It grows so bad that Patsey even approaches Solomon about taking her own life to end her misery (a form of rebellion against the slavocracy). "I ain't got no comfort in this life," she tells him.

Patsey's suffering climaxes, ironically, in the film's climax. In a sign of subtle rebelliousness (something slaves never show in *Gone with the Wind*), Patsey travels to a neighboring plantation, apparently without her master Edwin Epps's permission. When she returns, Epps violently confronts Patsey, forcing her to tell him where she went. Patsey relents, her voice crackling and trembling as she explains that she left to obtain a bar of soap not even the size of her palm—something Epps's jealous wife would not give her. "I stink so much, I make myself gag," she cries. "Five hundred pounds of cotton. Day in, day out! And for that, I will be clean." For that, Solomon—whom Epps forces to whip Patsey, threatening to shoot him if he refuses—rips open Patsey's back one lash at a time. Each lash against her back creates an even deeper impression on the viewer's mind.

Where *Gone with the Wind* falls short of the mark in its portrayal of slavery, *12 Years a Slave* transcends it, almost as if the filmmakers believed the film's violence must be excessive to begin chipping away at the common misperceptions of the institution that *Gone with the Wind* and other films firmly cemented in the public psyche. Both films serve memorable scenes for their audiences to consider. Aforementioned scenes of Georgia plantation scenery with content slaves in the cotton fields are cinematographically unforgettable but can be countered with similar scenes of Epps's plantation in *12 Years a Slave*. Only, in those latter scenes, the beauty of the scenery is broken by the crack of a whip or, in one scene, the crumpling of one of those exhausted field slaves. And no matter how gruesome the scene, how can anyone wipe from their minds the scene of Solomon's near lynching, as he dangles at the end of a rope, staying alive only by the tips of his toes as white people look on from the porch of the plantation home while slave children play in the background as if this were nothing new? Never, in all of my years of watching movies in a public theater, did I feel such an air of uneasiness pervade me and the audience around me as I did during that seemingly endless scene.

Lists of the scenes of violence, snapshots of unhappy slaves, and words describing the complexities and crimes of slavery could go on and on from watching McQueen's piece. When approached about including some of these gruesome scenes in his film, McQueen simply said, "Either I was making a movie about slavery or I wasn't, and I decided I wanted to make a movie about slavery," implying that these scenes of violence were needed to rightly depict the peculiar institution.[8]

To be sure, the violence depicted in the film did not detract from its popularity, though some did believe it went too far. "To reduce [slaves'] lives to violence misses far too much of the story," said one critic. "It threatens to swing the pendulum too far the other way." Yet another claimed the film's triumph was "resounding" when it came to depicting the horrors of slavery.[9] It seems that the second assessment caught more traction with the public, the group most susceptible to be swayed and influenced by the Civil War in popular culture. The popularity of Solomon's memoir soared, especially in the wake of *12 Years a Slave*'s three Academy Awards, including Best Picture.

When asked why he wanted to make the film, Steve McQueen was blunt: "I just felt there was a hole in the canon of cinema."[10] It was a hole that has long existed, and it continually shifts as more movies are released to the public on this tough-to-approach topic. The popularity and success of *Gone with the Wind* will probably never be eclipsed by another motion picture illustrating Civil War America. However, films like *12 Years a Slave*, though perhaps going too far in its violent depictions of slavery, as some believe it did, can slowly build a more accurate telling of our nation's past through one of our greatest mediums of communication.

Since the film's release in 2013, the book on which McQueen based his movie has been republished in countless new editions in more than half a dozen different languages, and sales for the book rose with the film's success. Public fascination with *Gone with the Wind* has likewise only increased, and the film is still being shown in select theaters on a limited basis today. With its seventy-fifth anniversary behind us, newly remastered editions of the film still sit on store shelves. Cinematically, "slavery is like the elephant in the room," McQueen said. "We have to confront this topic in a real way. No one's blind anymore. No excuses. That's the power of cinema."[11] So it is, and such is the beauty of the Civil War in pop culture. It gets people talking, and it piques their interest to look more deeply into the truth behind the silver screen stories. And so, the conversation will continue.

Notes

1. Carlton Jackson, *Hattie: The Life of Hattie McDaniel* (Lanham, MD: Madison Books, 1990), 51–52. Transcriptions of Fay Bainter's introduction and Hattie McDaniel's acceptance speech can be found at Andre Soares, "Hattie

McDaniel: Oscar Speech That Made History and Effortless Scene Stealer," Alt Film Guide, accessed 26 October 2016, http://www.altfg.com/film /hattie-mcdaniel/.

2. Bruce Chadwick, *The Reel Civil War: Mythmaking in American Film* (New York: Alfred A. Knopf, 2001), 187.

3. *Paternalism* is a term used to describe slave owners and their views toward their slaves. The term characterizes a system of enslavement "in which masters took personal interest in the lives of their slaves." In return for their paternalistic treatment of their slaves, owners expected slaves to return the favor with their "loyalty and work." Peter Kolchin, *American Slavery: 1619–1877* (New York: Hill and Wang, 1993), 60, 111–12.

4. Chadwick, *Reel Civil War*, 87.

5. Steven E. Woodworth, review of *Gods and Generals*, directed by Ron Maxwell, *Journal of American History* 90, no. 3 (December 2003): 1123–24.

6. This scene can be found at https://www.youtube.com/watch?v=hvVlkKD dSp4. As of the date of this writing, this video alone has over fifty-three thousand views.

7. Solomon Northup, *Twelve Years a Slave: Narrative of Solomon Northup, a Citizen of New-York, Kidnapped in Washington City in 1841 and Rescued in 1853, from a Cotton Plantation near the Red River in Louisiana* (Auburn, NY: Derby and Miller, 1853), 188–89.

8. Henry Louis Gates Jr. and Steve McQueen, "12 Years a Slave: A Conversation with Steve McQueen," *Transition* 114 (2014): 192.

9. "Film Roundtable: 12 Years a Slave," *Civil War History* 60, no. 3 (September 2014): 314, 311.

10. Gates and McQueen, "12 Years a Slave," 186.

11. Ibid., 188.

17. ❧ The Civil War in Prime Time:
The TV Miniseries *Roots*, *The Blue
and the Gray*, and *North and South*

Andrew Brumbaugh

The age of Watergate, the defeat in Vietnam, and the evolution of cultural norms ushered untold change into American society. While the social themes of the American Civil War remained ever present, television reflected the dramatic transitions of the baby boomer era. Television executives replaced the wholesome rural programming with new urban settings. A new format for programs came to fruition. The miniseries attempted to tell a story in a predetermined number of episodes, often in consecutive weeks or even nights. This format worked exceptionally well for novel adaptations, providing more time than films and maintaining the serial nature of television. Three popular miniseries of the era looked back to the events that transpired in America over a century earlier. ABC started the trend of historical miniseries with *Roots* in 1977. The 1980s saw *The Blue and the Gray* by CBS in 1982 and the return of ABC with *North and South* in 1985. The three miniseries presented the Civil War period through the perspectives of three different classes of society: slaves, middle-class white people, and white elites.

The story of *Roots* began a year before broadcast with the release of Alex Haley's novel *Roots: The Saga of an American Family*. It told the story of Kunta Kinte, a warrior from West Africa who is captured and sold into slavery. The story follows his life as well as the lives of his descendants down to the author, Haley. The novel surged to the top of the *New York Times* best seller list, where it stayed for twenty-two weeks.

ABC quickly jumped on the opportunity to adapt the successful novel into a television dramatization but maintained some concerns about the project. All the precedents indicated the network should be wary. The general belief in the industry was that white audiences simply would not tune into shows featuring predominantly black casts. NBC had experienced problems with

Southern affiliates in 1958 with *The Nat King Cole Show*. Many regional stations refused to air the show.[1] Since then, no other programs had changed the minds of the TV executives. *The Bill Cosby Show* ran for two seasons starting in 1969 before getting canceled. *The Jeffersons* was in the middle of the third season when *Roots* appeared in print, and the show's ratings indicated a decline in viewership.[2] On top of that, no sponsors were willing to advertise nationally on the show, fearing a boycott of their products.

ABC's qualms eventually led to the groundbreaking format of *Roots*. The network anticipated the broadcast of the show would be an uncomfortable flop that would need to be concluded as soon as possible. It avoided sweep months to prevent unfavorable statistics. Programmers decided to broadcast the show over consecutive nights to negate financial losses in case entire audiences tuned out or stopped watching the network.

To compensate for the relatively unknown leading black cast, well-known white actors were brought in to keep the audience watching. Ed Asner of *The Mary Tyler Moore Show* portrayed the remorseful captain of the slave ship—a character that did not originally appear in Haley's novel. His abusive crewman was portrayed by Ralph Waite, the family patriarch of *The Waltons*. At auction in America, Kunta Kinte was sold to John Reynolds, a fictional Virginian planter played by Lorne Greene of *Bonanza*. Reynolds renames Kunta Kinte "Toby" and trades him to his brother, Dr. William Reynolds, to settle a debt. To round out the ensemble of Hollywood father figures, Robert Reed of *The Brady Bunch* was selected to play Dr. Reynolds.

The show premiered the night of January 23, 1977, so it could be over and done with before the sweeps month of February. However, deciding to run the show consecutively over the course of a week may have helped the show achieve success. The first night started off strong with a solid 40.5 rating—meaning 40.5 percent of homes with televisions tuned in to watch. Aside from episodes four and seven, the viewership steadily increased, peaking with the finale at a record-breaking 51.1 rating. More than 100 million people in America gathered around their television sets to find out the final chapter of the descendants of Kunta Kinte.

The immediate impact of *Roots* rippled across society. Tom Bradley, the only African American mayor in the history of Los Angeles, declared the week of January 23 "Roots Week." "In telling the story of [Haley's] family heritage, he has told the story of all Americans," he proclaimed.[3] More than two dozen other mayors of major cities across the country followed his move and set decrees for the week. The night of the finale, movie theaters in some cities closed early because it would be useless to compete against television that night. Leslie Uggams, the actress who played Kizzy Reynolds, was performing in Las Vegas the week of broadcast and was amazed at what she saw. Casinos were effectively shut down, with guests fleeing to their rooms to watch *Roots* instead of gambling.

Meg Greenfield praised the show in a *Newsweek* column, claiming, "The last publishing event in this country that was in any way comparable to the phenomenon of *Roots* occurred in 1851."[4] She was referring to the publication of *Uncle Tom's Cabin* by Harriet Beecher Stowe, the novel that fueled the abolitionist cause.

Roots aired some of America's dirtiest laundry on national television. The chapter of history dealing with slavery was previously taboo for all realms of media. Historian and civil rights leader Roger Wilkins was amazed by the series. He placed the series alongside the Montgomery bus boycott and the Selma-to-Montgomery march for doing something remarkable. For the first time, white people were able to identify with African Americans as people through the eyes of Kunta Kinte.[5]

When it came time for awards and accolades, *Roots* cleaned the house. The series ended up claiming nine Primetime Emmy awards, a Golden Globe, and a Peabody Award. The astounding thirty-seven Emmy nominations are still a record today for a limited series.[6]

LeVar Burton, the nineteen-year-old actor who portrayed the young Mandinka warrior, was not prepared for the impact of the series. "In every history unit I ever had in school, slavery was always referred to as an economic unit," he said. "It was an economic engine upon which this country was built. The human cost was never a part of that module in school. We got schooled through *Roots*."[7] Before the series, people knew about slavery, but *Roots* provided a chance to actually see it. Colleges and universities added more courses on the history of slavery and *Roots*. Slavery became a part of the legacy of all races, especially that of white Americans.

Of course, *Roots* could not have happened without controversy and irate viewers. Haley's novel was attacked for discrepancies and misrepresentation. Haley faced two different charges of plagiarism; one he disproved, the other was settled out of court.[8] Critics and historians questioned the authenticity of the novel, with some condemning Haley for marketing fiction as fact. Haley eventually admitted that he used a concoction of archival research, oral tradition, and fiction to create the narrative of his ancestors and slavery.[9]

When it came to the public reception of the series, not all were impressed. *Newsday*, the suburban New York City newspaper, had some qualms about the show. "The whites are particularly offensive stereotypes," columnist Marvin Kitman wrote. "But I'm glad for those pat stereotypes. TV viewers know what whites are really like."[10] The *New York Times* relayed a similar tale from a conversation with a Queens family. The wife called for more decent white people to balance out the show, although the husband disagreed, claiming, "No, the good whites had their day with *Gone with the Wind*."[11] Robert Schickel at *Time* found the lack of sympathetic white characters "dramatically vulgar and historically preposterous."[12] The negative views of the series reached places like Cincinnati, which was once a critical stopping point on the trail of escaping slaves fleeing to Canada. In 1977, nearly a third of the city was African American, yet the local ABC affiliate received calls holding the network responsible for the next race riot.

Regardless of race, *Roots* changed how people viewed their personal history. America had just celebrated its bicentennial. *Roots* tapped into that same thirst for history, using Haley's quest for his ancestry as a model. Libraries experienced an increase in visitors searching for family history. The National Archives received 300 percent more inquiries on genealogical records.[13]

Previously, Americans had viewed the continent of Africa as an exotic and dangerous place. "For centuries, we were led to believe that Africa was a country belonging to wild animals," said poet Maya Angelou, "where naked, primitive human beings spent their time either climbing trees, leading safaris, or eating each other."[14] The series in which Haley traced his bloodline back to Africa redefined the image of the continent and forged a relationship with it. Manthia Diawara viewed *Roots* as a critical factor in the phenomenon of people of color changing their identification from black to African American: "Africentricity could not have existed without *Roots*."[15] On top of that, many changed their names or gave their children African names, inspired by Kunta Kinte's refusal to adopt the assigned name of Toby.

Roots changed television and society through its representation of slavery. The civil rights era had started a separation from the established myths created by the Lost Cause, but *Roots* enabled a modern analysis of slavery, the war, and the Confederacy. The romanticized visions of the South containing happy and cordial slaves were indisputably false. This misrepresentation permeated early Hollywood, making it appear to be fact. Thanks to *Roots*, the story was set straight and the memory corrected.[16]

Two years later, ABC adapted the last seven chapters of Haley's novel into a sequel, *Roots: The Next Generations.* It covered the descendants of Kunta Kinte from 1882 to Haley's journey to Africa in 1969. It achieved considerable success, reaching a Nielsen average rating of 30.1 for the series.[17] In 2016, the History Channel remade the original *Roots* to share the story with a new generation. Some changes were made to the story for the contemporary audience, such as the removal of the sympathetic slave ship captain. In an era of a more fractured television audience because of a greater number of channels and programming choices, the remake nonetheless had a respectable average of 6.9 million viewers a night over its four-night run.[18]

* * *

Five years later, CBS was the top broadcast network behind its flagship series, *M*A*S*H.* The iconic show was winding down, leading the network to search for its next big program. Hoping to match the success of *Roots,* CBS invested approximately $17.6 million in a Civil War miniseries called *The Blue and the Gray.* One CBS executive said it was "the most ambitious project the network has ever undertaken."[19] The network was spending three times the budget of *Roots* to create a sweeping epic of the Civil War filled with period wardrobe and large battles by reenactors. Cast members with household names, such as Gregory Peck and Lloyd Bridges, increased the appeal of the series.

The series used Lincoln's "House Divided" speech as a theme and sought to show the effect of the Civil War on ordinary citizens instead of focusing on leaders and generals found in history books. The story followed fictional John Geyser of Virginia, who traveled north to work for his uncle's newspaper in Gettysburg. At the outbreak of war, Geyser remained in the North, where he worked as a wartime illustrator for *Harper's Weekly.* His cousins, the Hales, enlisted in the Union army, while his own brothers enlisted in the Confederate army. Coincidentally, both sides of the family found each other at various points in the war, including an instance where the Hales traveled behind Confederate lines to a barn dance hosted by Luke Geyser.

The idea behind the series came from a story cowritten by the late Bruce Catton and drew on the story of John Geyser of the 7th Pennsylvania Reserves. Serving from spring 1861 to fall 1863, the real Geyser maintained a sketchbook and recorded the war through the eyes of a volunteer infantryman.[20]

The series presented passing overviews of the period by touching on important moments. John Geyser's first assignment was to head to the trial and execution of John Brown. Over the ensuing years of the war, viewers were swept away to a variety of battles and sieges, including First Bull Run, Vicksburg, and the Wilderness. Peck as Lincoln provided perhaps best scene of the series when he delivered the full Gettysburg Address.

The series introduced slavery as a cause of the war and included the Emancipation Proclamation but failed to offer context beyond touchstone moments. In regard to black characters, the series opened with a freedman living near the Geyser family. It later returned to him, only to have him lynched for hiding some runaway slaves in his shack.

The lack of focus on slavery was in part because the Geyser and Hale families were middle-class families swept up in the war. Neither owned slaves, yet neither was abolitionist.[21] No one was ideologically committed to a cause, but the men of both families were willing to enlist immediately to fight. The series closed out with John Geyser's wedding, where he insisted on taking a family portrait. Both sides came together, with some members missing due to the brutality of the war.

Despite being such a massive endeavor, *The Blue and the Gray* failed to achieve the success and impact of *Roots*. While the series was popular with television audiences when it premiered over three nights in November 1982, historians and critics did not view it well. Most bashed the series for the acting of the leading roles, which was in part due to a lackluster script. Others cited the historical clichés and awkward battlefield choreography. Entire segments and plot lines were distractions. A long scene of cockroach racing in a Union camp served no purpose to the overall plot. A historically disproportionate portion of the series was dedicated to observation balloons on the battlefields. Considering the scope of the project, that time could have been better used elsewhere.

Some did, however, recognize *The Blue and the Gray* was on the right path of accurately telling the story of the Civil War. Historian James McPherson called the series twice as good as the Lost Cause–ridden *Gone with the Wind*.[22]

Perhaps the greatest contribution *The Blue and the Gray* made was the addition of Civil War reenactors in the production. The series used hundreds of men to give the battle scenes a sense of authenticity. While the size of engagements pales in comparison to the likes of *Gettysburg* and other films that would come in the following decade, the series took a step in the right direction by setting the precedent of using living historians to supplement a production.

* * *

To reclaim the top spot in television, ABC brought back producer David Wolper, who had previously worked on *Roots* and related projects. The program this time was another novel-to-television conversion but vastly different than *Roots*. Author John Jakes had experienced immediate success with his multipart novel *North and South*. *Book I* was released in 1985 and *Book II* in 1986. *Book I* ran from 1842 to the opening fire on Fort Sumter; *Book II* covered the entirety of the Civil War.

The story met all the requirements for a success in Wolper's eyes: a best-selling costumed epic, a story of significance, and a major historical event.[23] Given Wolper's confidence and the achievements of *Roots*, ABC invested $25 million and allocated twelve hours of programming in a single week for the first novel, with plans to air an adaptation of the second novel a few months later. (A third novel was released in 1987 but was not adapted to television until 1994.)

North and South told the tale of the Main and Hazard families. As with *The Blue and the Gray*, one family was from the North and one from the South. The Main family was a plantation family from outside Charleston, South Carolina. The Hazard family was from Lehigh Station, Pennsylvania, where they owned a successful ironworks. Orry Main and George Hazard first met on their way to West Point, where they became best friends and roommates. After serving together in the Mexican War, the two became even closer because they had brothers who attended West Point together. The Mains and Hazards ended up being united through marriage but then have the war tear the families apart. Similarly to *The Blue and the Gray*, family and friends found each other at the business end of their pistols numerous times though the war.

With the amount of money invested in the project, everyone expected the series to match the success of *Roots*. An up-and-coming actor named Patrick Swayze was persuaded to play the lead role of Orry Main, a gig that would propel his career. Producers also cast some of the biggest names in Hollywood. Gene Kelly, Robert Mitchum, Johnny Cash, Jimmy Stewart, and Olivia de Havilland all made appearances in the series; even Elizabeth Taylor showed up for a few minutes as a New Orleans madam.

The Nielsen ratings of *Book I* came in at a respectable 26 in November 1985, although the producers and network had hoped to hit at least a third of the market. *Book II* recorded similar success six months later. For comparison, *Roots* recorded an average rating of 45 across its week of broadcast in 1977.[24]

Unlike *The Blue and the Gray* and *Roots*, *North and South* featured the point of view of elites from the era. Orry Main became the master of a seventeen-thousand-acre cotton plantation and built a cotton mill, something the South desperately lacked. Main was always conflicted about slavery, knowing its evils, yet insisted on defending his way of life. George Hazard, meanwhile, became the manager of the family ironworks, which produced the majority of the North's cannons for the war. Each friend served as the stereotypical model of Southern and Northern ideals. Both men ended up having an important role in their respective wartime governments before requesting battlefield assignments.

North and South followed myths set by the Lost Cause when it came to the issue of slavery. The Main family treated their slaves with respect and dignity, and Orry Main stopped an evil overseer from whipping one of the field hands. That overseer, Salem Jones, served as the cliché slave driver like Jonas Wilkerson of *Gone with the Wind* and Simon Legree of *Uncle Tom's Cabin*.[25] Main even accused George Hazard of being just as bad as Southern plantation owners whenever it came to the treatment of the wage laborers in the ironworks. When Main first met Robert E. Lee, the general proclaimed secession unconstitutional and slavery a moral evil. The only reason he joined the Confederacy was for the noble act of fighting for the state of Virginia. The series' abolitionists are fiery fanatics, including Hazard's sister, played by Kirstie Alley.

The largest problem historians had with *North and South* was the inaccuracies of the women's clothing of the period. The producers had played it fast and loose with multiple aspects, lowering necklines and tightening corsets on the elegant ball gowns to provide as much cleavage as they were allowed to show on network television. The scenes dealing with sex were some of the most explicit of the time.[26] Characters maintained their 1980s hairstyles, including Swayze's signature flow. The result was more along the lines of people playing dress-up instead of a historical sweeping epic. When it came to the opinion of the audience and entertainment community, though, the wardrobe was excellent. The series' lone Primetime Emmy win was for the costuming, with nominations in makeup and hairstyling.

The intent of *North and South* was established from the beginning. In an article in the *Washington Post*, Wolper noted, "I did not intend for there to be an incisive historical lesson in *North and South*. Basically it's just a good, juicy story."[27] A combination of Patrick Swayze and a soap opera–like story appealed to an audience the other series did not. Women all over fell in love with the plot—and with Swayze. Years later, even author John Jakes was receiving mail from enamored fans. He said in the *Los Angeles Times* in 1994, "I still get the occasional letter from a 14-year-old Danish girl asking me if I have Patrick Swayze's address."[28] *North and South* did not forget about the audience that tuned in for the war.

The Battle of Antietam sequence served as the climax of *Book II*, telling the battle from both sides and including panoramic views. Bodies filled the Sunken Road, and the only things missing were the blood and scattered limbs that primetime television prohibited.[29]

In *North and South*, the legendary actor Lloyd Bridges portrayed Jefferson Davis, the leader of the Confederacy. Earlier, in *The Blue and the Gray*, he had appeared as Ben Geyser, the family patriarch who remained unsympathetic about the lynching of a freedman on his property. In *Roots*, he was Evan Brent, a member of the Ku Klux Klan. Bridges was the actor who had to whip Tom Harvey, an experience that emotionally challenged him as an actor.[30] Multiple actors and actresses appeared in two of the series, but Bridges was the only one to work with all three.

North and South and *The Blue and the Gray* were popular and showed respectable success but still did not come close to the juggernaut of *Roots*. The three miniseries each offered a way for all Americans to reflect and learn about the Civil War era in a digestible, popular format. But *Roots*, in particular, took decades of romanticized history and sought to tell the correct story. Broadcast during the era of the bicentennial, when history seemed more important than ever, it served as a significant step in how America, regardless of race, looked back at its own origins.

Notes

1. David Zurawik, "Impact of Haley's *Roots* May Never Be Equaled," *Baltimore Sun*, 11 February 1992.
2. Pam Dean, "The Jeffersons," Museum of Broadcast Communications, 3 February 2018.
3. Joshua Glick, *Los Angeles Documentary and the Production of Public History, 1958–1977* (Oakland: University of California Press, 2018), 153–74.
4. Zurawik, "Impact of Haley's *Roots* May Never Be Equaled."
5. Alison Landsberg, *Prosthetic Memory: The Transformation of American Remembrance in the Age of Mass Culture* (New York: Columbia University Press, 2004), 101–6.
6. J. B. Bird, "Roots," Museum of Broadcast Communications, 22 January 2018.
7. Leslie Uggams and LeVar Burton, "Digging Deeper with *Roots*: Let's Talk," television interview transcript, *Pioneers of Television*, PBS, 5 February 2013.
8. Betsy Peoples, "Revisiting *Roots* after 25 Years," *Crisis* 109, no. 1 (2002): 10–11.

9. Matthew Delmont, *Making Roots A Nation Captivated* (Oakland: University of California Press, 2016), 5–7.

10. Marvin Kitman, "With 'Roots,' Very Few Nits to Pick," *Newsday*, 27 January 1977.

11. Charlayne Hunter-Gault, "'Roots' Getting a Grip on People Everywhere," *New York Times*, 28 January 1977.

12. Richard Schickel, review of *Roots*, *Time*, 24 January 1977.

13. William Aspray and Barbara M. Hayes, eds., *Everyday Information: The Evolution of Information Seeking in America* (Cambridge, MA: MIT Press, 2011), 162–63.

14. Landsberg, *Prosthetic Memory*, 101–6.

15. David J. Leonard and Lisa A. Guerrero, *African Americans on Television: Race-ing for Ratings* (Santa Barbara, CA: Praeger, 2013), 75–80.

16. Bruce Chadwick, *The Reel Civil War: Mythmaking in American Film* (New York: Knopf, 2009), 263–66.

17. Win Fanning, "*Roots* Rating Dips," *Pittsburgh Post-Gazette*, 28 February 1979.

18. Lisa de Moraes, "'Roots' Premiere Crowd On A+E Networks Grows to 6.9M in Live+3 Stats," *Deadline*, 7 June 2016.

19. John J. O'Connor, "'The Blue and the Gray' Often Loses Sight of the Civil War," *New York Times*, 14 November 1982.

20. M. Paul Holsinger, ed., *War and American Popular Culture: A Historical Encyclopedia* (Westport, CT: Greenwood Publishing Group, 1999), 87–88.

21. Barbara A. Gannon, *Americans Remember Their Civil War* (Santa Barbara, CA: Praeger, 2017), 111.

22. Holsinger, *War and American Popular Culture*, 87–88.

23. John J. O'Connor, "'North and South,'" *New York Times*, 7 November 1985.

24. Jane Sumner, "'North and South' Rises Again," *Los Angeles Times*, 27 February 1994.

25. Douglas Brode, Shea Brode, and Cynthia Miller, eds., *The American Civil War on Film and TV: Blue and Gray in Black and White and Color* (Lanham, MD: Lexington Books, 2017), 195–99.

26. Ibid.

27. Michael Hill, "'North and South,'" *Washington Post*, 3 November 1985.

28. Sumner, "'North and South' Rises Again."

29. Brode, Brode, and Miller, *American Civil War on Film and TV*, 195–99.

30. Meredith Blake, "For the Original Cast of 'Roots,' It Was a Mind-Blowing Series," *Los Angeles Times*, 26 May 2016.

18. ❀ The Civil War Trifecta: How Three Films Shaped Our Perceptions of America's Bloodiest Conflict

Jared Frederick

The Civil War Centennial of the 1960s was an era of widespread celebration as Americans marked one hundred years of national unity. While that commemoration failed to recognize the conflict in all its dark intricacies, it nonetheless instilled a popular image of the desperate struggle in the national consciousness. However, that fad was eclipsed thirty years later with the release of three iconic film depictions of the 1860s: *Glory* in 1989, Ken Burns's PBS documentary *The Civil War* in 1990, and the saga *Gettysburg* in 1993. Combined, these productions kindled widespread fascination among the public at large—giving birth to the next generation of Civil War scholars.

Glory, director Edward Zwick's masterful epic portraying the esteemed 54th Massachusetts Infantry, openly defied the standard patterns of Civil War cinema. In portraying the African American regiment as the embodiment of all that was righteous in the Union cause, the producers forged a new silver screen interpretation of the conflict. Absent was the romanticized aura of the plantation, the sense of Southern martyrdom, and the parody of the contented slave seen all too often in films such as *Gone with the Wind*.

While grossing a modest $28 million at the box office, the film received universal acclaim and garnered three Oscars—including a Best Supporting Actor win by Denzel Washington for his memorable performance. In accepting his gold statuette, Washington concluded, "I would like to pay homage to the men of the 54th, the black soldiers who helped make this country free."[1] The remarks raised international awareness of the tale of a long-ignored chapter of American history.

While the film is not a flawless historical portrayal of the 54th Massachusetts, scholars nonetheless found it useful as a platform of discussion. The movie is less an interpretation of the New England regiment and more emblematic of the black experience as a whole during the war. Perhaps most important, a major motion picture at last purged itself of the wholly inaccurate Lost Cause tendencies that permeated postwar literature and earlier films such as the virulently racist *The Birth of a Nation*. One critique of the film, however, was that it fell within the "white savior" paradigm, in which filmmakers focus on minority challenges through the eyes of a Caucasian protagonist (in this case, via Matthew Broderick's admirable portrayal of regimental commander Robert Gould Shaw). Films following this same pattern, such as *Mississippi Burning* and *Dances with Wolves*, bookended *Glory*'s 1989 release.

Adding to the savior element in the film's climactic scene at Fort Wagner is faint religious symbolism when Shaw is killed. "He decides it is time," said media expert Mark Golub of this scene, "he stands and advances, knowing he will die, and when he is shot in the chest he falls backward, arms extended as Christ's on the cross."[2] English professor Paul Haspel of Penn State University noted that this scene "bears comparison with the death of the Sergeant Elias character in Oliver Stone's *Platoon* (1986)." In both films, "overtly Christian symbolism is utilized to make the death of a sympathetic character symbolically redemptive."[3] Beyond the artistic merit of such choreography, this degree of nobility was never before ascribed to the Union cause in cinematic depictions of the war—a cause usually shown as that of a malevolent invader.

Accordingly, contemporary experts found the movie an evocative learning tool in linking the past and present. "I think the movie *Glory* accomplished a remarkable feat in sensitizing a lot of today's black students to the role that their ancestors played in the Civil War in winning their own freedom," said historian James McPherson in a May 1994 C-SPAN interview. "Another thing, by the latter half of the war many Northern soldiers, but not all, found themselves fighting for the freeing of the slaves."[4] Elsewhere, historians, educators, and corporations fully intended to invoke the themes of *Glory* to combat growing urban crime, poverty, and drug use at the end of the beleaguered 1980s.

In 1990–91, Pepsi-Cola initiated a nationwide campaign to bring the movie into America's classrooms. An edited PG-rated version of the film on videocassette and accompanying poster were made available to one thousand random contestants and twenty thousand teachers. An advertisement promoting the initiative in *Jet* magazine (with M. C. Hammer on the cover) touted, "African-Americans know better than anyone that freedom isn't free. That's why, from the Revolutionary War to Vietnam, African-Americans have always been willing to pay the price whenever their country called. Pepsi-Cola salutes these heroes."[5] The same ad appeared in copies of *Ebony* and *Black Enterprise* in recognition of Black History Month.

The limited-edition videocassette featured a special introduction by television personality Montel Williams (sporting his naval uniform). Williams explained to the young viewers their civic obligation to build on the standard of excellence and selflessness established by those in the 54th and other units. "Try to draw inspiration from them as you face challenges in your everyday life," he concluded.

Furthermore, many hoped the film would nurture an easing of racial tensions in the 1980s. The director of Boston's Museum of Afro-American History said as much following a benefit premiere of the film. The tale of the 54th continued to carry cultural sway in the regiment's hometown of Boston. Yet the racially charged Charles Stuart murder case in 1989 highlighted ongoing challenges in race relations in that city. The museum director lamented, "I'm hoping that this [movie] helps the process of healing."[6]

The movie also offers other insights frequently overlooked in Civil War cinema, according to teacher Daniel A. Nathan. "*Glory* shows a side of racism that most of my students (who are overwhelmingly white and come from above the Mason-Dixon Line) infrequently consider: northern racism," he said. Depictions of verbal and physical harassment inflicted on members of the 54th do not stray far from reality. Even Shaw referred to himself "as a Nigger Col." in his own correspondence. This uncomfortable truth adds an effective level of understanding of 1860s society and reveals to audiences that views on race between Northerners and Southerners were not always at odds. For this reason and more, Nathan used the movie for classroom discussion. "I continue to use *Glory* because students find it entertaining and enlightening," he explained, "because it tells an important and still relatively neglected story, and because it is a mature, creative (though not unproblematic) example of film as public history."[7]

Much the same can be said for Ken Burns's enduring PBS documentary *The Civil War*, which debuted less than a year after *Glory*'s theatrical release. Following the success of his Academy Award–nominated documentaries *Brooklyn Bridge* and *The Statue of Liberty*, Burns sought to tackle the Civil War in a comprehensive manner. Family and colleagues alike chuckled at the scale of the project, but Burns ultimately enjoyed the last laugh. More Americans watched *The Civil War* the week it aired than they did *Monday Night Football* with Howard Cosell—and Americans love football. Over the course of several days in September 1990, television viewers removed themselves from the tumult, politics, and human drama of their own day and inserted themselves into the world of 130 years prior. The filmmaker effectively used period images and words to evoke not the statistics of war, but its emotions—sentiments that viewers found highly resonant. The documentary remains a hallmark of the genre and spurred far-reaching conversations about how we interact with our national past.

James Lundberg of Lake Forest College semifacetiously praised *The Civil War* in a 2011 article titled "Thanks a Lot, Ken Burns." The subtitle of his article was "Because of you, my Civil War lecture is always packed—with students raised on your sentimental, romantic, deeply misleading portrait of the conflict." Lundberg's article brims with mixed emotion on the film and its legacies. He faulted the production for its nostalgic flair, its skimming of racial complexities, and its dependence on the folksy yarns of celebrated Southern novelist Shelby Foote. However, the author conceded the film had a profound impact on citizens' perspectives of the rebellion.[8] Furthermore, the country's battlefield parks witnessed a massive spike in visitation after the documentary's release. Gettysburg National Military Park saw a 175,000-person boost in 1991 compared with the previous year.[9]

Americans in the 1990s craved the rosewater interpretation of America's costliest war in the era of Reagan idealism. Transition was apparent as the recently initiated Persian Gulf War was the nation's first post–Cold War challenge. President George H. W. Bush sought solace in Burns's film, looking to the guidance of Lincoln's example as commander in chief. As Lundberg explained, "The film was perfectly calibrated to please most every constituency in the post-Vietnam culture wars. While many noted an antiwar crosscurrent in its brutal images of mangled limbs and bloated corpses, the film's dominant notes present an unapologetic patriotism." The show's theme underlined a perseverance of national fortitude—that we may overcome our challenges to make ourselves anew. The allure of Sullivan Ballou's final letter to his wife combined with the poetic heartache of the song "Ashokan Farewell" is irresistible to a society wishing to find hope and beauty amidst misery. For these reasons and more, Lundberg contended, "some 40 million people chose to forego *Cheers*, *Roseanne*, *The Wonder Years*, and *America's Funniest Home Videos* for a PBS documentary."[10]

Actor Tom Hanks was among the masses tuning in to Burns's runaway hit. Recently emerging from lackluster films such as *Joe versus the Volcano*, Hanks, like the nation as a whole, may have been conducting some soul-searching. In this regard, *The Civil War* was a revelation to him personally. He commented in a *Time* interview with historian Douglas Brinkley in March 2010, "The writing [of history] is often too dull to grab regular people by the lapel." Yet Burns's artistry revealed how the past could be vividly shared with broader audiences. "I watched that with my son," Hanks reflected. "There was nothing but great music married with talking heads, pan and scan of old photographs and get to the creeks at sunset. But I wept at the end of almost every hour of that incredibly powerful entertainment. So I thought there might be some other ways that HBO could also make history interesting for people."[11]

This epiphany resulted in the highly successful historical miniseries *From the Earth to the Moon* and *Band of Brothers*. Additionally, it is perhaps no coincidence that the majority of Hanks's films throughout the rest of the decade were set in historical time periods. Thus the Ken Burns Effect became more than a trait of cinematography; it was a cultural phenomenon that morphed history and popular culture in ways that still ripple through society.

On more philosophical grounds, *Washington Post* columnist George Will appraised the documentary as a triumph of the ages:

> If better use has ever been made of television, I have not seen it and do not expect to see better until Ken Burns turns his prodigious talents to his next project. . . . He is the filmmaker five of whose 37 years went into the making of this masterpiece of national memory. Our Iliad has found its Homer: he has made accessible and vivid for everyone the pain and poetry and meaning of the event that is the hinge of our history.[12]

Despite its reliance on anecdotes, its neglecting of Reconstruction, and the claim that Robert E. Lee "disapproved" of slavery, Burns's masterwork revived a sense of place and meaning for an often bewildered American public.

The Civil War has since enjoyed many lives on public television and on home video. A best seller on VHS, it reaired for its tenth anniversary in 2000—and again for the Civil War Sesquicentennial, when it was repackaged in a commemorative DVD set. The series debuted once more in September 2015 after receiving a frame-by-frame restoration to ultrahigh definition. The program has not become obsolete. Rather, it has evolved with technology and the tastes of consumers.

Even more so, the film offers testimony to America's painful record on race. "A quarter century ago, America wasn't in as good a place on race as it is now, although that's hard for many to believe," writer Matthew Cooper opined in a September 2015 *Newsweek* piece. "After all, *The Civil War* aired at a rotten time in race relations a year after Spike Lee's *Do the Right Thing* and the first ugly David Dinkins–Rudy Giuliani election battle in New York."[13] MSNBC host Joe Scarborough echoed some of these sentiments in a conversation with Ken Burns a month prior. Scarborough said of the film, "It not only changed the way we watched television, it changed the way we look at history." Yet when Scarborough pressed Burns on some of Foote's dubious commentary regarding slavery, Burns replied that "it would be unfair to tar Shelby with that brush." In the end, the director vocally defended the talking head that was the centerpiece of his work.[14]

Educator Kevin Levin reflected on the mixed emotions historians felt regarding Burns's film when it was rereleased in 2015:

> I see *The Civil War* as a wonderful example of the split personality of Civil War memory. On the one hand Burns embraced and even antici-pated a robust narrative that deals directly with the tough questions re-lated to slavery and race—one that we've seen blossom during the Civil War 150. At the same time Burns's film reminds us of the difficulty of fully reconciling this narrative with a lingering Lost Cause narrative.[15]

Those same specters of the past lingered in the 1993 epic *Gettysburg*. For fifteen years, director Ronald F. Maxwell languished in his attempts to bring to the screen Michael Shaara's Pulitzer Prize–winning novel *The Killer Angels* (the book that inspired Burns in his own cinematic quest). Maxwell initially tried to cast Paul Newman to play Robert E. Lee and Charlton Heston to portray James Longstreet. A young Russell Crowe auditioned for the part of Joshua Chamberlain. Maxwell sold his home in New York to keep the project afloat. He considered filming in Europe to save money. Shaara died in 1988. ABC network picked up the project but soon after dumped it. Going by its initial track record, the production never should have taken flight.

But Maxwell persisted. The success of Burns's film offered salvation for the withering hopes of *Gettysburg*. The studios "couldn't overlook that 30 million people stayed home for a week to watch still photographs with sound-over narration," according to Maxwell. Media mogul Ted Turner, a lifelong Civil War buff, was intrigued by the prospects of the project. After meeting Ken Burns, the public television director encouraged Turner to further investigate the potential of *Gettysburg*. Turner signed on and fed $20 million into the film's development. In addition to reaping the financial rewards of a popular histor-ical topic, Turner also had other ambitions. "This film will help contribute to world peace," he claimed. It "will be another nail in the coffin of war. We're going to get that behind us. We're going to start acting like human beings."[16] Filming began in the summer of 1992.

In addition to being the first major motion picture to film within Gettysburg National Military Park, the movie used the expertise of Civil War reenactors. Actor Jeff Daniels was surprised by the immersive qualities and

Fig. 18.1. Actors Patrick Gorman as John Bell Hood and Tom Berenger as James Longstreet rest under the shade of an umbrella during the filming of Gettysburg. *Gettysburg National Military Park.*

eccentricities of those weekend warriors. He remarked in a *Baltimore Sun* article:

> You're sitting there in a T-shirt, jeans, drinking a Diet Coke, and [the reenactors are] walking by saluting and saying, "Sir." The first time, you want to say, "Get a life." But then it keeps happening, and you realize the importance of the war, of Gettysburg, to them, and you realize this ain't just a job. . . . It was like a Broadway play. . . . They were right there. You had to reach down and pull out these big heroic emotions. It was different than being the hero in *Die Hard*.[17]

Like many of his fellow actors, he felt a great allure—even a sense of mysticism—in filming on the actual battleground, which was "like a cathedral," Daniels confessed. Actor Sam Elliott echoed that sentiment in saying, "When you get back and spend some time in Gettysburg with people who are really consumed by it, it's overwhelming. It's living history."[18]

Indeed, reenactors were emotionally involved while filming in the national park. Extra Brian James Egen reflected in 2012, "I have never had a more intimate experience with history as I did the day we filmed that scene on the actual battlefield. . . . As we proceeded toward the Emmitsburg Road (our stopping point for filming), I was brought to tears—overwhelmed by the inculcation of the moment, location, and facile understanding of the historical event we were replicating."[19] Ken Burns himself made a cameo as one of General Hancock's aides and exclaimed to coproducer Robert Katz of the cast and crew scale, "How do you guys do this? I could never do this."[20]

While the end product—the longest American movie theatrically released, at 254 minutes—received generally positive reviews, some were quick to criticize the stuffy language and technical minutiae. Film critic Gene Siskel called the film "bloated Southern propaganda," while historian Gary Gallagher said, "The thing that bothered me the most was there were too many overweight Confederate soldiers. . . . By 1863, they were a pretty lean bunch." Reenactor Bill Holschuh wrote in the *Camp Chase Gazette*, a living-history magazine:

> We [reenactors] are hard to please [and] are extremely fussy. . . . We shaped this film, through our participation, our expertise and our passionate desire to see it done right—at least our own version of right. Could it be that we had so much input and influence in creating the final product that they made a film that is mainly just for us?[21]

Acclaimed film critic Roger Ebert probably agreed, writing:

This is a film that Civil War buffs will find indispensable, even if others might find it interminable. I began watching with comparative indifference, and slowly got caught up in the majestic advance of the enterprise; by the end, I had a completely new idea of the reality of war in the 19th century, when battles still consisted largely of men engaging each other in hand-to-hand combat. And I understood the Civil War in a more immediate way than ever before.[22]

Most viewers concurred. Turner was so impressed with his pet project that he released it in theaters before debuting it as a TNT miniseries as was originally planned. When the film aired on television in June 1994, more than 30 million people watched—a viewership near equal to Burns's film. Accordingly, the movie captured the imagination of the public at large with similar energy.

Michael Shaara's novel became a *New York Times* best seller five years after his death. Shaara's son, Jeff, was moved to continue his father's literary work with the prequel novel *Gods and Generals* (which Michael Shaara had intended to be the original title of *The Killer Angels*). Visitation to Gettysburg National Military Park jumped to nearly 1.7 million in 1994, in contrast to barely 1.3 million visitors the year prior. That high number remained steady throughout the 1990s as *Gettysburg* successfully reared on TNT summer after summer. The soundtrack became a best seller, opening the Super Bowl and used by Olympic skater Todd Eldredge at the 1998 games in Japan.

But as with most cultural phenomena, there is a cost to pay. To this day, some licensed battlefield guides at Gettysburg are miffed by Chamberlain's celebrity originating from both *The Civil War* and *Gettysburg*. His likeness adorns shot glasses, magnets, T-shirts, calendars, nutcrackers, and every form of tourist kitsch conceivable. Other notable commanders deserve equal fame, in the estimation of some historians, and they are right. But no form of scholarship can defeat Hollywood. Burns, who himself made Chamberlain a focal point of his examination of Gettysburg, noted that the Maine colonel offered "a different kind of heroism there that we need so desperately to be aware of today." Yet the fact that visitors sojourn to the park's national cemetery seeking out the burial plot of Chamberlain's fictional sidekick, Buster Kilrain, speaks to the power of cinema in creating our interpretations of the past.[23]

Most important, *Gettysburg* forged a whole new generation of historians who otherwise may not have chosen that profession. Supervisory historian

Christopher Gwinn of Gettysburg National Military Park was among them. "I first saw the film *Gettysburg* when I was ten years old. . . . The movie, regardless of its historical inaccuracies, captured my imagination in a way that nothing, short of the battlefield itself, had previously," he said. "It made the past, at least the Hollywood version of it, a place inhabited by real people and not just two-dimensional characters."[24]

In 2014, British journalist Martin Pengelly admitted that Maxwell's movie remained his guilty pleasure in life. The "film is of a rare genus: the cheap epic," he said.

> Essentially, *Gettysburg* is for children. Particularly, it may be for boys— or overgrown ones. It is no surprise to learn that it is used in U.S. schools. . . . They believe this stuff. And they believe *in* it. After living in the U.S. for almost two years, so do I. Show me, for the thousandth time, Joshua Lawrence Chamberlain on Little Round Top, exhorting his exhausted men to make one last charge to win the day for freedom . . . and I will feel a thrill and a catch in the throat.[25]

And who can blame him? Society often seeks inspiration from history as much as it yearns for the past's guidance. Artistic license, questionable commentary, and *truly* atrocious fake beards aside, the trifecta of Civil War cinema released between 1989 and 1993 continues to sway our collective imagination regarding America's defining conflict. The ghost of Buster Kilrain surely approves.

Notes

1. "Denzel Washington Wins Supporting Actor: 1990 Oscars," 12 May 2010, video, https://www.youtube.com/watch?v=_jbHwmvg7Rk.
2. Lawrence A. Kreiser Jr. and Randal Allred, eds., *The Civil War in Popular Culture: Memory and Meaning* (Lexington: University Press of Kentucky, 2014), 165.
3. Paul Haspel, "Antietam, James Island, and Fort Wagner: The Battle Sequences in Edward Zwick's *Glory*," *Studies in Popular Culture* 30, no. 1 (2007): 78.
4. James McPherson, "What They Fought For, 1861–1865," interview by Brian Lamb, C-SPAN Booknotes, 21 March 1994, https://www.c-span.org/video /?55946-1/what-fought-for-1861-65.
5. Pepsi-Cola advertisement, *Jet*, 18 February 1991, 34–35.

6. Haspel, "Antietam, James Island, and Fort Wagner," 80.

7. Daniel A. Nathan, "The Massachusetts 54th on Film: Teaching *Glory*," *OAH Magazine of History* 16, no. 4 (2002): 38–42.

8. James M. Lundberg, "Thanks a Lot, Ken Burns," *Slate*, 7 June 2011.

9. National Park Service, "Visitor Use Statistics," accessed 4 October 2016, https://irma.nps.gov/Stats/.

10. Lundberg, "Thanks a Lot, Ken Burns."

11. Douglass Brinkley, "How Tom Hanks Became America's Historian in Chief," *Time*, 6 March 2010.

12. George F. Will, "A Masterpiece on the Civil War," *Washington Post*, 20 September 1990.

13. Matthew Cooper, "Ken Burns's Merciful Portrayal of the South in 'The Civil War' Is a Good Lesson for 2015," *Newsweek,* 11 September 2015.

14. "Burns on Anniversary of Civil War Film," *Morning Joe*, MSNBC, 20 August 2015, video, https://www.msnbc.com/morning-joe/watch/burns-on -anniversary-of-civil-war-film-509304387899.

15. Kevin M. Levin, "The Split Personality of Ken Burns's 'The Civil War,'" *Civil War Memory* (blog), 31 August 2015. http://cwmemory.com/2015/08 /31/the-split-personality-of-ken-burnss-the-civil-war/.

16. Paul Willistein, "The Battle Royal: Civil War's Turning Point Comes to Screen in 4-hour *Gettysburg*," *Allentown (PA) Morning Call*, 8 October 1993.

17. Drew Jubera, "*Gettysburg*: Ted Turner, a Cast of Thousands and the Ghosts of the Past," *Baltimore Sun*, 9 October 1993.

18. Willistein, "Battle Royal."

19. Brian James Egen, "Part I: My Experience on Set of the Movie 'Gettysburg,'" *O Say Can You See?* (blog), National Museum of American History, 17 October 2012, https://americanhistory.si.edu/blog/2012/10/my-experience -on-set-of-the-movie-gettysburg-1.html.

20. *Gettysburg* motion picture soundtrack companion booklet (New York: Milan Records, 1998).

21. Bill Holschuh, "*Gettysburg*: A Movie Just for Us?" *Camp Chase Gazette* (November–December 1993): 32–35.

22. Roger Ebert, review of *Gettysburg*, 8 October 1993, https://www.rogerebert .com/reviews/gettysburg-1993.

23. Thomas A. Desjardin, *These Honored Dead: How the Story of Gettysburg Shaped American Memory* (Cambridge, MA: Da Capo, 2003), 150–51, 178–79.

24. Christopher Gwinn, email interview with the author, 18 October 2016.

25. Martin Pengelly, "My Guilty Pleasure: *Gettysburg*," *Guardian*, 21 March 2014.

19. ❖ One Giant, Forgotten Leap: The Life, Death, and Resurrection of the *H. L. Hunley*

Brian Hicks

They boarded the boat just after dusk on February 17, 1864.[1]

There was no fanfare that evening on Sullivan's Island, a quiet, slender ribbon of sand just outside Charleston Harbor. There was no anticipation of momentous events among the troops at Battery Marshall. There was only a crew of eight men climbing into an iron craft that, for lack of a better term, they called the "fish boat."

After all, that's what it looked like.

The *H. L. Hunley*—its official name—was a forty-foot cylindrical iron warship that rode low in the water. Its hull was oval, forty-two inches at its widest, each end tapering to a point. Its exterior features were minimal—a seventeen-foot spar off the bow, a propeller and rudder on the stern, two long, slender fins on its flanks. The crew boarded through two squat hatches on top of this strange contraption, which later generations would recognize as a submarine.

The *Hunley* could dive beneath the waves, cruise underwater at four knots, and resurface again. It could pass beneath ships undetected, allowing its crew to spy on unsuspecting fleets anonymously. Other boats had accomplished these tricks with varying degrees of success over the years, but that night the *Hunley* would become the first to carry out the task for which all submarines that followed were built: it would sink an enemy ship.

That night, in the waning days of the Civil War, the *Hunley* made history. But no one would realize it for years.

Sometimes history unfolds in epic fashion, witnessed by thousands of people. The men and women who watched the first shots of the war fired on Fort Sumter from the Charleston Battery realized they were witnessing the story of their country as it was being written—though some complained

173

it was taking too long.[2] The spectators at the First Battle of Bull Run knew they were present for an important, if shocking, chapter of that same history.

But the *Hunley*'s achievement passed largely without notice. It happened four miles offshore with no Southern spectators. The Confederates did not realize what had transpired for several days, and when they did learn of the attack, they attached no particular significance to it. The fish boat was just one of many strange contraptions the South aimed at the U.S. Navy during the war. And because of the secrecy surrounding the project, newspaper accounts were vague and purposely misleading. One report claimed the crew that sank an enemy blockader was safely back in Charleston.[3] In truth, no one knew where the crewmen were, who they were, or what, exactly, they had done.

The crew of the *H. L. Hunley* accomplished a historic first in the last full year of the Civil War. But those men were quickly lost to time. Some of their names remain anonymous today, but their actions are no longer forgotten. It took a twentieth-century adventure novelist to secure their place in history, to make them famous.

* * *

When the *Hunley* was launched in July 1863, its builders had been through two years of what would be considered research and development in the twenty-first century. Even though the boat had a primitive propulsion system—seven men simply turned a crank attached to the propeller—it included design features that would endure in submarines for more than a century. The sub was one of the first to include ballast tanks, dive planes, and conning towers, as well as innovations such as an intricate plumbing system that moved water through the submarine to give it balance. By any measure, the *Hunley* was a great technological advance over any underwater craft that preceded it—not that the bar had been set very high.

Perhaps because it was the first of its kind, no one recognized the *Hunley*'s innovativeness or importance. It was, at the time, merely another experiment. Even some of the men who participated in its construction later said it was little more than a converted steam boiler.[4]

That is the only narrative, such as it was, that endured: A group of men added fins and a propeller to an old boiler, then went out and sank a ship. In that version of the story, the crew comes off as a lucky band of amateurs. Nothing could be further from the truth.

In part, the frustrating lack of official records led to the *Hunley*'s historic sleight. Although it was often called the CSS *Hunley*, the submarine was actually a privateer—a privately owned ship built to collect government bounties for sinking enemy ships. The boat was only briefly controlled by the Southern military, when it was seized in August 1863 by a frustrated Charleston command. After a Confederate navy crew sank it at the dock, an incident that claimed the first five men who died inside it, the *Hunley* was declared a failure and promptly returned to its owners.

The myth of the converted ship's boiler has robbed James McClintock of the credit he deserves as one of the fathers of the modern submarine. McClintock, a former steamboat captain, was running a machine shop in New Orleans when Horace Lawson Hunley hired him to build a boat that could attack navy ships from underwater. Hunley didn't come up with the idea, nor was he particularly patriotic—he actually held a barely disguised disdain for the Confederacy and the war.[5] He was most interested in making money and securing his reputation as a man of substance. But he never saw a dime from his investment and never knew fame in his lifetime. As his relatives warned, his greatest get-rich-quick scheme was his last.

McClintock and Hunley launched their first effort in the spring of 1862, around the same time the USS *Monitor* and CSS *Virginia* (nee *Merrimack*) faced off at Hampton Roads. They later reported their tiny boat leaked, had trouble maintaining an even keel, and was dreadfully slow. Still, it worked well enough to sink an old barge during tests on Lake Pontchartrain. The *Pioneer*, as it was christened, was the only underwater boat to receive a letter of marque—that is, a privateer license—from the Confederate government during the war.[6] But it never saw action. The *Pioneer* was ultimately scuttled to avoid discovery when the Union invaded New Orleans that spring.

Fleeing to Mobile, the pair built a second sub with the assistance of the Confederate army. McClintock overcompensated for his mistakes on the *Pioneer*, but the *American Diver* was by most accounts no improvement. The sub was cramped and so weak that the one time it sailed unassisted into the Gulf of Mexico, it was nearly swept away by the current. The *Diver* was lost under tow a few weeks later, taking with it the last of Horace Hunley's money.

A year later, the pair's third-generation sub—financed by investors that included an heir to the Singer sewing machine fortune—disappeared as well. The story of this curiosity shows up sporadically in histories of the war. The historian Shelby Foote, who mentioned the *Hunley* briefly in his three-volume series *The Civil War*, focused more on its shortcomings than its innovation, even repeating an oft-told legend that the sub was found lying alongside its victim at the bottom of the sea.[7] Still, this was the most notable appearance of the sub in the war's history—and it would remain that way for decades.

That is a shame, for the men who built and tested and piloted the *Hunley* were the fathers of one of the great inventions of their century, an inspiration to Simon Lake's submarines and the U.S. Navy's first sub, the *Holland*.[8] Their imagination and ideas stretched the reach of their day's technology. The *Hunley*'s design was ahead of its time by three decades.

Just as important, the men who sailed the *Hunley* were the nineteenth-century equivalent of astronauts—men willing to risk their lives to test an unproven science. Ultimately, twenty-one men died in those endeavors. The *Hunley* sank twice in Charleston Harbor on training exercises, the first time killing five men and in the second incident, less than two months later, another eight—including Horace Hunley himself. When it finally disappeared, the sub was under the command of Lieutenant George E. Dixon, the man most responsible for its success. Because the *Hunley* was supposed to be a secret, newspapers vaguely attributed the deaths to boating accidents. The men weren't hailed as pioneers; they were simply more casualties of the deadliest period in American history.

They were promptly forgotten.

* * *

The story of the *Hunley* could have been culled from a Clive Cussler novel: a fantastic ship disappears after a remarkable feat, only to be discovered a century later. Cussler ran across the submarine's tale in the 1970s while reading documents from the Civil War. At the time, he was an up-and-coming novelist whose books all focused on a character named Dirk Pitt—a sort of American James Bond attached to a government marine agency. Cussler's books were making enough money that he set out to create his own adventures at sea, hunting for lost ships simply for the fun of it and perhaps for inspiration.

Cussler began searching for the *Hunley* in 1980. The on-again, off-again expedition became an obsession that would last fifteen years. Living in Colorado, he faxed charts of the areas he wanted surveyed to his divers in South Carolina. At one point, his crew feared he would have them searching the entire Eastern Seaboard. The sub had become a white whale for Cussler.

Fig. 19.1. Author Clive Cussler, famous for his maritime adventure novels, helped spearhead the effort to recover the *Hunley* from the waters outside Charleston Bay. *Kellen Butler Correia/Friends of the Hunley, Inc.*

When his team, led by maritime archaeologist Ralph Wilbanks, finally found the sub in May 1995, they not only recovered one of the most complete artifacts of the Civil War, but they also rescued it from obscurity. The *New York Times* broke the news of the sub's discovery.

Cussler's first nonfiction book, *The Sea Hunters*, was published a year later and included the author's account of searches for dozens of lost ships, many of them relics from the War between the States. Not only did the *Hunley* rate several chapters, but it was also featured on the cover. Without a doubt, the Civil War submarine was Cussler's most significant discovery.

"For someone like me, addicted to the mysteries of the sea, *Hunley* cast a spell that I found about as irresistible as a starving cat staring at an overweight rodent exercising on a treadmill," Cussler wrote. "Through the decades after she triumphed and vanished into oblivion, many tried to find the little sub that could, and all failed."[9]

Cussler introduced the submarine to his legion of fans, which number in the hundreds of thousands. Aside from that brief mention in Foote's epic account of the war, *The Sea Hunters* marked the first time the *Hunley* appeared in a popular, nationally published book. Between Cussler and the news stories his discovery generated, Hollywood soon took notice. This was no accident, for the author had stumbled on a true rarity: an unmined story from history.

Ted Turner, the Southern cable television mogul with ties to Charleston, was enchanted by the submarine and ordered his Turner Network Television to make a movie about it. The producers hired Donald Sutherland to star as General Pierre Gustave Toutant Beauregard, the Charleston commander who allowed the *Hunley* to sail despite strong misgivings. Sutherland's appearance gave the movie more status than the average TV movie when it premiered in July 1999, and his portrayal of Beauregard was spot-on.

Fig. 19.2. After the success of *Gettysburg* and *Andersonville*, Ted Turner's media empire turned to the *Hunley* for its next Civil War story. *Friends of the Hunley, Inc.*

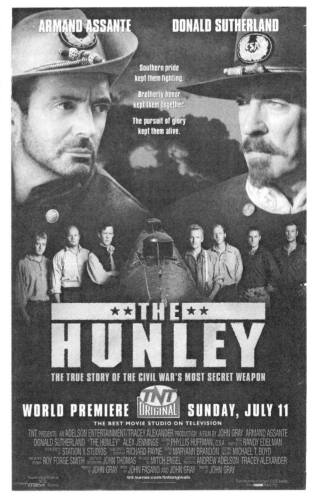

Because so little was known about the *Hunley*, writer-director John Gray had to fictionalize much of the movie. He based the main subplot on a legend surrounding *Hunley* captain George E. Dixon, portrayed by Armand Assante. Dixon had been wounded during the Battle of Shiloh when he was shot in the thigh. The injury likely would have killed him, but the bullet miraculously struck a gold twenty-dollar piece in his pocket. That story is verified in letters written by soldiers from the 21st Alabama Volunteers, but an early twentieth-century Mobile newspaper story—published without sourcing—added a romantic element.[10] The story claimed Dixon's sweetheart gave him the gold coin for luck before he left for Shiloh.[11] Gray built the movie *The Hunley* around this legend, painting Dixon as a widower so despondent he took on a suicide mission.

"I thought, this poor, haunted guy is going to use this submarine to deliver himself back to this woman," Gray told the *Los Angeles Times*. "Once I had this idea, the rest just fell into place."[12]

Dixon was not married, and there is no proof of any romantic entanglements. But the story of the gold coin endured and even became the most popular legend surrounding the *Hunley*—especially after the coin was found inside Dixon's pocket, engraved with his initials, the date of the Shiloh battle, and the haunting words "My life preserver."

Even before Dixon's coin was discovered, the *Hunley* had become a story that translated into sales and ratings, and national news outlets exploited its popularity. Stories appeared in the Chicago papers and the *Wall Street Journal*, which reported, "Forget the *Titanic*; this sub wreck is hot."[13] By the time the *Hunley* was raised from the floor of the Atlantic on August 8, 2000, CNN carried the event live.

Within months, one of the most in-depth maritime archaeological excavations began, and the story of the *Hunley* slowly took on greater depth. Scientists soon discovered the submarine was a much more advanced, complex piece of machinery than anyone had reported. This was no converted boiler; it was a craft ahead of its time. History was rewritten. Books and television specials by National Geographic and the Discovery Channel followed. Over the course of a few years, the *Hunley* went from Civil War footnote to one of its most daring, inspiring tales of courage.

The *Charleston Post and Courier* assigned two reporters to the submarine and published a story about the archaeological dig inside the *Hunley* each day during the five-month excavation. Often those stories were picked up by the Associated Press and wound up in newspapers across the country. The submarine was like a time capsule from the Civil War, and each new find only seemed to increase its popularity. Soon TV crews from Germany and Australia were visiting the Warren Lasch Conservation Center to report on the sub.

The *Hunley* provided endless amounts of information for history buffs and scientists, but it was coy. The sub presented as many new mysteries as it answered. Why did one of its crewman wear the medallion of a Union soldier from Connecticut? Why was there a rudimentary battery in one of the ballast tanks? And more than two decades after its discovery, no one can say exactly why the submarine disappeared after the attack on the USS *Housatonic*. These mysteries have lured historians and investigative journalists back into the scant historical record to try to chronicle a tale of one small step in naval warfare.

* * *

The entire battle lasted only a few minutes.[14]

The night of February 17, 1864, was just another in the routine and, frankly, boring life aboard the USS *Housatonic*. The sloop of war had been attached to the South Atlantic Blockading Squadron off Charleston for more than a year. It held the northernmost post in the fleet, tasked mainly with chasing blockade-runners that tried to sneak into the city. The *Housatonic* crew had sunk a couple of these ships, but by 1864, most blockade-runners had given up on Charleston. One of the South's most important ports had been all but shut down.

At 8:00 that night, the second watch came on duty. There were nine men on deck, six of them lookouts—not that there was much to see. The South Carolina coast was dark, and the low-lying barrier islands and the crumbling mass of Fort Sumter were little more than black silhouettes set against a dark sky. It had been four months since the Southerners had ventured into the Atlantic to engage the U.S. fleet.

Around 8:30, a black landsman on bow watch named Robert Flemming spotted something on the water less than five hundred feet from the ship. The fleet had been warned about the South's stealth boats—intelligence gleaned from various deserters and the Union army's own discovery of the *Pioneer* in a New Orleans channel. But Flemming's warning was initially ignored by his commanding officers. Precious seconds passed as they argued.

"It's a log," Flemming was told.

While the deck watchman tried to convince his supervisor of the threat, the *Hunley* drew closer. Soon officers stationed on the *Housatonic*'s stern caught sight of the mysterious craft, one describing it as a "porpoise coming to the surface to blow." The captain was called to the deck, and he immediately started firing on the mysterious object in the water—joined by several members of his staff. The *Hunley* kept coming, apparently impervious to small-arms fire. The ship's cannons could not be trained on the tiny ship because, by the time it was spotted, the boat was too close to aim the big guns at it.

In less than a minute, the fish boat came to a stop less than twenty feet from the *Housatonic*'s rear quarter, and the ship disappeared beneath the feet of its officers in a silent, but fatal, blast. The *Hunley* had blown a hole ten feet wide into its side. The *Housatonic* began to take on water. In five minutes, it would sink.

The first versions of the story maintained that the *Hunley* carried a bomb with a rope trigger at the end of its spar. The theory held that the sub would ram the ship, planting the barbed torpedo in its hull. Then the sub would back away, and when it was at a safe distance, the crew would pull the line to detonate the package. One of the most meaningful discoveries of the twenty-first-century examination of the sub has found this wasn't the case. The torpedo was bolted to the spar; it was a contact mine. When the *Hunley* collided with the *Housatonic*, the explosion was instantaneous. The navy is still conducting tests to see what, if any, effect this had on the *Hunley* crew. Accounts from *Housatonic* crewmen suggest this was no suicide mission, however—another myth culled from a nineteenth-century account.

The explosion killed 5 of the 155 men aboard the *Housatonic*, all of them sailors below deck who were too close to the blast. The ship sank in just twenty-four feet of water, barely enough to cover its deck. That allowed the survivors to climb into the ship's rigging and avoid the frigid February Atlantic. There they awaited rescue as a small launch set out for help from a nearby blockader.

While hanging off a yardarm on the foremast, forty-five minutes after the explosion, Flemming thought he spotted the strange boat on the water, shining a light toward the shore. The bow watchman who had recognized the submarine on its approach was the only living soul to see firsthand that the crew of the *Hunley* survived the battle.

He repeated that story in the U.S. Navy's inquiry into the *Housatonic*'s sinking more than a month later, an investigation in which nearly twenty of the witnesses recounted the attack. Flemming's sighting was mostly ignored, but it lent credibility to articles published in Charleston newspapers that claimed the torpedo boat had survived and was still stalking the blockading squadron. The navy remained on alert for months, all the while searching the waters off Charleston for the South's newest secret weapon.

When no second attack followed, the story was eventually forgotten. One year to the day later, Charleston fell—a precursor to the war's end. By that time, most people in the city had forgotten whatever they knew of the *Hunley*; they had bigger problems, and the sub's one minor victory had made little difference in their lives.

Even though the *Housatonic*'s crew witnessed a historical first, they did not recognize it as such. Unlike those folks who watched Fort Sumter bombarded and saw the carnage at Bull Run, they gave no great significance to what they had seen. They simply considered themselves victims of a sneak attack.

Sometimes it takes distance and perspective to recognize a historic event. Serious scholars long viewed the *Hunley* through the lens of nineteenth-century accounts and wrote it off as a group of men who got lucky with a floating iron boiler. In truth, visionary engineers and brave test pilots changed the course of naval history, if not the Civil War's. The *Hunley*'s success was the culmination of a quiet arms race between the North and South, the sort of tale that an adventure novelist might imagine or, in this case, recognize as significant.

That is just one great irony of the *Hunley*'s legacy: it languished in obscurity for more than a century and then became one of the most popular stories of the Civil War. It took the power of popular culture, and an eye for adventure, to grant the world's first successful attack submarine its proper place in history.

Notes

1. Report of O. M. Dantzler, 19 February 1864, reprinted in *Official Records of the Union and Confederate Navies in the War of the Rebellion*, ser. 1, vol. 15 (Washington, DC: Government Printing Office, 1921), 335.

2. *Charleston Mercury*, 12 April 1861.

3. *Charleston Daily Courier*, 29 February 1864.

4. William Alexander, a Mobile engineer who helped build the *Hunley* and tried to revive its legacy in the early twentieth century, had a faulty memory of the sub's construction and operations. He claims the sub was a modified ship's boiler in at least two of his accounts: "The Heroes of the Hunley," *Munsey's Magazine*, August 1903, 748; and "The True Stories of the Confederate Submarine Boats," *New Orleans Picayune*, 29 June 1902.

5. Horace Hunley's unvarnished opinion of the Confederacy and the war comes from a letter his sister, Volumnia Hunley Barrow, wrote to her husband, Robert Ruffin Barrow, 13 March 1862, reprinted in Ruth H. Duncan, *The Captain and Submarine CSS H. L. Hunley* (Memphis: S. C. Toof, 1965). A notebook carried by Hunley, now held by the Louisiana Historical

Society in New Orleans, contains many of his grand schemes and ideas in the years before he became a submarine financier.

6. *Official Records of the Union and Confederate Navies*, ser. 2, vol. 1, 399–400.

7. See Shelby Foote's *The Civil War: A Narrative*, vol. 2, *Fredericksburg to Meridian* (New York: Random House, 1963), 896–98.

8. Simon Lake studied the *Hunley* while designing his first submarines. He even interviewed Charles Hasker, a man who survived the *Hunley*'s first sinking. Letter from Lake to Horatio L. Wait, 6 February 1899, Augustine Smythe Papers, South Carolina Historical Society, Charleston.

9. Clive Cussler and Craig Dirgo, *The Sea Hunters: True Adventures with Famous Shipwrecks* (New York: Simon and Schuster, 1996), 198.

10. A couple of accounts of Dixon's miraculous coin saving his life are included in John Kent Folmar, ed., *From That Terrible Field: Civil War Letters of James M. Williams, Twenty-First Alabama Infantry Volunteers* (Tuscaloosa: University of Alabama Press, 1981).

11. "George E. Dixon's Submarine. Details of How Brave Man Lost His Life—Sons of Mobile Honor Him," *Mobile Daily Item*, 26 April 1910.

12. Susan King, "Hunley's Tragic Tale Surfaces," *Los Angeles Times*, 10 July 1999.

13. "Forget the Titanic: Everybody Really Wants a Piece of the Hunley," *Wall Street Journal*, 23 March 2001.

14. The story of the *Hunley*'s battle with the USS *Housatonic* is taken entirely from Proceedings of a Naval Court of Inquiry into the Sinking of the *Housatonic*, 26 February–7 March 1864. The entire court of inquiry was held on the USS *Wabash* off Charleston.

20. ❀ Abraham Lincoln: Freedom Fighter, Vampire Hunter, and Zombie Killer

Ashley Webb

The year 2012 brought out three separate Abraham Lincoln movies, one year into the sesquicentennial anniversary of the Civil War. The best known of these is Steven Spielberg's critically acclaimed *Lincoln*, with Academy Award–winning powerhouses Daniel Day-Lewis, Tommy Lee Jones, and Sally Field, as well as star power from actors Lee Pace and Joseph Gordon-Levitt. Released a few months earlier, *Abraham Lincoln: Vampire Hunter*, produced by Timur Bekmambetov and Tim Burton, included a number of recognizable actors—but ones whose names you can never seem to remember, including Rufus Sewell, Benjamin Walker, Jimmi Simpson, and Alan Tudyk. A further B-listed horror movie, *Abraham Lincoln vs Zombies*, also appeared in 2012.

The first two films follow a series of historical events in Lincoln's life, as well as within American history, but with two wildly different plots and outcomes. The third badly butchers any semblance of history, creating a "mockbuster" film that is borderline absurd. Out of the three, which captured the legend the best? History buffs and avid moviegoers will say Spielberg captured the characters, the time period, and the politics best, especially since large portions of *Vampire Hunter* and *Zombies* are glaringly false. However, artistic license played a large role in all the movies, and the attention to detail within *Lincoln* and *Vampire Hunter* make the two movies more similar than one might realize in light of their immediate differences.

In case one or more of these movies were not on your watch list, here's a quick recap:

Lincoln, a dramatic and historical biopic based on a portion of Doris Kearns Goodwin's biography, *Team of Rivals: The Political Genius of Abraham Lincoln*, focuses solely on Abraham Lincoln's push to get the Thirteenth Amendment through Congress before the end of the Civil War. While the war plays a role in the movie, Spielberg instead emphasizes the backroom dealings and political schemes behind Lincoln's advocacy of abolishing slavery and his interpersonal dealings with the lame-duck Congress.

Abraham Lincoln: Vampire Hunter is an epic adventure based on Seth Grahame-Smith's novel of the same name, pitting Lincoln against century-old vampires conspiring throughout the Southern states. From an early age, Lincoln learns the art of identifying and killing vampires with his silver-tipped ax. The movie follows his quest to kill the vampire that ended his mother's life, which leads him to discover the widespread underground vampire problem plaguing the South. As Lincoln rises to the presidency, he must put a stop to the vampires, who have created an army of undead to defeat the Union.

In *Abraham Lincoln vs. Zombies*, Abraham Lincoln wields a scythe instead of his notorious ax, which he uses to behead a host of zombies under a Confederate stronghold. Lincoln teams up with Stonewall Jackson, a young Theodore Roosevelt, two prostitutes, and John Wilkes Booth (under the pseudonym John Wilkinson) to combat the undead and reunite the Union. *Zombies* is supposed to be a mockery of *Abraham Lincoln: Vampire Hunter.*

Of course, only one of these films sounds remotely plausible, but each, to varying degrees, uses artistic license to take liberties with the historical record. Because that record sometimes lacks necessary details, the directors and screenwriters created scenes to make the stories coherent—a common and long-standing industry practice. With historical films, memory and firsthand accounts are researched, developed, and—where memory fails—fabricated to move the story. Steven Spielberg, in a speech given on the 149th anniversary of Lincoln's Gettysburg Address at Soldiers' National Cemetery in Pennsylvania, commented on this process in relation to *Lincoln*:

> Nothing matters more than memory. Without memory, we learn nothing, without memory there's no coherence, no progress. I'd imagine that's why historians ultimately write history and why human beings hunger for history and, I have to add, for fiction based on history. It's the hunger we feel for coherence, it's the hunger we feel for progress for a better world. . . . History forces us to acknowledge the limits of memory. . . . It tells us that memory is imperfect, that no matter how much of the past we've recovered, much of what once was or has been, now is lost to us.[1]

Where there are no firsthand accounts, imagination takes over. Historians may weave facts into cohesive and spellbinding retellings, but movie directors rely on imagination and creativity to weave that history and memory into a viewable format. Additionally, directors and producers use art to "go to the impossible places that other disciplines such as history must avoid," enlisting "the imagination to bring what's lost back to us, to bring the dead back to life." For Spielberg, Lincoln and his unfortunate, untimely death was always a fascination: one of the reasons for making his 2012 masterpiece was that he "wanted—impossibly—to bring Lincoln back from his sleep of one and a half centuries even if only for two and a half hours, and even if only in a cinematic dream."[2]

Many of the events recounted in the movie occurred in 1865, but Spielberg had to use creative license in the small details, conversations, and visual artistry of the movie to connect the viewer with the significance of those events. These are minor fabrications, such as Mary Todd Lincoln sitting in on the votes for the passage of the Thirteenth Amendment; Caucasian and African American soldiers together reciting Lincoln's Gettysburg Address; Tad Lincoln viewing glass negatives of Alexander Gardner's various images of the Civil War; the portrait behind Lincoln's desk of the ninth U.S. president, William Henry Harrison (who died thirty-two days into his term as president); or jokes being made about Lincoln's likeness on the fifty-cent piece. Harold Holzer, the dean of modern Lincoln scholars, who served as content consultant to the movie, wrote an article concerning these fabrications and others, feeling as if he were to blame for the inaccuracy of these small details. He commented:

> [*Team of Rivals*, written by Doris Kearns Goodwin,] tries to tell the real story of passage of the 13th Amendment, but where Tony Kushner's extraordinary, beautiful screenplay was concerned, not all of my suggestions were adopted. Not all of my advice was taken. . . . In pursuit of broad collective memory, perhaps it's not important to sweat the small stuff.[3]

With *Abraham Lincoln: Vampire Hunter*, however, the small stuff matters the most. Author and screenwriter Seth Grahame-Smith worked small details and events from Lincoln's life into the movie, so that while the overall plot of Lincoln being a vampire hunter is silly and impossible, there is some truth behind the madness. One example is the opening scene involving the kidnapping of several free African Americans in the state of Illinois. (The Northwest Ordinance of 1787 prohibited slavery throughout the territory, and in 1818, the Illinois Constitution reiterated this prohibition.) Another is the brief courtship of Stephen Douglas, Lincoln's political opponent in the presidential election of 1860, and Lincoln's soon-to-be-wife, Mary Todd. A third example is Lincoln meeting and subsequently subletting from eventual lifelong friend Joshua Speed in Springfield, Illinois. And while all these small historical details add to the flow of the story, the ultimate outcome illustrates Lincoln as the savior of the country over slavery, with vampirism being a metaphor for slavery: "a metaphor for an evil that is almost incomprehensible—that such a brutal, inhuman thing was allowed to exist and grow generationally."[4]

Small details, as those mentioned above for both *Abraham Lincoln: Vampire Hunter* and *Lincoln*, create character development and set the scenery in which the characters are placed. This emphasis on the character development and actor portrayal is another area where artistic license excels. From extensive research of personal communication, diaries, and other forms of primary sources, we can guess at what Lincoln might have been like. However, it is only that: a guess. Spielberg and Daniel Day-Lewis portray the sixteenth president as gangly and birdlike, with a wheezy drone that occasionally exudes force. In their rendition, Lincoln often uses little anecdotes to get his point across, which grate on the nerves of some of the people around him but calm others. This physical portrayal is very similar to Alexander Gardner's portrait of Lincoln four days before his death. The weight of the war combined with the fate of the large African American population physically altered Lincoln's appearance, as if the burdens of the entire country rested on his shoulders.

Day-Lewis won an Oscar for his portrayal of Lincoln, far surpassing the countless imitations of the sixteenth president in film since the early 1900s. Next to Daniel Day-Lewis, Hal Holbrook, who portrayed Lincoln several times in TV miniseries including *North and South* (1985–94), won critical acclaim for his portrayal of Lincoln throughout the 1980s. However, Sam Waterston, who also portrayed Abraham Lincoln several times in film, earned an Emmy nomination for his depiction, and up until Day-Lewis's representation, critics declared Waterston's performance of Lincoln as the most definitive, giving life to Lincoln's shrewd political nature as well as his humorous side.

On the other side of the spectrum, in *Abraham Lincoln: Vampire Hunter*, producer Tim Burton's Lincoln is a force to be reckoned with. Benjamin Walker's portrayal of Lincoln is confident, much like Nicholas Shepherd's 1846–47 photograph of the congressman-elect. Grahame-Smith's character becomes legend, not only for his fight for African Americans and the reuniting of the country but also for the physical attributes Lincoln exemplifies: he chops down a tree in a single swing, battles across the backs of stampeding horses, and sprints across the top of a train that struggles across a burning, collapsing bridge. While these attributes are absolutely and utterly fantastical, the character captivates viewers, and the scenes don't fall short on the cinematography or special effects. Compared with other, more traditional Lincoln portrayals, Walker's performance illustrates the decisive Lincoln that most people associate with the historical figure. Walker's depiction of Lincoln's commanding presence is similar to that of Gregory Peck in *The Blue and the Gray* (1982) or Henry Fonda in *Young Mr. Lincoln* (1939).

While Spielberg was fascinated by the untimely death of Lincoln and time limit on his greatness, Grahame-Smith professed a different fascination with Lincoln:

> His life was so incredibly dark and fraught with peril and misfortune. His baby brother died, his mother died when he was nine, he was estranged from his father. With no worldly possessions or education, he dusted himself off and became a man of letters, married a woman of high station, and gained the highest office in the land, and then saved this land while burying two of his sons. His story is dark and gothic. It's like a super hero origin story: the outcast, disadvantaged youth who possesses some secret skill. With great power comes great responsibility. ... When he achieves this power, he finds himself in the middle of the Civil War, taking the whole country on his shoulders and wrestling it into shape and then paying the price for doing this with his life.[5]

Vampire Hunter illustrates this sense of macabre, not only in the plot but also in the costume design, the special effects, and the character analysis.

In all three movies, the cinematic dream and imaginative vision of each director push forward the stories, creating intriguing interactions among characters, conflicts, and the landscape. *Lincoln* pulls in viewers with its portrayal of the characters and poignant view of America at a critical turning point. *Vampire Hunter* pulls in viewers with its mash-up between the plausible and the impossible and its use of special effects. Out of the three, though, the artistic license in *Zombies* takes a dramatic turn away from historical accuracy and into the realm of a movie made solely for entertainment. It badly befuddles historical fact, completely altering well-known events to create fictional and outlandish conflicts. The Asylum studio, best known for the *Sharknado* series, backed the film with director Richard Schenkman and a budget of $150,000—a tiny budget compared with *Lincoln*'s $65 million and *Vampire*

Hunter's $99.5 million. When asked about whether Schenkman had watched, read, or peeked at the plot of the movie he was mocking, he replied, "No. I specifically avoided it until I was done. I never read the book. If there are any similarities at all, they're an unfortunate accident. I honestly know nothing about it."[6] Schenkman used imagination alone to create this movie.

A majority of the main players in the movie have little reference to the Civil War or little significance in Lincoln's life. Teddy Roosevelt is an example of this: he would have been five years old when the movie takes place, yet he plays a critical role in the destruction of the zombie Confederate stronghold.

Although *Vampire Hunter*'s plot is just as unrealistic as that of *Zombies*, it follows a credible line of research, making the movie closer to *Lincoln* in terms of historical accuracy. Both *Vampire Hunter* and *Lincoln* resonate from Doris Kearns Goodwin's Lincoln biography, *Team of Rivals: The Political Genius of Abraham Lincoln*, and both films used *Team of Rivals* to create the film world in which Lincoln resides. Despite the necessary fabrication of conversations and exchanges where firsthand accounts and memory could not define the scenery, the screenwriters for both movies immersed themselves in the research on Lincoln's life and politics, attempting to create an accurate portrayal of both the character and the time period.

Tony Kushner, *Lincoln*'s screenwriter, conducted his own research to adapt Spielberg's vision into a screenplay, as *Lincoln* portrays only a few pages of the original biography. His additional research attempted to capture the themes and major players for the movie and included reading several Lincoln biographies in addition to *Team of Rivals*, as well as Lincoln's speeches and letters, a few general histories of the Civil War, and several American novels of the period in order to accurately reproduce nineteenth-century language.[7] Seth Grahame-Smith did likewise. In addition to using Goodwin's *Team of Rivals*, Grahame-Smith heavily researched Lincoln's life, speeches, and personal correspondence to become "a mini-Lincoln scholar" so the ridiculous idea of Lincoln being a vampire hunter would seem plausible. In one interview, Grahame-Smith said, "The more audacious the title or concept you're trying to get across, the more you really have to put in the work, the research, [and] the time to make it unexpectedly make sense. When I wrote *Abraham Lincoln: Vampire Hunter*, on its surface, it was a very ridiculous proposition." Now, the biggest compliment Grahame-Smith receives from readers is "that they say they forget while they are reading the book that it never happened and it's absolutely absurd. That's really the fun for [him], to pull a book-length sleight-of-hand trick on the reader."[8] Grahame-Smith did this sleight of hand so well that even Harold Holzer thought Grahame-Smith created a believable plot: "Parts were so credibly formulated, one fear I had was that people would believe the conceit."[9]

"I think any period in history can be adapted into interesting fiction, as long as you approach the actual history with respect," Grahame-Smith explained. "I went into this respecting Lincoln enormously, and I came out respecting him even more, because I did so much research on his actual life."[10]

While *Lincoln* pulls in viewers for the acting and artistry, *Abraham Lincoln: Vampire Hunter* uses vampires to tap into millennial interest. It's arguably more fun but is aimed at a different audience than Spielberg's *Lincoln*. With such a ridiculous plot, it's hard to take *Vampire Hunter* seriously, but the artistic license makes the movie more intriguing. The same could be said for *Lincoln*, where the viewer is pulled into the unfolding events from the very beginning. The greatest accomplishment of creating and releasing these movies during the sesquicentennial of the Civil War is the resurgence of interest in Abraham Lincoln, the War between the States, and the resulting amendments, as well as a resurgence of political and racial problems that resonated with those of the 1860s that have had long-standing repercussions on today's society. And while interest in the Civil War has seen a spike in growth, movies such as these continue to keep individuals relevant and alive for future generations to study and admire.

Notes

1. Steven Spielberg, "Keynote Address on 149th Anniversary of Gettysburg Address," C-SPAN, 19 November 2012, https://www.c-span.org/video/?309433-1/steven-spielberg-149th-anniversary-gettysburg-address.
2. Ibid.
3. Harold Hozler, "What's True and False in *Lincoln* Movie," *Daily Beast*, 22 November 2012, http://www.thedailybeast.com/articles/2012/11/22/what-s-true-and-false-in-lincoln-movie.html.
4. Chris Lee, "'Abraham Lincoln: Vampire Hunter': Seth Grahame-Smith on Its Real-Life Origins," *Daily Beast*, 22 June 2012, http://www.thedailybeast.com/articles/2012/06/22/abraham-lincoln-vampire-hunter-seth-grahame-smith-on-its-real-life-origins.html.
5. Seth Grahame-Smith, "Modern Gothic Master Seth Grahame-Smith Talks 'Abraham Lincoln: Vampire Hunter,' 'Pride and Prejudice and Zombies,' 'Dark Shadows,'" interview by Maggie Lange, *IndieWire*, 12 June 2012, http://www.indiewire.com/2012/06/interview-modern-gothic-master-seth

-grahame-smith-talks-abraham-lincoln-vampire-hunter-pride-and-prejudice
-and-zombies-dark-shadows-181213/.

6. Richard Schenkman, "Inmate at the Asylum," interview by R. Emmet
   Sweeney, *StreamLine: The Filmstruck Blog*, 15 May 2012, http://movie
   morlocks.com/2012/05/15/dtv-action-items-part-3-inmate-at-the-asylum-an
   -interview-with-director-richard-schenkman/.

7. Tony Kushner and Harold Holzer, "Lincoln: The Screenplay," interview
   by Daniel Weinberg, C-SPAN Book TV, 15 February 2013, https://www.
   c-span.org/video/?311074-1/lincoln-screenplay&start=456.

8. Seth Grahame-Smith, "Interview: Seth Grahame-Smith Talks 'Pride and
   Prejudice and Zombies,'" interview by Tim Lammers, Direct Conversations: Tim Talks Hollywood, 5 February 2016, http://directconversations
   .com/2016/02/05/interview-seth-grahame-smith-talks-pride-and-prejudice
   -and-zombies/.

9. Lee, "'Abraham Lincoln: Vampire Hunter.'"

10. Seth Grahame-Smith, interview by Eric Spitznagel, *Vanity Fair*, 26 Feb-
    ruary 2010, http://www.vanityfair.com/hollywood/2010/02/qa-abraham
    -lincoln-vamire-hunter-author-seth-grahame-smith.

Part Three
FOR YOUR LISTENING PLEASURE: THE CIVIL WAR IN SONG

All history proves that music is as indispensable to warfare as money; and money has been called the sinews of war. Music is the soul of Mars.

—*New York Herald*, 1862

Scan to see exclusive online material related to this part of the book.

21. ❄ "Dixie"

Dan Welch

> If I had known it was going to be so popular, I would have written it better.
>
> —Daniel D. Emmett

I t was fall of senior year in high school. The leaves were changing, the morning and evening air was crisp, and the Friday night football game was the most talked-about event of the week. A studious few in the senior class worked on ballots for the class to vote on our motto, song, color, and other symbolic representations that would appear in the yearbook and in graduation profiles for years to come. I pushed hard to get my favorite song on the ballot and have it win. I had always shied away from mainstream "anything" during my high school career, and that included music, as well. In the end, my campaign for Lynyrd Skynyrd's "Free Bird" made it to the ballot but lost by several votes. The loss did nothing to deter my musical obsession with the Southern rock band, however.

The holiday season that year brought two memorable gifts from the Skynyrd catalog. The first was a video recording of the band's August 1976 performance at the Knebworth Festival, while the second was the audio soundtrack. Both the video and audio performances ended with a full-length studio cut of one of the South's enduring anthems, "Dixie." The South's leading rock band had commercialized and capitalized on one of the most powerful and iconic songs from the era of the Confederate States of America. The once-martial song of the Confederacy had descended from a revered, yet unofficial, national air into the popular culture of the American rock-and-roll era. And there, with strong staying power, it continued to permeate further into popular forms of expression in modern society.

The year I pushed for Lynyrd Skynyrd to represent my senior class—and discovered the band's version of the Confederate classic—was not in the late 1970s, when the song was first recorded, but rather the early 2000s. Clearly, the simple, memorable melody had remained entrenched in popular culture well into the twenty-first century. But had "Dixie" really descended from its once-vaunted status into popular culture, where it resides today—or had it always been part of popular culture, generation after generation?

Many people who know "Dixie" know its ironic history. The future Confederate melody was written by a Northerner—and even more scandalous, a New Yorker at that—several years before the American Civil War erupted. But for almost all, the history of the song and its composer ends there.

"Dixie" was actually composed not by a native New Yorker, but by a native Ohioan. Daniel Decatur Emmett's roots in the Buckeye state ran strong. His father was an ardent abolitionist in the then-frontier state and participated in the establishment of further stops along the Underground Railroad.[1] But as he neared his thirties, Emmett, who had taught himself to play the fiddle at a tender age and had learned the art of popular music of the day from his mother, found himself living in New York City. His experiences by that age had been vast and varied. For a brief period, he apprenticed as a printer, but he soon enlisted in the army, where he excelled as a fife and drummer. Military service was nothing new in the Emmett familial line. Daniel's father had served in the War of 1812, and his grandfather had fought with the colonists during the American Revolution.[2] Following his time in the military, Emmett joined another popular pastime that allowed him to hone his musical skills: the circus. Performing with the Cincinnati Circus Company, Emmett further experienced what crowds of the day looked for in musical entertainment. It was his next career change that ultimately led him on a path to "Dixie."

In addition to the circus and many other forms of entertainment of the period, musical performances by minstrel groups in blackface had come into vogue by the 1840s. Blackface performances, where white singers and instrumentalists blackened their face and hands and performed as caricatures of African Americans, had become a staple in musical variety shows, which typically featured one or two pieces performed in that manner. Emmett entered the scene in 1840 and, not long thereafter, formed what became a widely touring act in the genre, the Virginia Minstrels. Musicians Billy Whitlock, Dick Pelham, and Frank Brower rounded out the ensemble. Ever the showman, with an understanding of audiences, popularity, and success, Emmett put together an entire performance in the blackface style with his group, instead of just one or two pieces. The idea caught on and, because of its novelty, became successful. The group traveled and performed throughout New York and England.

By 1857, Emmett, entrenched in the pop music and blackface performances of minstrel shows, had moved on to another traveling group, Bryant's Minstrels. Bryant, a stage name for the brothers who had founded the group, was extremely successful in New York City, a town also familiar with Emmett. After two years with the group, in 1859, the Bryant brothers approached him to write a new piece in the style of a walk-around for their show. The show had been running for an extended period of time and needed a new, exciting piece to spruce it up and bring back previous attendees. Emmett was no stranger to composing lyrics that were easy to remember and setting them to tunes with a hummable melody. Several origin stories of the song "Old Dan Tucker," for instance, credit Emmett as its lyricist.

Emmett set to work. The meeting that had taken place between the brothers and Emmett had occurred on a Saturday evening, and a new piece was needed for the next performance just forty-eight hours later. According to historian Wayne Erbsen, Emmett described the origin of "Dixie" as follows:

> I went to my hotel and tried to think out something suitable, but my thinking apparatus was dormant; rather than disappoint Bryant, I searched through my trunk and resurrected the manuscript of "I Wish I Was in Dixie's Land," which I had written years before. I changed the tune and rewrote the verses, and in all likelihood, if Dan Bryant had not made that hurry-up request, "Dixie" never would have been brought out.[3]

Thus the song's origins were never of the martial and national type: "Dixie" had been written by a known pop musician of the day for an audience that consumed pop music. This was just one of numerous versions of the origin of "Dixie" told by Emmett during his later years.

According to yet another version, Emmett said he wrote the first verse and chorus in less than an hour. Two nights later, an audience at Mechanics' Hall in New York City received the performance of the new piece enthusiastically. It took off and quickly became part of the city's pop music scene.

Within a year, Emmett sold the rights to "Dixie" to Firth, Pond and Co., making three hundred dollars from the sale. Just a scant four weeks before blood was spilled on the plains of Manassas, the company had the first score printed for distribution. During the intervening time, however, the song's popularity grew outside of the regional performances of Bryant's Minstrels. In New Orleans, an orchestra conductor at a local theater, Carlo Patti, added the tune to a march and drill routine by forty female Zouaves. The song was an overnight smash in the Louisiana town. "Dixie" quickly spread across "the land of cotton."[4]

Although it was never officially declared as the newly formed Confederate States of America's national anthem, it surely was one of its most popular patriotic songs during the late war, if not its unofficial official anthem. Emmett's hasty work was now elevated from pop status to a musical symbol of a burgeoning country with very different ideals from those of the United States.

Helping hurry this transition from pop song to musical symbol was Henry Hotze. A Swiss-born journalist who emigrated to the United States to become

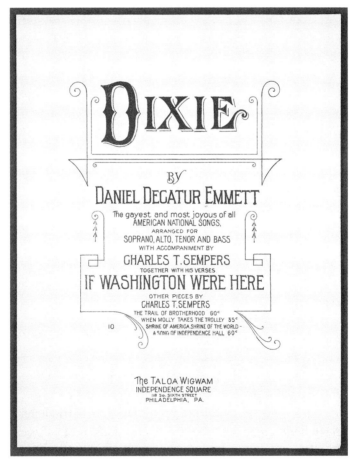

Fig. 21.1. Sheet music for a vocal arrangement of "Dixie" proclaims it to be "the gayest and most joyous of all American national songs." *Library of Congress.*

a citizen, Hotze accepted a commission in November 1861 as a commercial agent for the Confederate State Department. Working as a Confederate propagandist in London throughout the war, his weekly journal, *The Index*—circulation 2,250—had the largest impact of any publication in spreading pro-Confederate propaganda and culture.[5] In June 1862, Hotze commented on the popularity of the South's new favorite song:

> It is marvelous with what wild-fire rapidity this tune of "Dixie" has spread over the whole South. Considered as an intolerable nuisance when first the streets re-echoed it from the repertoire of wandering minstrels, it now bids fair to become the musical symbol of a new nationality, and we shall be fortunate if it does not impose its very name on our country. Whether by a coincidence simply accidental, or from some of those mysterious causes which escape our limited intelligence, its appearance in its present form was the knell of the American Republic, and as such it seems to have been instantaneously received by the masses in the South everywhere.[6]

As the war dragged on, myriad versions of "Dixie" proliferated across the South for a variety of ensemble settings. Between 1860 and 1866, one chronicler of the song's popularity tallied thirty-nine different versions "arranged for piano, violin, minstrel band, plantation dance, polka, reel, rondo, caprice, cornet band, olio, and all vocal combinations—solo, duet, quartet, quintet, chorus (mixed, male, and female), and minstrel walk-around." Of that count, during the postwar era, one organization fighting for Confederate memory, the United Daughters of the Confederacy, listed twenty-two exclusively Southern versions.[7]

With the Confederate experiment failed, and no more need for an unofficial national anthem, "Dixie" once again returned to its pop status from its short-lived stint as a vaunted nationalistic symbol. The reclamation happened almost immediately, triggered by none other than President Lincoln himself. On April 10, 1865, one day after the surrender of the Army of Northern Virginia, thousands of jubilant citizens in Washington chanted for an audience with Lincoln. When the president finally obliged, he noted a "band of music" in the crowd. He proposed closing his remarks with a piece of music, "a particular tune which I will name," to be performed by the band. The tune was "Dixie," and according to Lincoln, it was "one of the best tunes I ever heard." With Lee's surrender at Appomattox, Lincoln felt they had bagged not only one Confederate field army but also the unofficial national anthem of the Confederacy. Just to make sure it was fairly appropriated, Lincoln joked, "I presented the question to the Attorney General, and he gave it as his legal opinion that it is our lawful prize."[8]

By the close of the nineteenth century, there it still remained, firmly in the popular national consciousness. Emmett, dragged out of retirement in Mount Vernon, Ohio, hit the road for a minstrel show farewell tour in 1895–96 and played his biggest hit to ovations at every stop. Several years later, just before his death, he performed it for the last time in front of an audience.

Since Emmett's passing in 1904—when "Dixie" was performed at his funeral—the song has remained where it began, in popular culture. With the development of marching bands in the early part of the twentieth century, the lively tempoed piece became a staple of the repertoire of numerous high schools and universities across the South. As the century rolled on, many musical acts added the piece to their records and live shows—Jan and Dean, Bob Dylan, Lynyrd Skynyrd, and Charlie Daniels, to name a few. It has appeared in movies and documentaries retelling the Civil War era, such as *Gone with the Wind* and Ken Burns's *The Civil War*. "Dixie" has appeared on television as well, providing a soundtrack to cartoon *Foghorn Leghorn* and serving as the musical horn for the car named the General Lee on *The Dukes of Hazzard.*

The song's popularity and its place in popular culture have not come without criticism, however. Many feel that with its racist overtones, caricatures of African slaves, and continued symbolism of a militant white South, "Dixie" is unsuited for a place in popular culture and should be avoided. As a young college student enrolled in a music education program, I had a field experience where I taught music of the Civil War era. The class was diverse in its student makeup and composed of those who chose neither band nor choir for their music elective. The lesson went well, even for an emerging educator, but when I played "Dixie," two students started calling me racist. Like the Confederate flag controversies of the 2010s, "Dixie" can stir up trouble.

In that particular moment, though, I had presented the song within its historical context. If we refrain from presenting or performing pieces of music from our musical history just because they have controversial overtones, we lose a part of our short musical heritage. Compared with world history, our country's history is infinitely smaller, and this applies to our musical traditions as well. As painful as some of that history—including our musical history—may be, we must ensure that future generations can learn from what defined us in the past. The only way to do this is by ensuring that the iconography from this time period is not lost, but rather taught in proper historical context. Performing "Dixie" as a marching band arrangement on Friday nights at a high school football game as a "fight" or "spirit" song does nothing to further our collective understanding of the famed antebellum and Civil War–era tune; rather, presenting the piece in a concert series focusing on American marches or walk-arounds does.

With its long and complex history, one can see that "Dixie" never truly descended into popular culture from an elevated place as an unofficial national anthem and rallying cry of an entire populace; rather, it has always belonged to pop culture and pop music from the mid-nineteenth century to today. By the time of Dan Emmett's death, he had seen "Dixie" take on numerous roles in culture and popularity. Ultimately, it was the song's association with the Confederacy and its supporters that increased the work's influence and stature. Witnessing the growth and renown of his piece throughout his own lifetime, Dan Emmett wrote, "If I had known it was going to be so popular, I would have written it better."

Notes

1. Wayne Erbsen, *Rousing Songs and True Tales of the Civil War* (Asheville, NC: Native Ground Music, 1999), 26–31.
2. Willard A. Heaps and Porter W. Heaps, *The Singing Sixties: The Spirit of Civil War Days Drawn from the Music of the Times* (Norman: University of Oklahoma Press, 1960), 41–61.
3. Wayne Erbsen, "Dan Emmett: The Man Who Wrote Dixie," *Banjo Newsletter*, February 1980.
4. Erbsen, *Rousing Songs and True Tales*, 26–31; Paul Glass, *Singing Soldiers (The Spirit of the Sixties): A History of the Civil War in Song* (New York: Grosset and Dunlap, 1968), 8.
5. James J. Horgan, "Henry Hotze," *Encyclopedia of the Confederacy* (New York: Simon and Schuster, 1993), 2:798.
6. Heaps and Heaps, *Singing Sixties*, 41–61.
7. Ibid., 45–46.
8. *Daily National Intelligencer*, 11 April 1865.

22. ❀ "The Battle Hymn of the Republic": Origins, Influence, Legacies

John Stauffer

Origins

"The Battle Hymn of the Republic" is far more popular today than it was during the Civil War. It has become the nation's unofficial anthem—beloved by Northerners and Southerners, conservatives and radicals, white people and black people.[1] Yet the song's origins have long been shrouded in obscurity. Benjamin Soskis and I discovered that the "Battle Hymn" tune actually dates back to early nineteenth-century Southern camp meetings.[2] It was adapted from "Say, Brothers, Will You Meet Us on Canaan's Happy Shore?" a Southern camp-meeting spiritual. The "Say, Brothers" hymn was first published in an 1807 Virginia hymnbook by the Methodist circuit-rider minister Stith Mead, who was known for preaching to slaves. Originally titled "Grace Reviving in the Soul," it became the "Say, Brothers" or "O Brothers" hymn. A folk hymn, it adapted sacred words to a secular tune and circulated orally.[3]

What's especially fascinating about this first-known publication of "Say Brothers" is that it includes call-and-response directions:

> *Question*: O brothers will you meet me [repeat 2X],
>   On Canaan's happy shore?
> *Ans*: By the grace of God I'll meet you [repeat 2X],
>   On Canaan's happy shore.

Such directions between minister and congregants typified the basic form and structure of African American spirituals. The black roots of the "Say, Brothers" hymn are further supported by eyewitnesses, who described slaves singing "Say, Brothers" in a ring shout, an African religious ritual in which

202

participants gathered in a circle and sang (or shouted) while dancing in a counterclockwise direction and using a call-and-response structure. Additionally, the "Glory, glory Hallelujah" chorus, which soon replaced "We'll shout and give him glory," was especially popular in black spirituals. The hymn's call-and-response structure, the interracial makeup of camp meetings, Mead's documented preaching to black people, and eyewitness observers' descriptions of slaves singing the hymn in a ring shout all suggest that the origins of "Say, Brothers" were as much African as white American.[4]

The "Say, Brothers" hymn began circulating in the North via hymnbooks in the 1840s. By the late 1850s, it was popular especially in Boston, then the cultural and publishing center of the nation. Northerners were introduced to it through hymnbooks, without the call-and-response structure. They understood it as a white spiritual and associated it with Methodists, owing to the sect's explosive growth.[5]

In 1861, one Northerner would become closely associated with the "Say, Brothers" hymn: John Brown, the abolitionist famous for his raid on the federal arsenal at Harpers Ferry, Virginia, with an interracial army in October 1859. Federal troops led by Robert E. Lee captured or killed Brown and his men, tried the survivors for treason and murder (except for five who escaped), and executed them in December 1859 and March 1860. Brown's influence and memory would transform and disseminate the "Say, Brothers" hymn in the form of "John Brown's Body."

In April 1861, following the South's bombing of Fort Sumter, the 2nd Battalion, known as the "Tigers," garrisoned Fort Warren in Boston Harbor. The soldiers talked of John Brown, as did almost every other Bostonian, for Brown's raid was widely considered a major catalyst leading to secession and war, with most Bostonians regarding Brown as a martyr.[6] One Tiger—a Scottish immigrant also, coincidentally, named John Brown—joined a choral group with other soldiers at the fort. Brown's comrades needled him about his famous name, quipping, "This cannot be John Brown! John Brown is dead." Another soldier added, "His body lies mouldering in the grave." As a result of such ribbing, the singing group created "John Brown's Body," set to the "Say, Brothers" hymn, one of the Tigers' favorite tunes.

In May 1861, the Tigers Battalion merged with the Massachusetts 12th Regiment, and "John Brown's Body" (also known as the "John Brown Song") became the unit's signature anthem. In June, the Boston abolitionist C. S. Hall published the "John Brown Song" as a penny ballad, including six verses and the "Glory, glory Hallelujah" chorus. Hall's sheet quickly sold out. On

July 18, the 12th sang "John Brown's Body" on Boston Common while under review.

When members of the regiment sang it again a week later, while marching down Broadway in New York City, observers reportedly went "crazy with enthusiasm and delight." A reporter for the *New-York Tribune* published the lyrics, and by August 1861, "John Brown's Body" was the most popular song in the Union army.[7] Its popularity coincided with the first Confiscation Act, authorizing the Union army to confiscate all slaves of rebel masters who had managed to reach Union lines, effectively freeing them.[8]

Perhaps it wasn't coincidental that "John Brown's Body" became a mascot of the Union at the moment the conflict became a war for emancipation, for the lyrics are unambiguous in their abolitionist message. They portray John Brown as martyr: his body "lies a mouldering in the grave," but his soul is "marching on." The second stanza is even more explicit:

> He's gone to be a soldier in the army of the Lord,
> He's gone to be a soldier in the army of the Lord,
> He's gone to be a soldier in the army of the Lord,
>   His soul's marching on.

The fifth stanza seeks vengeance against slaveholders: "We will hang Jeff Davis to a sour apple tree." And the last stanza calls for "three rousing cheers for the Union"—at a moment in which a war for the Union had been transformed into a fight for emancipation.

* * *

Despite its immense popularity, "John Brown's Body" was not considered a national anthem. The words were too coarse and needed to be elevated. That happened in November 1861, after Julia Ward Howe traveled to Washington, D.C., with her husband, Samuel Gridley Howe, who had joined the U.S. Sanitary Commission, in company with her Unitarian minister James Freeman Clarke and Massachusetts governor John Andrew—all of whom had known John Brown. Julia had hosted Brown in her home.[9]

While in Washington, she witnessed a review of troops across the Potomac being broken up by a Confederate raiding party, resulting in the nineteenth-century equivalent of a traffic jam. To pass the time, she joined soldiers in singing "John Brown's Body." The troops were impressed with her beautiful

Fig. 22.1. Portrait of Julia
Ward Howe, circa 1861,
by Josiah Johnson Hawes.
Author's collection.

voice, shouting "Good for you!" The Reverend Clarke suggested that she "write some good words for that stirring tune." Julia replied that she had often thought of doing so but had not yet received the inspiration.[10]

Inspiration came that same night at the Willard Hotel, where Julia was staying. As she later recalled, "I awoke in the gray of the morning twilight; and as I lay waiting for the dawn, the long lines of the desired poem began to twine themselves in my mind." She jumped out of bed and scrawled her verses on Sanitary Commission stationery. In Julia's telling, her inspiration resembled that of Harriet Beecher Stowe, who had frequently declared, "I didn't write" *Uncle Tom's Cabin*; "God wrote it."[11]

Howe's lyrics are deeply indebted to the Book of Revelation. The first stanza comes directly from Revelation 14, in which an angel "gathered the vine of the earth, and cast it into the great winepress of the wrath of God."[12] Throughout that section, God or his angels cast lightning bolts and thunder into the earth, inducing an earthquake. Howe places the narrator of her poem *within* Revelation, personalizing its phantasmagoric imagery and turning it into a narrative lyric:

Mine eyes have seen the glory of the coming of the Lord:
He is trampling out the vintage where the grapes of wrath are stored;
He hath loosed the fateful lightning of His terrible swift sword:
His truth is marching on.

Howe's familiarity with Revelation's verses was representative, reflecting the degree to which most Americans interpreted the Civil War in apocalyptic terms. Revelation explained the ravages of war in religious terms and offered hope for the future. If the war was the apocalypse, then a new age of peace and harmony was not far away.[13]

The version of "Battle Hymn" published in February 1862 on the front page of the *Atlantic Monthly* was largely unchanged from Howe's original scrawl, with one notable exception: she had omitted the sixth and last stanza—appropriately, I think, because in doing so, the song ends with the climactic power of the fifth stanza.

Influence

The "Battle Hymn" was never as popular during the Civil War as "John Brown's Body," largely because the "Battle Hymn" had more sophisticated lyrics that soldiers on the march found more difficult to memorize. (Even today, few people know the whole song by heart.) Moreover, Howe squeezed a lot of words into each bar of music, requiring singers to enunciate them quickly. The words are almost too big for the music.

The wartime popularity of "John Brown's Body" stemmed partly from the fact that it is a simple ballad, easy to memorize and soothing to march to. Then, too, by 1860, sheet music was the most profitable printed medium. Publishers realized that "John Brown's Body" would make money; as a result, the ballad rolled off the presses in countless variations.

The "John Brown" song was also open-ended enough to be interpreted in a variety of ways. It was a heroic song, an inspirational song, a revenge song, and a comradeship song. It inspired soldiers to fight, and possibly die, for the abstract causes of freedom and Union. But it also helped build esprit de corps, encouraging troops to seek revenge for a friend who had been killed. One Union officer said that the ballad "made heroes of all his men," while another officer required his troops to sing it every day, in hopes of imbuing them with "Cromwellian earnestness." A New Hampshire lieutenant noted, "The effect of 'John Brown's Body' when heard in camp or on the march was simply indescribable."[14]

There is one final explanation for the popularity of a song that enshrined an abolitionist hanged for murder and treason. "John Brown's Body" became popular when the war, initially waged to preserve the Union, had been transformed into a war to abolish slavery. The two discrete aims had converged into one: preserving the Union *required* abolishing slavery and vice versa.[15]

"John Brown's Body" was especially popular among African Americans. The soldiers of the 1st Arkansas (Colored) Regiment created a new adaptation, which Sojourner Truth sang to inspire recruits. Then in February 1865, when the Massachusetts 55th Colored Regiment marched triumphantly into Charleston, South Carolina, the troops were cheered on by thousands of freedmen and women as they sang "John Brown's Body." For many Northerners, that marked the symbolic end of the war.[16]

The "Battle Hymn" also had its adherents. It was widely promoted by Charles McCabe, a Methodist minister and chaplain of the 122nd Ohio Volunteer Infantry, who was so taken with Howe's poem in the *Atlantic* that he memorized it. But it was not until McCabe heard the "Battle Hymn" sung at a war rally that he realized the poem had been written to accompany the tune of "John Brown's Body."

In 1864, McCabe turned Abraham Lincoln into an ardent fan of Howe's song. He sang the "Battle Hymn" at a Christian Commission meeting at the U.S. Capitol, with the president in attendance. Lincoln was reportedly quite moved by the fifth stanza, which equated Christ's sacrifice on the cross with the Union troops' sacrifice on the battlefield.[17]

Legacies

Before the "Battle Hymn" could become a *national* anthem, it first needed to be embraced by Southerners and Northerners. This transformation began in the 1880s, which coincided with the quest for reconciliation and reunion between white Northerners and Southerners and the uncoupling of the "Battle Hymn" from "John Brown's Body," with which it had been closely associated.

This uncoupling opened the way for the "Battle Hymn" to be reinterpreted. Whereas "John Brown's Body" evokes the memory of a militant abolitionist and calls for hanging Jeff Davis, the lyrics of "Battle Hymn" are wonderfully vague and thus adaptable. God is the main actor, advocating freedom. Southerners believed that they, too, had fought for God and freedom. In the 1890s, the University of Georgia adopted the "Battle Hymn" as its anthem, and it remains the school's anthem today.

In 1911, an early silent film, *The Battle Hymn of the Republic*, gained popularity especially in the South. The movie focused on the hymn's millennialist themes, and its aesthetic innovations, both visually and aurally, helped revitalize the "Battle Hymn" for a modern age.[18]

The "Battle Hymn" enjoyed many other legacies. At the turn of the century, it became a Progressive Party anthem. Theodore Roosevelt treated it as his personal anthem, encapsulating his advocacy of a sacred, strenuous life. Roosevelt led a campaign to adopt the song as the official national anthem, but he could not persuade enough Southern politicians to make that a reality.[19]

America's entry into World War I further helped nationalize, and indeed, internationalize, the hymn. It became the anthem of countless Northern and Southern soldiers who fought in that conflict, as well as Britons.[20]

The "Battle Hymn" was also transformed into the workers' anthem in 1915, when Ralph Chaplin, a leading Wobbly (the common name for Industrial Workers of the World, or IWW) wrote "Solidarity Forever" to the tune of "John Brown's Body" and "Battle Hymn." Wobblies defined themselves as "the modern abolitionists, fighting against wage slavery." Like the abolitionists, they were racial egalitarians and millennialists. Chaplin retained the note of millennialism in his version of "Solidarity Forever," reflected in the song's last lines before the refrain: "We can bring to birth the new world from the ashes of the old, / For the Union makes us strong."[21]

Throughout the twentieth century, the "Battle Hymn" was also used as an evangelical anthem, serving as the theme song of both Billy Sunday and Billy Graham, the two greatest evangelists in American history. It was the perfect anthem for Sunday's revivals, for it fit his militant, triumphant, and patriotic style of "muscular Christianity." A former professional baseball player, Sunday brought his athleticism to his sermons, shadow-boxing Satan, sliding home to Jesus, and climbing atop the pulpit to wave an American flag while his orchestra performed "Battle Hymn"—garnering a terrific response. During Sunday's 1917 revival in New York, he preached to one-quarter of the city's population.[22]

For several decades, millions of listeners also heard "Battle Hymn" on Billy Graham's weekly radio program, *Hour of Decision*. Graham's love of the song reflected his background as a Southerner haunted by the Civil War. Both grandfathers had been wounded as Confederate soldiers: his maternal grandfather lost a leg and an eye at Seminary Ridge at Gettysburg, and his paternal grandfather died with a Yankee bullet in his leg. The young minister's mother had recommended the "Battle Hymn" as his theme song. Just as the hymn had transcended its Northern, abolitionist origins, it also helped Graham transcend his roots to become a world-renowned revivalist rather than just another Southern preacher.[23]

The "Battle Hymn" was also a civil rights anthem and one of Martin Luther King Jr.'s favorite songs. In March 1965, after King led a group of twenty-five thousand black and white people from Selma to Montgomery, Alabama, he delivered a speech ending with a millennialist vision of racial justice: "How long?" King asked. Not long, because

> Mine eyes have seen the glory of the coming of the Lord
> He is trampling out the vintage where the grapes of wrath are stored;
> He has loosed the fateful lightning with his terrible swift sword;
> His Truth is marching on.[24]

Progressives, Wobblies, evangelicals, and civil rights activists were never united in their vision of America. Many evangelicals (though not Graham) opposed Wobblies and civil rights radicals, and Progressives hated the Wobblies.[25] Despite their lack of unity, however, all these movements are the legacies of the abolition movement—legacies that have largely been ignored or downplayed. Yet members of these groups, like the abolitionists, saw themselves as holy warriors, uniting religious faith with their visions of social reform. And much like abolitionists, they spoke truth to power and were willing to sacrifice themselves for the cause of freedom. Wobblies and civil rights activists also advocated, as abolitionists had, equality under the law for all people.

These legacies highlight the degree to which the "Battle Hymn" has become America's unofficial anthem. Indeed, for the past several decades, it has been sung as the finale of the National Democratic and Republican conventions. It was performed at the funerals of Presidents Kennedy, Johnson, Nixon, and Reagan, as well as those of Robert and Teddy Kennedy. More recently, the Brooklyn Tabernacle Choir performed "Battle Hymn" at President Obama's Second Inaugural.[26]

Then, too, the hymn served as the finale of the 9/11 memorial service at Washington National Cathedral, where Billy Graham delivered one of his last public sermons. The "Battle Hymn" also has a *physical* presence in the National Cathedral: in the Lincoln Bay, seven ornamental keystones depict the hymn's most vivid images, including grapes of wrath being trampled and lightning loosed, trumpets sounding forth, lilies growing where Christ was born, and soldiers singing the Hallelujah chorus.[27]

Why has the "Battle Hymn" served as a national anthem for so long? There are several reasons. First, it manages both to unite and divide Americans, distinguishing "us" from "them" and clarifying a sense of national identity. It is an ideal hymn for a nation at war, which is when it has been most popular—and the United States has been at war for most of the last century. Like the Gettysburg Address, it encourages individuals to sacrifice themselves for a greater, collective good. The fifth stanza brilliantly emphasizes the theme of sacrificing oneself for freedom:

> In the beauty of the lilies Christ was born across the sea,
> With a glory in his bosom that transfigures you and me:
> As he died to make men holy, let us die to make men free,
> His truth is marching on.

Second, the "Battle Hymn" has long functioned as a template of the United States' "civil religion," in which Americans act out what they believe is God's will for their country. As the fifth stanza implies, Christ is both an exemplar and an object of faith. He (rather than humans) is the catalyst of social change, thus lightening reformers' burdens.[28]

Third, the song is immensely adaptable. It has served violent and nonviolent, postmillennial and premillennial, Northern and Southern, conservative and radical ends.

Fourth, it exploits the millennialist strain in American culture, revealing the degree to which the United States stands apart from Europe and Canada in its religiosity.[29]

Fifth, it is aspirational, much like the Declaration of Independence. The "Battle Hymn" envisions a future good society, a reign of peace and harmony. It is sublime, which some critics have called an *American* aesthetic; it evokes terrible delight, uniting present afflictions with future joy.

Perhaps most important, the "Battle Hymn" is a musical masterpiece, especially when performed in largo—a slow, dignified tempo—as it was recorded by the U.S. Army chorus, for example. In arrangements such as this, the melody notes have been expanded to allow the words the chance to express themselves. Even listeners who disagree with the song's apocalyptic message cannot help but be transported by its aesthetic power.

Notes

1. This essay is adapted from my coauthored book, John Stauffer and Benjamin Soskis, *The Battle Hymn of the Republic: A Biography of the Song That Marches On* (New York: Oxford University Press, 2013).

2. Stauffer and Soskis, *Battle Hymn*, 17–21; Dickson D. Bruce, *And They All Sang Hallelujah: Plain-Folk Camp Meeting Religion, 1800–1845* (Knoxville: University of Tennessee Press, 1974); Christine Leigh Heyrman, *Southern Cross: The Beginnings of the Bible Belt* (New York: Knopf, 1997); Ellen Jane Lorenz, *Glory, Hallelujah! The Story of the Campmeeting Spiritual* (Nashville: Abingdon, 1980).

3. Stauffer and Soskis, *Battle Hymn*, 17–22; Stith Mead, *A General Selection of the Newest and Most Admired Hymns and Spiritual Songs, Now in Use* (Richmond, VA: Seaton Grantland, 1807), 2, 80–81.

4. Mead, *General Selection*, 80–81; Stauffer and Soskis, *Battle Hymn*, 23–25, 306n22.

5. Stauffer and Soskis, *Battle Hymn*, 26–27; George Pullen Jackson, *White and Negro Spirituals: Their Life Span and Kinship . . .* (New York: J. J. Augustin, 1943), 119–23; Bruce, *And They All Sang Hallelujah*, 56–57; Charles A. Johnson, "The Frontier Camp Meeting: Contemporary and Historical Appraisals, 1805–1840," *Mississippi Valley Historical Review* 37 (June 1950): 98–99.

6. John Stauffer and Zoe Trodd, eds., *The Tribunal: Responses to John Brown and the Harpers Ferry Raid* (Cambridge, MA: Harvard University Press, 2012), 126–27; Henry Greenleaf Pearson, *The Life of John A. Andrew: Governor of Massachusetts, 1861–1865* (Boston: Houghton, Mifflin, 1904), 1:95–101.

7. Stauffer and Soskis, *Battle Hymn*, 3; *New York Times*, 25 July 1861; *New York Tribune*, 28 July 1861.

8. James Oakes, *Freedom National: The Destruction of Slavery in the United States, 1861–1865* (New York: W. W. Norton, 2013), ch. 4.

9. Stauffer and Soskis, *Battle Hymn*, 74–81.

10. Ibid., 82–83; Julia Ward Howe, *Reminiscences, 1819–1899* (Boston: Houghton, Mifflin and Company, 1899), 274–75 (italics added).

11. Stauffer and Soskis, *Battle Hymn*, 83–84; Howe, *Reminiscences*, 275; Harriet Beecher Stowe, "The Author's Introduction," *Uncle Tom's Cabin*, vol. 1, *The Writings of Harriet Beecher Stowe* (Boston: Houghton, Mifflin and the Riverside Press, 1896), xxxv–xxxvi; Annie Fields, ed., *Life and Letters of Harriet Beecher Stowe* (Boston: Houghton, Mifflin, 1897), 377.

12. Rev. 14:19 (King James Version).

13. Stauffer and Soskis, *Battle Hymn*, 83–84; Ernest Lee Tuveson, *Redeemer Nation: The Idea of America's Millennial Role* (Chicago: University of Chicago Press, 1968), 187–214; James H. Moorhead, *American Apocalypse: Yankee Protestants and the Civil War, 1860–1869* (New Haven, CT: Yale University Press, 1978), 79–81.

14. Stauffer and Soskis, *Battle Hymn*, 44, 53–59, 63–71; Henry A. Beers, "Literature and the Civil War," *Atlantic Monthly* 88, no. 530 (December 1901): 759–60; Fred Winslow Adams, "Our National Songs: 'Battle Hymn of the Republic,'" *Zion's Herald*, 27 July 1898, 938; Christian McWhirter, *Battle Hymns: The Power and Popularity of Music in the Civil War* (Chapel Hill: University of North Carolina Press, 2012), 43–44.

15. Stauffer and Soskis, *Battle Hymn*, 44.

16. Ibid., 59–62; "'Marching On!': The Fifty-Fifth Massachusetts Colored Regiment Singing John Brown's March in the Streets of Charleston," *Harper's Weekly*, 18 March 1865; Henry Mayer, *All on Fire: William Lloyd Garrison and the Abolition of Slavery* (New York: St. Martin's Press, 1998), 577.

17. Stauffer and Soskis, *Battle Hymn*, 93–94.

18. Ibid., 106–39, 144–45.

19. Ibid., 140–43, 145–61, 165–75.

20. Ibid., 11, 162–64.

21. Ibid., 176–207; Melvyn Dubofsky, *We Shall Be All: A History of the Industrial Workers of the World* (Chicago: Quadrangle Books, 1969), 160; "Solidarity Forever," *I.W.W. Songs: To Fan the Flames of Discontent* ["Little Red Songbook"] (Chicago: Industrial Workers of the World, 1923), 25–26; Upton Sinclair, *The Jungle*, ed. Clare Virginia Eby (1906; repr., New York: W. W. Norton, 203), 299.

22. Stauffer and Soskis, *Battle Hymn*, 208–12.

23. Ibid., 128–29; William Martin, *A Prophet with Honor: The Billy Graham Story* (New York: William Morrow, 1991), 52–62; Cliff Barrows, interview by the author.

24. Stauffer and Soskis, *Battle Hymn*, 255–58, 262–71.

25. Ibid., 225–26.

26. Ibid., 282–92.

27. Ibid., 3–8.

28. Robert N. Bellah, "Civil Religion in America," *Daedalus* 96 (Winter 1967): 1–21; Bellah, *The Broken Covenant: American Civil Religion in Time of Trial*, 2nd ed. (Chicago: University of Chicago Press, 1992).

29. Paul Boyer, *When Time Shall Be No More: Prophecy Belief in Modern American Culture* (Cambridge, MA: Harvard University Press, 1992), 1–18.

23. ✳ Bobby Horton and Sam Watkins: All along "The Kennesaw Line"

Chris Mackowski

On summer evenings when I was a boy, back in the late seventies, my father often loaded my brother and me and his pound dog Eela into the cab of his Chevy, and we'd go out for a ride. We'd eat whoopie pies and drink too much sugary soda too close to bedtime as night fell. Dusk would grow thick among the miles of pine trees that lined the empty back roads of eastern Maine. A coyote might flash green eyes in our headlights, or a moose might loom up out of the dark forest. Maybe we'd see a bear black as night.

The soundtrack for these excursions was always classic country music broadcast from some far-off AM station that only nighttime would let us hear—plaintive voices like Hank Williams Sr. and Patsy Cline. Roger Miller sang "King of the Road," and Claude King sang "Wolverton Mountain." They all seemed to be having a tough go of it. The weak glow from the analog face of the radio made everything feel all the lonelier.

This was the note "The Kennesaw Line" struck for me years later when I first heard it. Written by singer-songwriter Don Oja-Dunaway in the 1960s and later appearing on his 1989 Civil War–themed album, *Kennesaw*, the song first showed up on my playlist—perhaps—in the late nineties from Bobby Horton's 1986 CD *Homespun Songs of the C.S.A.* (vol. 2). I say "perhaps" because the song blends in so completely with those classic country balladeers from AM radio that I feel as if I've known the song for ages. I've *always* felt as if I've known the song for ages.

The narrator, a soldier named Sam, relays the dying words of a comrade wounded during the Battle of Kennesaw Mountain on June 27, 1864. "Sammy, I think I'm hurt really bad," the mortally wounded soldier says. "Ain't this a hell of a day. You'd best go and leave me now. I think I need time to pray."

It was, Sam says, "The day that hell broke loose just north of Marietta / all along the Kennesaw line."[1]

213

"I knew Sam," Bobby Horton told me on the phone one day. "I met him back in the sixties, when I was a kid."[2]

Bobby was referring to Sam Watkins, author of the Civil War memoir *Co. Aytch: A Side Show of the Big Show*—the inspiration for the song. "When you read Sam's book—which he wrote in the 1880s, about twenty years after the war—once you read his book, he's your friend. You feel like you know him," Bobby explained. "And everybody who reads the book pretty much has the same reaction."

Bobby said Don Oja-Dunaway wasn't any different. "So when Don read it, he took that book as inspiration and loosely based the song on the Dead Angle, where Sam was with Company H, First Tennessee, on the Kennesaw Line, and that is the premise of the song."

As Watkins described his position, the Confederate line at Kennesaw formed "an angle, a little spur of the mountain, or rather promontory of a range of hills, extending far out beyond the main line of battle, and was subject to the enfilading fire of forty pieces of artillery of the Federal batteries. It seemed fun for the guns of the whole Yankee army to play upon this point."[3]

"That's what moved Don so hard," Bobby said. "Sam inspired that song; the book *Co. Aytch* inspired it. Some of the words in there come directly out of the book." That's how Bobby recognized Sam in the song. "I was drawn to it because, when I heard it, I was like, 'That's Sam Watkins,'" he said with a laugh. "I recognized his language, you know? And so, naturally, I've loved the song because I've just loved the book."

First published in 1883, *Co. Aytch* has long been recognized by historians for its soldier's-eye view of the western theater, but Sam Watkins found his widest readership in the late twentieth century after Ken Burns featured the book in *The Civil War*. Burns chose Watkins as his typical western Southerner, just as he chose Elisha Hunt Rhodes of the 2nd Rhode Island as his typical eastern Northerner.

"Talk about other battles, victories, shouts, cheers, and triumphs," Watkins wrote of the fight at the Dead Angle, "but in comparison with this day's fight, all others dwarf into insignificance." "My pen is unable to describe the scene of carnage and death that ensued," he added. Although he was "unable to describe the scene," the section about the battle manages to go one for some thirty-five hundred words and covers about ten pages.

"It's about a man who's stuck in the position he's in, and he's not glorifying it at all," Bobby explained. "He's glorifying the people who didn't want to be there that did their duty. In fact, he even points that out about those poor Yankee boys coming up that hill. That's humanity. That's getting down to the human part."

At the Dead Angle, attacking federals had to ascend a steep slope to get at the Confederate position. "I will ever think," wrote Watkins, "that the reason they did not capture our works was the impossibility of their living men passing over the bodies of their dead. The ground was piled up with one solid mass of dead and wounded Yankees. I learned afterwards from the burying squad that in some places they were piled up like cord wood, twelve deep."

A line from the song—from a verse Bobby did not include but that appeared in the original—sums up Watkins's feelings perfectly: "I pity those poor Yankee bastards / Who died so far from home."

"Don paraphrased some of Sam's words and made it work," Bobby said. "He did such a beautiful job. He's a *fine* songwriter, just an amazing songwriter, and a good guy."

Bobby, too, is a *good guy*. Every conversation I've ever had with him feels as if we've known each other forever, although I only first met him through an interview in 2002. He was "raised Southern" and lives in Alabama—"I'm very, very strongly Southern, and I always will be," he's told me—but he had ancestors on both sides of the war. He's proud of them all. "I refuse to be embarrassed by them," he said.

For forty-seven years, he's played with the same band, a group first formed in college that still tours regularly. Aside from his lengthy catalog of recordings, he's worked with Ken Burns on the soundtracks for eighteen films, and he's done extensive work for the National Park Service. "I have five or six balls in the air all the time, working, and I'm just so thrilled," he admitted. He's a man living the dream.

Like me, Bobby isn't sure where he'd first heard "The Kennesaw Line." "When I first recorded the song, in '86 or something, I'd known the song a couple years, but I don't remember where I first heard it," he said. "I heard it from somebody who's friends with Don. That's how I came to know and love that tune."

In the thirty years since, "The Kennesaw Line" has come to be one of Bobby's best-known songs. A Google search brings up dozens of results with his name attached (a 2007 version by Claire Lynch also pops up, although less frequently). "There are a lot of people who used to play the song," Bobby said. "I don't know if they do anymore, but for a long time they did." Bobby's version on *Homespun Songs* features his own arrangement—"my own little spin on it with a guitar, messing around with a double-D tuning and stuff," he explained. People would call him up and ask him how to play it. "I'd walk 'em through it over the phone," he said. "But Don wrote the tune and I give him all the credit—him and Sam. And *Don* credited Sam, too."

Bobby's had his share of criticism about "The Kennesaw Line"—mostly from die-hards who say he shouldn't have recorded it because it wasn't an authentic period piece. "It's only one of two nonperiod songs I've recorded in my series of Civil War–era stuff, but I felt justified in it because I'm using Sam's words—because Don did," Bobby told me. "Especially now, with people downloading the songs, they don't read the liner notes. I explain it thoroughly in the liner notes—who wrote the song and why I chose to do it. They don't read them, so I get a lot of criticism from purists. But that's OK. Those things happen."

Bobby invites doubters to do what he—and Don—have both done: visit Kennesaw's Dead Angle with *Co. Aytch* in hand and read it on the spot. "You can go there and see everything Sam saw that's described in the book. Everything

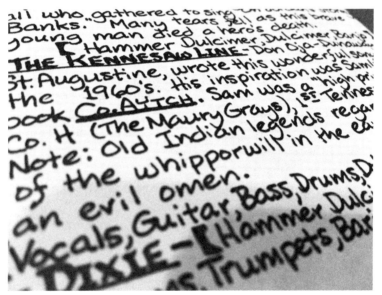

Fig. 23.1. Liner notes from volume 2 of Bobby Horton's *Homespun Songs of C.S.A.* offer some background to the story—but nobody reads the liner notes anymore, Horton laments. *Chris Mackowski/Bobby Horton.*

he writes about, you can envision what those fellas went through," Bobby said. "It's one of the most touching things I've read in my whole *life*."

I visit the Dead Angle myself on an early March day, gray with drizzle but warm with the first hint of spring. At Bobby's suggestion, I bring a copy of *Co. Aytch* to read on the spot, although the rain and the book don't mix well. From the Cheatham Hill parking area, a gravel path runs past an artillery position and along the outside of the Confederate works. The trees—tall, brown, bare—stand like dark slashes against the overcast sky. It's a stark look different from the one Watkins described, where "even the little trees and bushes which had been left for shade, were cut down as so much stubble." An occasional jogger plods along, sneakers scuffing in the gravel, but I'm mostly alone as I reach the tip of the trail that wraps around the Dead Angle.

The day could not be more different from June 27, 1864. As Watkins recalled:

> The sun beaming down on our uncovered heads, the thermometer being one hundred and ten degrees in the shade, and a solid line of blazing fire right from the muzzles of the Yankee guns being poured right into our very faces, singeing our hair and clothes, the hot blood of our dead and wounded spurting on us, the blinding smoke and stifling atmosphere filling our eyes and mouths, and the awful concussion causing the blood to gush out of our noses and ears, and above all, the roar of battle, made it a perfect pandemonium.

However, if not for the signs and the monuments and markers, one might not ever guess a battle took place at the Dead Angle. The landscape does not evoke the frightful carnage as Watkins described it in his memoir but, rather, the elegiac mood as Don and Bobby have captured it in their song. The landscape itself is an elegy.

Maybe it's the drizzle or the Gibraltar-like solitude. Maybe it's the earthworks, covered with leaf litter and melancholy. Maybe it's the gloom and the gray. Maybe it's the late-night, back-road lonesomeness I feel, even in the daylight, even with the occasional jogger here and gone. But I don't think so. I've visited the Dead Angle when Cheatham Hill bulged with full-summer green and dozens of tourists and hikers, and I could hear the elegy then, too. This stretch of the Kennesaw Line has resigned itself to its heartbreak. If you listen, careful, quiet, you can hear its song.

Notes

1. Don Oja-Dunaway, "The Kennesaw Line," circa 1960s.

2. Bobby Horton, interview by the author, 9 January 2018. All subsequent quotes from Horton come from this interview.

3. Sam Watkins, "Dead Angle," *"Co. Aytch," Maury Grays, First Tennessee Regiment, or a Side Show of the Big Show*, 2nd ed. (Chattanooga, TN: Times Print Co., 1900), chap. 12, http://www.gutenberg.org/cache/epub/13202/pg13202-images.html. All subsequent quotes from Watkins come from this source.

24. ✦ Not from This Century:
A Longing Melody from a Modern
Time—"Ashokan Farewell"

Dan Welch

A black screen with a sweeping wind accompaniment gives way to large, bold, white opening credits. The screen blackens again, then a lone cannon appears on the horizon, swirled in a stormy sky of gray and purple clouds and glowing embers of the sun's light; a voice from the past cuts through in ringing clarity. The words, those of Oliver Wendell Holmes, given two decades after the war, echo back to that tumultuous time. "We have shared the incommunicable experience of war, we have felt, we still feel, the passion of life to its top. In our youth our hearts were touched with fire." While the sentiments and the wind fade, the viewer is left with images of the destruction and cost of this war. Faces of youth and the dead of the battlefield are juxtaposed with burned-out buildings and the detritus of war on the farms and lands of America's civilians. And there the musical pickup notes of A and C# lead the listener into the tonic of the key of D major and the first measure of what became one of the most iconic and memorable parts of the landmark documentary film *The Civil War*, by Ken Burns.

In the fall of 1990, the eleven-hour, five-night miniseries event attracted record viewership. The filmmakers explored the causes of the war, memorable reminiscences and images of the conflict, and a chronological examination of the military campaigns. Behind it all stood a pantheon of American folk melodies of the period. Unforgettable airs such as "Battle Cry of Freedom," "When Johnny Comes Marching Home," "Dixie," and many others that the men in the ranks and those on the home front played and sang during the war supported the images, reminiscences, and historians' commentary on the screen. All listeners—those of the mid-nineteenth century and those watching the documentary in the comfort of their homes—would have been familiar with those melodies, except one. Blending a twentieth-century composition with the sounds and style of a longing, plaintive melody in the vein of "The Vacant Chair," composer and folk musician Jay Ungar had introduced his work "Ashokan Farewell" to its largest audience yet.

By the time Burns's series premiered on PBS, Jay Ungar had been in the American folk and bluegrass music scene for nearly two decades. Born in Brooklyn, and raised on the sounds of 1940s and 1950s pop music, Ungar frequently visited Greenwich Village during the height of its musical influence. Ungar later traveled through North Carolina and Tennessee as he sought to learn from traditional fiddle players. From there, the emerging folk musician performed with several bands and ensembles, but it was his meeting with another musician that later led him on the path to "Ashokan Farewell." In what was described as a "chance meeting," Ungar was performing at a club in New York where bassist Molly Mason was also performing. The two later worked together on and off throughout the 1970s. The opportunity arose for Ungar to perform with Mason regularly after Ungar and several other musicians formed a new group, Fiddle Fever, and brought on Mason as a bassist. Ungar and Mason, along with Evan Stover, Matt Glaser, and Russ Barenberg, went on to record two LPs as Fiddle Fever. Unger and Mason also eventually married.[1]

As Fiddle Fever continued to perform and record, the members also separately began work on other projects. For Ungar, it was working on the establishment of the Ashokan Fiddle and Dance Camp. The camp was a haven for fiddlers, as well as those who reveled in early Americana dance and music. By 1982, the summer arts camp, held at the Ashokan Field Campus of SUNY New Paltz, became a special annual event for Ungar and Mason. In the Catskill Mountains not far from Woodstock, New York, the camp took its name from the town of Ashokan. Today most of the town is covered by the serene Ashokan Reservoir—the water source from which those in New York City receive their drinking water. Ungar, in a short essay on the history of the now-famed song, recalls discussing the origins of the name Ashokan with the late local historian Alf Evers. He "once told me that the name Ashokan first appeared as a place name in 17th century Dutch records. He thought it was probably a corruption of a local Lenape Indian word meaning, 'a good place to fish.'"[2]

Earlier in the summer of 1982—according to an interview with the *Atlantic* in 2015, the twenty-fifth anniversary of the Burns documentary—the fiddler had traveled to Scotland. Back in Ashokan, as his annual camp was coming to an end, and with it the happiness of music-making, creativity, and friendships that would be paused for another year, he drew inspiration from his trip weeks earlier and the musical stylings and history of Scotland to compose a piece

Fig. 24.1. Jay Ungar and Molly Mason's haunting "Ashokan Farewell" has become part of the musical canon of the Civil War, even though it's not of the era. *Ungar/Mason.*

of music that captured his sadness at the time. The stage was set for work on his next composition.[3]

Although it was sadness at the end of another Ashokan Camp that drove Ungar to compose, he later noted, "The tune was my attempt to get back to a feeling of connectedness."[4] As Ungar explained:

> I was feeling a great sense of loss and longing for the music, the dancing and the community of people that had developed at Ashokan that summer. I was having trouble making the transition from a secluded woodland camp with a small group of people who needed little excuse to celebrate the joy of living, back to life as usual, with traffic, newscasts, telephones and impersonal relationships.[5]

Pulling out his fiddle, "maybe in the first 20 to 40 minutes, I had most of it," he recalled. As "it's very easy to drift away from your initial inspiration," he said, referring to the musical composition process, Ungar pushed the Record button on a nearby cassette player to ensure his ideas weren't quickly lost during those inspirational moments. "Maybe after an hour or so, I put it away [the fiddle] and then listened." Ungar continued to work on his new piece, and after getting to a place where he was happy with it, he sat on it. For the time being, the now-iconic fiddle tune was not destined to be heard.[6]

A year went by, and with Ungar and Mason's group, Fiddle Fever, heading back into the studio, Ungar finally shared the composition with the rest of the group for the first time. The fiddler recalled the group's need of another slow number for the album: "We tried my yet unnamed lament. The arrangement came together in the studio very quickly with a beautiful guitar solo by Russ Barenberg, string parts by Evan Stover and upright bass by Molly Mason."[7] Supported by his fellow musicians, it went from a demo on a cassette to a recording for the group's 1983 album, *Waltz of the Wind*. All that was needed for Ungar's work was a name. It was Mason who suggested "Ashokan Farewell." Ungar liked it. The song, and thus the album, was complete. Group members moved on to other projects. Two members of the group in particular, Matt Glaser and Russ Barenberg, were working with a young documentary filmmaker named Ken Burns. While collaborating on a project with Burns on the Brooklyn Bridge, they gave Burns a copy of *Waltz of the Wind*. Burns was instantly drawn to Ungar's work and asked to use it in his next documentary, *Huey*, about Louisiana governor Huey Long. Ungar and Mason's collaboration with Burns did not end there. They continued to work on other projects, the height of which would be Burns's *The Civil War*.[8]

By the time of its completion, Burns's documentary of the American Civil War had clocked in at more than eleven hours in run time. Although Ungar, along with Mason, other members of Fiddle Fever, and pianist Jacqueline Schwab, worked on much of the traditional nineteenth-century period pieces as well, it was Fiddle Fever's recording of Ungar's longing melody that became the focal point of the musical score and the only contemporary work included on its soundtrack. The group's original recording would not be the only version of "Ashokan Farewell" that would be heard, however. Several other variations of the piece were also included in the final production. In total, Burns's love of Ungar's lament placed the Scottish-style work in the film twenty-five times. The slow, plaintive fiddle melody occupied fifty-nine minutes and thirty-three seconds of audio space during the miniseries—one-tenth of the total run time.[9]

The Civil War, by Ken Burns, has become a touchstone in the Civil War community since its release in 1990. The film reignited the study of our past and inspired a generation of historians and enthusiasts alike to reexamine this period. Similarly, the musical centerpiece "Ashokan Farewell" revolutionized musical scores for period pieces on the Civil War, from documentaries to films based on historical fiction and adaptations of true stories. A plaintive melody performed with a haunting timbre of a well-played violin became the hallmark of musical scores in the subsequent decades. Songs such as "Going Home" by Mary Fahl and "You Will Be My Ain True Love" by Alison Krauss, from the movies *Gods and Generals* and *Cold Mountain*, respectively, serve as emotional and musical themes throughout the works. Pieces throughout the scores of John Williams and Mark Isham, for *Lincoln* and *The Conspirator*, also feature the string section with the predominance of a lead violin. All these works were not of the turbulent period, but they try to channel its emotion through timbre and instrumentation to blend it seamlessly into a soundtrack of musical works from over 150 years ago. It was "Ashokan Farewell" that had been the first to successfully accomplish this, however.

Since its release, the song has taken on a life of its own. It has been played, covered, and recorded by fiddlers, classical musicians, Her Majesty's Royal Marines, James Galway, Charlie Byrd, Jerry Garcia, and David Grisman, to name a few. Ungar and Mason even performed the piece with Galway in the East Room of the White House for President George W. Bush. Its popularity also led to an Emmy nomination for Ungar and a Grammy for the overall soundtrack of the film.[10]

But why did this modern, simple fiddle tune blend so well into a soundtrack of nineteenth-century folk songs and resonate with so many people over the last twenty-seven years? As the tunes of the 1860s were "living thing[s]" to those of the period, "Ashokan Farewell" became a living piece as well, but Ungar believes that was because "the music had connected us to our past in important ways." It continues to do so today.[11]

Notes

1. Jay Ungar, "Bio," *Jay Ungar and Molly Mason*, accessed December 8, 2017, http://jayandmolly.com/about/.
2. Jay Ungar, "Ashokan Farewell FAQ," *Jay Ungar and Molly Mason*, accessed December 7, 2017, http://jayandmolly.com/ashokan-farewell/ashokan-farewell-faq/.

3. Megan Garber, "'Ashokan Farewell': The Story behind the Tune Ken Burns Made Famous," *Atlantic*, 25 September 2015, https://www.theatlantic.com /entertainment/archive/2015/09/ashokan-farewell-how-a-20th-century -melody-became-an-anthem-for-the-19th/407263/.
4. Ibid.
5. Ungar, "Ashokan Farewell FAQ."
6. Garber, "'Ashokan Farewell.'"
7. Ungar, "Ashokan Farewell FAQ."
8. Ungar, "Bio"; Garber, "'Ashokan Farewell.'"
9. Ungar, "Ashokan Farewell FAQ."
10. Ungar, "Bio."
11. Garber, "'Ashokan Farewell.'"

25. ❈ *The Civil War*: American Epoch, Nashville Album, and Broadway Musical

Rebecca S. Campana

In 2016, an unlikely musical based on American history grossed more than $1.9 million per week.[1] Lin-Manuel Miranda's *Hamilton*, a hip-hop biography, brought Alexander Hamilton to the fore of the founding fathers. Now a generation of young theatergoers views early America in a new way, and they can rap about the details. For them, Hamilton is a flawed but sympathetic genius, and Thomas Jefferson is . . . well, Jefferson has not fared so well.

History has long been an inspiration for theater artists, and indeed, audiences can enter the past in a powerful way through musical theater. Well before *Hamilton*, in 1998, a team of artists assembled to take the Civil War to Broadway, encountering the challenges of making an epic musical of an American epoch.

The Civil War's story begins in Texas, which is not a surprising starting point. Artists often develop shows at not-for-profit professional theaters around the country. There new musicals can undergo multiple drafts with less risk. Then the show gets a test run in front of paying audiences before the producers invest millions.

The Alley Theatre in Houston was preparing to celebrate its fiftieth season. Its artistic director at the time, Gregory Boyd, wanted to commemorate the milestone by commissioning a world-premiere musical. What better subject than the American Civil War?

Boyd teamed up with Jack Murphy (lyrics and book) and writer-composer Frank Wildhorn (book and music). In 1990, the Alley had produced the world premiere of Wildhorn and Leslie Bricusse's musical adaptation *Jekyll & Hyde*. The show subsequently went to Broadway and on national tours. Wildhorn was also a successful pop music writer, who wrote Whitney Houston's international hit "Where Do Broken Hearts Go?" and songs for the likes of Natalie Cole, Kenny Rogers, Sammy Davis Jr., Bryan White, and Amy Grant.[2]

In this project, Boyd, Murphy, and Wildhorn wanted to explore history, but with contemporary sounds and aesthetics. The team decided early on that there would be no "Dixie" or "Battle Hymn of the Republic" in *The Civil War*. Instead, Wildhorn—a polarizing figure in musical theater—used his signature blend of soft pop, country, gospel, and R&B with swelling pseudo-operatic orchestrations. This sound is what his fans love and his critics loathe. A critic once branded Wildhorn's work "mere ice-skating music."[3]

Wildhorn didn't see that as a problem.

"If theater does not embrace the pop music of the day for the next millennium, what's it going to be?" Wildhorn asked a *New York Times* writer. "A museum for dead white guys?"[4]

With its score in the present, the team wanted to root the text in the past. Boyd, Murphy, and Wildhorn immersed themselves in research, reading diaries, letters, and firsthand accounts. Though excerpts from iconic speeches, such as the Gettysburg Address, became the mortar between scenes, it was personal accounts of everyday people that inspired the creative team most.

In an interview, Wildhorn shared his delight at discovering these stories:

> We took the diaries of many young nurses, and we wrote a song based on a nurse called Hannah Ropes. She said, "If I know the names of these kids that I have to take care of during the day, I will become too close with them and won't be able to do my job." So we wrote a song called "I Never Knew His Name" based on her writing.[5]

A letter from dying soldier Sullivan Ballou to his wife became the song "Sarah." Civil War buffs with a trained ear might also hear accounts from Mary Chesnut, 2nd Virginia infantryman Henry Kyd Douglas, and Henry H. Pearson of the 6th New Hampshire.

Central Civil War figures were incorporated, too. Frederick Douglass emerged as a quasi-narrator. The era's euphemism for slavery, "the peculiar institution," became the title of a song. Of course, there was also Abraham Lincoln.

With enthusiasm for the breadth and depth of their source material, the team sought to portray the experiences of all Americans and capture the full scope of the war in two acts, on one stage.

On September 16, 1998, the Alley Theatre premiered *The Civil War: Our Story in Song*.

The musical emerged as a series of more than twenty musical vignettes, a collage of archetypes singing the Civil War stories we know. Blue soldier, gray soldier, the young regimental drummer, the fugitive slave, the parted lovers, the bereaved mother, the cocky boy turned dying soldier—all the expected people appeared. The staging emphasized that one character represented many people. The same group of young men sang at one side of the stage and then ran to sing on the opposite side to show there is little difference but geography between North and South. Most characters were not addressed by name because they were meant to be universal.

The band was onstage, holding modern instruments. The actors wore headset microphones and costumes with only hints of period clothing. "Projections of photos, paintings and letters evoke[d] the period setting," wrote Joe Leydon in the *Variety* review. "Otherwise, however, *Civil War* is aggressively 'timeless' in its pursuit of universal truths."[6]

For some audiences, therein lies the beauty of the show, and for Wildhorn, that is its genius. "*The Civil War* is by far the most emotional and dramatic show I've ever written. You don't get back story, or development. A dying soldier singing to his father? We don't even have to know the guy's name and we get emotionally involved."[7]

However, sometimes knowing a character's name—and the details of his story—is exactly what gets audiences emotionally involved. The writers enjoyed learning about Hannah Ropes and Sullivan Ballou as individuals, but they denied the audience that personal introduction. When characters are ideas and not people, a show can feel generic and, by extension, cliché. Rather than tearing up, an audience can end up rolling its eyes as an anonymous soldier in blue holds his unremarkable dying brother in gray.

More like a concert, the musical had no spoken story connecting the scenes. The musical relied on loose chronology to hold it together, beginning with the men of the Union and Confederacy marching off with optimism ("By the Sword/Sons of Dixie") and concluding with songs about death ("Five Boys"), endings ("Last Waltz for Dixie"), and legacy ("The Glory"). The story of African Americans was shared—in shanties, on the auction block, in a church. "River Jordan," a gospel revival number, provided a catchy tune before intermission.

When the show ended with a full-cast number, it—for better or worse—hit all the expected notes. The creators reached for a show that showed everything, running the risk of conveying nothing new.

Audiences seemed to be on board. The Alley extended the show by three weeks.

Next, *The Civil War* took an unusual—and metaphorical—pit stop in Nashville. There Wildhorn used his mainstream music clout to drum up national excitement for the show before its Broadway premiere.

On November 3, 1998, Atlantic Records released *The Civil War: The Nashville Sessions*. The album features country music stars such as Trace Adkins and Trisha Yearwood singing fourteen songs that sound ready for windows-down, back-road, country-radio listening. Those songs also happen to be in the musical.

If you don't know it is about the Civil War, you can still enjoy the album without missing much. Some songs have nothing in their lyrics, melody, or instrumentation to suggest they were inspired by the Civil War. "Missing You (My Bill)," a wife's simple song about her husband who is away, could be a forgettable B-side to Deana Carter's hit "Strawberry Wine."

The songs suit country music's love of God, duty, country, and home—especially the South. Gene Miller sings "Virginia," a young man's elegy for a home he'll never see again:

> I can hear Virginia
> When the south wind sings
> And I see her shining
> On a blackbird's silver wings.

It's easy to picture old high school friends at a campfire, draping their arms around each other, holding cans of beer and toasting home, family, roots.

Or to imagine Travis Tritt stepping out, commanding but cool in his cowboy boots, plucking his guitar, solo, singing, "We were young and bound for glory / Itchin' for a fight . . ."

The drums come in—a steady snare, then full set. The bass and lead guitar join in. Orange and yellow lights burst onstage. The crowd is blinded, then goes wild. The songs sound at home.

Usually, after the high-profile release of a record, a show would open, but Wildhorn and company were not done yet.

On January 5, 1999, Atlantic Records released *The Civil War: The Complete Work*. *Playbill* magazine called this "*The Civil War*'s assault on U.S. record stores—both Union and Confederate."[8] The thirty-nine-track, two-disc "concept album" expanded to twenty-six songs, with artists such as Hootie and the Blowfish, Patti LaBelle, and "Broadway All Stars" joining those from *The Nashville Sessions*. Danny Glover is the voice of Douglass and James Garner is Lincoln. Dr. Maya Angelou reads quotes from Sojourner Truth and her own poem "Still I Rise."

The Civil War marched north to a brief pre-Broadway engagement at the Shubert Theatre in New Haven, Connecticut.

Finally, on April 23, 1999, *The Civil War* opened on Broadway at the St. James Theatre. This made Wildhorn the first American composer in twenty-two years to have three shows running on Broadway simultaneously: *Jekyll and Hyde*, *The Scarlet Pimpernel*, and *The Civil War*. He was only forty.

Under the direction of Jerry Zaks, the show became a big-budget commercial production, and it looked the part. Gone was the stripped-down look of the Alley production. The band was out of sight, and women in wide skirts and armed soldiers in full uniform filled the stage. Zaks added "strobe lights and slow-motion battle scenes to a set frame of ravaged classical columns and lots of projections."[9]

Critics hated the show. As he blasted Wildhorn's "pale variations on pop standards," Ben Brantley of the *New York Times* wrote:

> The problem isn't the form. It's that there's not one moment of insight or originality in the show's consideration of matters that have already been exhaustively written about and portrayed. The method of *The Civil War*, in its lyrics and historical allusions as well as in its music, is to strike chords with which even an elementary school student would be familiar.[10]

The *Houston Chronicle*'s reviewer called the musical Wildhorn's "latest and truly appalling effort," which "bathes the U.S. Civil War in more than two hours of pop songs, gospel, folk, country-and-western and adrenaline-soaked anthems. There's not a complex emotion or idea—musical or otherwise—to be found."[11]

The show closed on June 13, 1999, after only 61 performances. To put this in perspective, *Fosse*, which won the Tony Award for Best Musical that year, closed after 1,093 performances.[12] In addition to a nomination for Best Musical, Murphy and Wildhorn received a Tony nomination for Best Score. The show also received a handful of Drama Desk Award nominations.

However, Broadway was not the end of *The Civil War*. Soon after, it had a two-year national tour.

In 2006, the team reimagined the show as a concert–musical event at Gettysburg's Majestic Theater. They renamed it *For the Glory*, arranging the songs so the story culminated in the Battle of Gettysburg. Its new director, Vincent

Marini, said its mantra was "'no guns, no costumes.' Instead of trying to form a traditional narrative we're creating an emotional tapestry."[13]

In 2008, *The Civil War* became a gala at the National Theatre in Washington, D.C., a one-night-only performance for President George W. Bush and First Lady Laura Bush. The star-studded cast included many artists from the albums and newer talent such as Clay Aiken.

During its almost twenty-year history, creators and producers have called it a musical, a song cycle, a revue, an oratorio, a concert, and an emotional tapestry. They've changed its name and reworked the order. They've tried to carve out its place on the legitimate stage and radio airwaves. Critics hated the show, but the albums average reviews of four and a half stars (out of five) on Amazon. Does the show have an identity crisis or universal possibilities?

In 2015, to commemorate the 150th anniversary of Lincoln's assassination, Ford's Theatre announced it would produce "the new Frank Wildhorn musical *Freedom's Song: Abraham Lincoln and the Civil War.*" A quick look at the song list revealed that it was the latest configuration of *The Civil War*, now with text "drawn entirely from the written and spoken words of Abraham Lincoln."[14]

Director Jeff Calhoun and adapters Richard Hellesen and Mark Ramont made clear decisions, and the show began to take a more compelling shape. It became a tribute to Lincoln, performed in his house—not an artistic expression of the entire war.

The production maintained some of the concept elements of the original. The cast began in modern dress—a nod to the musical's origins—but they quickly changed into Civil War–era costumes. A flag fell to reveal a tilted house, which acted as many locations, including slave quarters and the White House—with all the complications therein. A stovepipe hat sat on the table. The recorded speeches were mostly gone. Instead, ensemble members said the words of Lincoln to the audience and each other with the warmth and reverence appropriate to the space, holding the president's hat and passing it along. The world was complete, and the actors could be characters within it. Careful casting helped create modest character arcs.

It's the same music, but in a clearer structure, where the actors can showcase the difference between a solo on an album and a song in a musical. A pop artist sings a song in a way that is meant for anyone at any time. In a musical, an actor sings that same song as a fully realized character. For that character, his or her story has been building up to singing that song at that moment—the only moment it could be sung. The song is a monologue and lets the audience in on a psychologically revealing moment. That's how audiences connect to a character, and in that specificity lies the potential emotional power of a musical.

Listen to Kevin McAllister sing the fugitive slave's "Father, How Long?"[15] *Freedom's Song* places that number and emancipation at the height of the show. Something about that choice gets to the heart and humanity of that moment in history.

As *Freedom's Song*, the show formerly known as *The Civil War* becomes a tribute to the man who preserved the Union, in the presence of the flag-draped presidential box. It is not a sweeping epic, but a humbler show that takes its opportunity to honor the past and educate its audience in the present.

Whether *The Civil War* has found its final shape or will continue its twenty-year metamorphosis is unclear. However, now that Broadway audiences are caught up on the Federalist Papers and the Whiskey Rebellion, perhaps the time is ripe for another Civil War musical.

Notes

1. Michael Paulson and David Gelles, "'Hamilton' Inc.: The Path to a Billion-Dollar Broadway Show," *New York Times*, 8 June 2016, https://www.nytimes .com/2016/06/12/theater/hamilton-inc-the-path-to-a-billion-dollar-show .html.

2. "Welcome," Official Site for Frank Wildhorn, accessed January 28, 2018, http://www.frankwildhorn.com.

3. Robin Pogrebin, "Broadway's Critic-Proof Composer Says This Is (Still) His Moment; Like His 'Scarlet Pimpernel,' Frank Wildhorn Keeps on Going," *New York Times*, 5 October 5, 1999, http://www.nytimes.com/1999/10/06 /theater/broadway-s-critic-proof-composer-says-this-still-his-moment-like -his-scarlet.html.

4. Ibid.

5. "Frank Wildhorn Discusses *The Civil War*," Music Theatre International, 3 September 2013, video, 05:35, https://www.youtube.com/watch?v=NDN SSQBGWhU.

6. Joe Leydon, review of "The Civil War," *Variety*, 28 September 1998, http:// variety.com/1998/legit/reviews/the-civil-war-1200454909/.

7. Bruce Weber, "A 'Musical Event' That's Bucking for, Yes, a Profit," *New York Times*, 26 September 1998, http://www.nytimes.com/1998/09/27/theater /theater-a-musical-event-that-s-bucking-for-yes-a-profit.html.

8. Robert Simonson, "Civil War 'Concept Album' to be Released Jan. 5, 1999," *Playbill*, 4 January 1999, http://www.playbill.com/article/civil-war -concept-album-to-be-released-jan-5–1999-com-79260.

9. Ben Brantley, review of "History Soldiering On," *New York Times*, 22 April 1999, http://www.nytimes.com/1999/04/23/movies/theater-review-history -soldiering-on.html.

10. Ibid.

11. Steven Winn, "New York Theater Review: 'Civil War' Loses the Battle," review of *The Civil War*, *Houston Chronicle*, 2 February 2012, http://www. chron.com/performance/article/NEW-YORK-THEATER-REVIEW -Civil-War-Loses-the-2934746.php.

12. "Longest-Running Shows on Broadway," *Playbill*, 4 January 2018, http:// www.playbill.com/article/long-runs-on-broadway-com-109864.

13. Kenneth Jones, "Gettysburg Welcomes Wildhorn's 'New' Civil War Musical, *For the Glory*," *Playbill*, 15 June 2006, http://www.playbill.com/article /gettysburg-welcomes-wildhorns-new-civil-war-musical-for-the-glory-com -133233.

14. *Freedom's Song: Abraham Lincoln and the Civil War*, directed by Jeff Calhoun, written by Frank Wildhorn, Gregory Boyd, and Jack Murphy, adapted by Richard Hellesen and Mark Ramont (Washington, DC: Ford's Theatre /Washington Area Performing Arts Video Archive, 2015), DVD.

15. "*Freedom's Song* Rehearsal: 'Father, How Long?' Featuring Kevin McAllister," Ford's Theatre Society, 10 March 2015, video, https://www.youtube .com/watch?v=su0D697XC9I.

Conclusion

Chris Mackowski

As my colleagues and I worked on this volume, two things happened that drove home our initial premise for this book.

The first incident occurred while I was ordering lunch from a strip-mall Chinese restaurant in Lexington, Virginia, in January 2017. I was in town to speak at a Lee-Jackson Symposium, and without time for a leisurely meal at the local microbrewery, I had fallen back on a quick lunchtime favorite. As I waited for my General Tso's chicken, my phone dinged with an incoming text. A swipe of my thumb revealed a message from my cousin Amy in Southern California and a photo of myself on TV.

"I came downstairs and Jack was watching his typical war history shows," she said of her ten-year-old, "and I turned around and I saw this and I said Holy Crap! LOL!"[1]

"Jack," she said to her son, "don't you know who that is?"

"Oh my gosh! It's my cousin!" he exclaimed, jumping to his feet and running upstairs to tell his father.

Jack had been watching *Blood and Fury: The American Civil War*, a six-part television documentary that aired on the American Heroes Channel. I was one of three talking heads featured in the episode about the Battle of Fredericksburg. Amy's husband, Ryan, said he'd been watching the show all week and, he joked, "have probably been watching Chris all week and didn't even realize it because it looked so legit."

And indeed, the production values looked beautiful. The reenactments looked dramatic, suspenseful, and action-packed. The interpretive angle—focusing on the stories of a few men to tell the tale of the larger battle—also proved effective. The result: an engaging, entertaining series. Everything emphasized action—even the cameras, as they filmed the talking heads, slid smoothly from side to side, always in motion.

But I cringed at the many historical inaccuracies in the film, where Union soldiers crossed the Rappahannock River in canvas boats instead of wooden pontoons and the Confederates defended a low row of piled rocks instead of a formidable stone wall of quarried rock. The urban combat on December 11, 1862, took place in a reconstructed pioneer village of log huts instead of downtown Fredericksburg. "Who knew the street fighting occurred in the woods?" a colleague asked. "Perhaps they'll make up for it by throwing in a few urban scenes when they do an episode on the Wilderness."[2]

Not only were such things beyond our control as historians, but we also didn't get to see what any of the rest of the production even looked like until we all saw it air.

Yet based on the dozens of emails and notes I got about the series—most of them from folks casually interested in the Civil War rather than die-hard buffs—no one mentioned any of the faux pas. They either didn't notice or didn't care. People found the series engrossing and even inspiring. A few emailed me with questions. At my next few speaking engagements—including the one in Lexington—sales of my Fredericksburg book ticked upward.

An email I received from someone who works at the same university as I do—someone I know casually but not well—typified the correspondence: "I wanted to tell you how wonderful your segment on Fredericksburg was," she wrote. "The series was so interesting as people in general tend to focus so much attention on the battles themselves and don't take into account the individuals who have to fight them. Think I'll need to get myself back to either Antietam or Gettysburg or maybe both."[3]

It was the story, not the historical details, that captivated her. Better still, she feels inspired enough to revisit a battlefield. And after all, isn't that what I want?

So, should I be bothered by the funky pontoon boats and the fieldstone wall? Or should I be glad that people are inspired to visit battlefields and read books and ask me questions? Can I feel both bothered *and* glad?

Did the artistic impact of the piece outweigh its historical inaccuracies, or do those historical inaccuracies negate the film's artistic value? This is no small thing when I think of the insidious effects of the original *Birth of a Nation*—a stunning artistic achievement for its day, but one that skewed national understanding of Civil War history in a deeply disturbing way. *Gone with the Wind* had a similar, albeit magnolia-scented, impact. The happy medium rests somewhere on this side of D. W. Griffith's and David O. Selznick's films—but where?

From a purely pragmatic perspective, my cousin Jack, who lives in Southern California, isn't likely to get to a Civil War battlefield anytime soon. Watching the Civil War on TV is as close as he's apt to get for a while. That he's choosing to spend his Saturday morning watching the Civil War instead of cartoons sure looks like a win in my book.

* * *

The second incident occurred on Wednesday, January 25, 2016: actress Mary Tyler Moore passed away. Moore, a beloved comedic actress, first charmed viewers on the *Dick Van Dyke Show* (1961–66) and later as the star of her own *Mary Tyler Moore Show* (1970–77). She pioneered roles for strong female characters at a time when television had few, making her an icon.

Most people didn't realize, though, that Moore had a number of personal Civil War connections. One of my colleagues, Eric Wittenberg, *did* know of those connections—so he drafted a quick post outlining them.[4] Moore's great-grandfather, Lieutenant Colonel Lewis Tilghman Moore of the 4th Virginia Infantry, served in the Stonewall Brigade, and Stonewall Jackson used Moore's home in Winchester, Virginia, as his office in the winter of 1861–62. Mary Tyler Moore later donated considerable resources to preserving the home, which is now a museum. She also preserved the home of her great-great-great-grandfather, Conrad Shindler, in Shepherdstown, (West) Virginia, which serves as the home of Shepherd University's George Tyler Moore Center for the Study of the Civil War. And as one final touch, Moore portrayed Mary Todd Lincoln in a 1988 TV miniseries based on Gore Vidal's *Lincoln*.

The Emerging Civil War website was first to "break the story," as it were, about Moore's Civil War connections, and overnight, the story went viral and the website exploded. Thousands of new visitors, seeing the link on Facebook and Twitter, came to ECW to read the details. "I never knew," one reader replied. "Thanks for this insight about MTM." The story kept its legs for a week, well after Moore's death faded from the headlines. Once more, pop culture connected people to the Civil War.

What brought this incident full circle for me, though, was a comment my colleague Kevin Pawlak made in a personal reflection he posted the day after Eric's. As a recent graduate of Shepherd University, he benefited directly from Mary Tyler Moore's generosity to the Civil War community, so I invited him to write something that would comment on that. "Diving into her biography," he wrote, "I was . . . stunned to see she was such a comedic actress. . . . To me,

Mary Tyler Moore was someone completely different."[5] Pop culture was not his thing, he admitted; he knew her solely as the benefactor who established the Civil War research center at his university. The Civil War, it turned out, connected Kevin back to an otherwise widely recognized icon of pop culture.

* * *

My hope, as editor of this volume, is that readers have been able to explore the *many* connections between the Civil War and popular media. The glamour of the big screen, the aura of our favorite authors, the catchiness of a great tune—we love these things in ways rational thought can hardly explain. That's art's special power, which transcends anything traditional history can do.

That doesn't necessarily put art and history in opposition, though. Both, as Shelby Foote suggested, seek to get at Truth, even if they take different approaches. The more perspectives we benefit from, the more complete the picture will be and the fuller our understanding.

We can be entertained *and* moved and inspired.

Notes

1. Amy Taber, text message to the author, 14 January 2017.
2. Don Pfanz, email to the author, 1 January 2017.
3. Nancy Ryan, email to the author, 28 January 2017.
4. Eric Wittenberg, "In Memory of Mary Tyler Moore," 25 January 2017, https://emergingcivilwar.com/2017/01/25/in-memory-of-mary-tyler-moore/.
5. Kevin Pawlak, "A Personal Reflection on Mary Tyler Moore," 26 January 2017, https://emergingcivilwar.com/2017/01/26/a-personal-reflection -on-mary-tyler-moore/.

Contributors

Index

Contributors

Amelia Ann is a writer originally from northwest Pennsylvania. Ann has degrees in journalism and English literature.

Paul Ashdown is an emeritus professor of journalism at the University of Tennessee, Knoxville. He previously worked as a newspaper and wire service journalist. In addition to his interest in the Civil War era, media, and popular culture, he specializes in the literary journalism of the writer James Agee.

Chris Barr is a native of Americus, Georgia, just ten miles from Andersonville National Historic Site. Before working at Andersonville, Chris taught social studies in the local school system and earned a master's degree in history education from Columbus State University. He is an interpretive park ranger at Chickamauga and Chattanooga National Military Park.

Sarah Kay Bierle graduated from Thomas Edison State University with a bachelor's degree in history. She enjoys American Civil War research, writing, and public speaking, often emphasizing the role of civilians during the conflict. Bierle's small business, Gazette665, publishes well-researched historical fiction and coordinates educational history events.

Chris Brenneman has been a licensed battlefield guide at the Gettysburg National Military Park since 2009. He is also an employee of the Gettysburg Foundation, the nonprofit group that oversees the visitors center and museum. He is a coauthor of *The Gettysburg Cyclorama: The Turning Point of the Civil War on Canvas*, in which he focuses on all the people and places depicted in the painting.

Andrew Brumbaugh is a 2017 history graduate of the University of Pittsburgh. Beyond participating in many World War II living-history projects throughout Pennsylvania, he has worked at Soldiers and Sailors Memorial Hall and Museum in Pittsburgh and at Fort Roberdeau Historic Site, a Revolutionary War frontier outpost in Altoona, Pennsylvania.

Rebecca S. Campana is a writer, teaching artist, and arts administrator. Now in her sixteenth season at Arena Stage, she devises autobiographical theater for social change with youth in the D.C. metro area. At the invitation of the U.S. Department of State, she has written and directed plays in India (Kolkata, Mumbai, Chennai, and Hyderabad) and Croatia. She is also a guest artist at the University of Notre Dame.

Ever since childhood, **Jared Frederick** has been captivated by the people and ideas that dramatically shaped American history. The author of *Dispatches of D-Day*, Frederick served as a seasonal park ranger at Gettysburg National Military Park for five years. Involved in various nonprofit organizations and public history initiatives, he is currently an instructor of history at Penn State Altoona. Visit his website at jaredfrederick.com.

Richard G. Frederick is the author of books on Warren G. Harding and William Howard Taft ("So I know about outstanding presidents," he says). He has taught history at the University of Pittsburgh at Bradford since 1979 and is a past recipient of the university-wide Chancellor's Distinguished Teaching Award.

H. R. Gordon is the director of marketing and publicity at Buffalo Heritage Press. Previously, she was the managing editor of the Emerging Revolutionary War Series, published by Savas Beatie. She earned her bachelor's degree in journalism and mass communication (2016) and her master's in integrated marketing communications (2018) from St. Bonaventure University. In 2018, Gordon earned a graduate certificate in book publishing from the Denver Publishing Institute.

Meg Groeling is a contributing writer for Emerging Civil War. A writer, teacher, and curriculum developer since 1987, she has taught at both the elementary and middle school levels for more than thirty years. She received her master's degree in military history with a Civil War emphasis in 2016 from American Public University. Her first book is *The Aftermath of Battle: The Burial of the Civil War Dead*, published in 2015 by Savas Beatie. She lives in Hollister, California.

Brian Hicks is a columnist with the *Post and Courier* in Charleston, South Carolina, and the author or coauthor of ten books. He has written extensively on the *Hunley* and the Civil War in *Raising the* Hunley, *City of Ruin*, and *Sea of Darkness*. His most recent work, *In Darkest South Carolina*, is the story of federal judge J. Waties Waring and his plot to force the U.S. Supreme Court decision in *Brown v. Board of Education*.

Mary Koik has been professionally involved in the battlefield preservation movement for more than fifteen years, including a decade spent as a spokesperson for the Civil War Trust. Under her editorship, the organization's membership magazine, *Hallowed Ground*, has won nine consecutive national niche publication awards and been recognized by the international Society of Publication Designers.

For more than fifteen years, **Ryan Longfellow** worked as a park guide at Fredericksburg and Spotsylvania National Military Park, interpreting the battlefields of central Virginia. By day, he works as a history teacher and chairs the social studies department at Spotsylvania (Virginia) Middle School and facilitates the World History Learning Community. He was chosen as the 2015 Spotsylvania County Mentor Teacher of the Year and 2019 Spotsylvania Middle School Teacher of the Year.

Chris Mackowski is the editor in chief of Emerging Civil War. The author of more than a dozen books, he is a writing professor at St. Bonaventure University's Jandoli School of Communication, where he also serves as the associate dean of undergraduate programs, and the historian-in-residence at Stevenson Ridge, a historic property on the Spotsylvania battlefield.

Kevin Pawlak is a historic site manager with the Prince William County Historic Preservation Division and a certified battlefield guide at Antietam National Battlefield. He is the author of *Shepherdstown in the Civil War: One Vast Confederate Hospital* and a coauthor of *To Hazard All: A Guide to the Maryland Campaign, 1862*, part of the Emerging Civil War series. He also contributed an essay about the Emancipation Proclamation to the first volume in the Engaging the Civil War series, *Turning Points of the American Civil War.*

Nick Sacco is a park ranger with the National Park Service at Ulysses S. Grant National Historic Site in St. Louis, Missouri. He holds a master's degree in history from IUPUI, is a regular contributor to *Muster,* the official blog of the *Journal of the Civil War Era,* and is a member of the board of directors for the Missouri Council on History Education.

John Stauffer is the author of nineteen books, including *The Battle Hymn of the Republic: A Biography of the Song That Marches On,* which he coauthored with Benjamin Soskis. Stauffer is the Sumner R. and Marshall S. Kates Professor of English and of African and African American Studies at Harvard University.

Ashley Webb, a contributor to Emerging Civil War, is a museums collections specialist and consultant based in Roanoke, Virginia. She is the curator for two Roanoke-area historical societies and can usually be found with her nose stuck in a good book.

Dan Welch serves as a primary and secondary music educator with a public school district in northeast Ohio and is a seasonal park ranger at Gettysburg National Military Park. Previously, Dan was the education programs coordinator for the Gettysburg Foundation, the nonprofit partner of Gettysburg National Military Park. He is a coauthor of *The Last Road North: A Guide to the Gettysburg Campaign.*

Index

An italicized page number refers to a figure or its caption.

ENGAGING
the
CIVIL WAR

Engaging the Civil War, a series founded by the historians at the blog Emerging Civil War (www.emergingcivilwar.com), adopts the sensibility and accessibility of public history while adhering to the standards of academic scholarship. To engage readers and bring them to a new understanding of America's great story, series authors draw on insights they gained while working with the public—walking the ground where history happened at battlefields and historic sites, talking with visitors in museums, and educating students in classrooms. With fresh perspectives, field-tested ideas, and in-depth research, volumes in the series connect readers with the story of the Civil War in ways that make history meaningful to them while underscoring the continued relevance of the war, its causes, and its effects. All Americans can claim the Civil War as part of their history. This series helps them engage with it.

Chris Mackowski and Brian Matthew Jordan, Series Editors

Queries and submissions
emergingcivilwar@gmail.com

Other books in Engaging the Civil War

The Spirits of Bad Men Made Perfect: The Life and Diary of Confederate Artillerist William Ellis Jones
Constance Hall Jones

Turning Points of the American Civil War
Edited by Chris Mackowski and Kristopher D. White

Where Valor Proudly Sleeps: A History of Fredericksburg National Cemetery, 1866–1933
Donald C. Pfanz